The Benefits of Learning

The Benefits of Learn ... is ... ... tematic and vivid account of the impact of formal and informal education on people's lives. Based on extended interviews with adults of all ages, it shows how learning affects their health, family life and participation in civic life, revealing the downsides of education as well as the benefits.

At a time when education is in danger of being narrowly regarded as an instrument of economic growth, this study covers:

- the interaction between learning and people's physical and psychological well-being
- the way learning impacts on family life and communication between generations
- the effect on people's ability and motivation to take part in civic and community life.

The book reveals how learning enables people to sustain themselves and their communities in the face of daily stresses and strains.

It will be a valuable resource for education researchers and of particular interest to education policy-makers, adult education practitioners, health educators and postgraduate students in education.

The authors are all members of the Research Centre on the Wider Benefits of Learning, University of London.

The Benefits of Learning

The impact of education on health,
family life and social capital

Tom Schuller, John Preston,
Cathie Hammond, Angela
Brassett-Grundy and
John Bynner

Routledge
Taylor & Francis Group

LONDON AND NEW YORK

First published 2004
by Routledge
2 Park Square, Milton Park, Abingdon, Oxon, OX14 4RN

Simultaneously published in the USA and Canada
by Routledge
270 Madison Ave, New York NY 10016

Routledge is an imprint of the Taylor & Francis Group

Transferred to Digital Printing 2008

Typeset in Goudy by
Wearset Ltd, Boldon, Tyne and Wear

British Library Cataloguing in Publication Data
A catalogue record for this book is available from the
British Library

Library of Congress Cataloging in Publication Data
A catalog record has been requested

ISBN 0-415-32801-2 (pbk)
ISBN 0-415-32800-4 (hbk)

Contents

List of illustrations   vii
Notes on contributors   viii
Acknowledgements   x

PART A
Background and approach   I

1 Studying benefits   3
   TOM SCHULLER

2 Three capitals: a framework   12
   TOM SCHULLER

PART B
Themes and case studies   **35**

3 The impacts of learning on well-being, mental health and
   effective coping   37
   CATHIE HAMMOND

4 Mental health and well-being throughout the lifecourse   57
   CATHIE HAMMOND

5 Family life and learning: emergent themes   80
   ANGELA BRASSETT-GRUNDY

6 Family life illustrated: transitions, responsibilities and
   attitudes   99
   ANGELA BRASSETT-GRUNDY

7 'A continuous effort of sociability': learning and social
capital in adult life   119
JOHN PRESTON

8 Lifelong learning and civic participation: inclusion,
exclusion and community   137
JOHN PRESTON

PART C
Drawing together   **159**

9 The benefits of adult learning: quantitative insights   161
JOHN BYNNER AND CATHIE HAMMOND

10 Reappraising benefits   179
TOM SCHULLER, CATHIE HAMMOND AND JOHN PRESTON

Appendix 1   Background characteristics of respondents   194
Appendix 2   Specification of outcome and control variables   196
References and bibliography   199
Index   210

Illustrations

Figures

2.1	Conceptualisation of the wider benefits of learning	13
2.2	Classifying the effects of learning	25
3.1	Mediators between learning and health outcomes	40
4.1	Experiences of learning: Gareth	62
4.2	Experiences of learning: Beryl	65
4.3	Experiences of learning: Denise	71
4.4	Experiences of learning: Consuela	77
6.1	Experiences of learning: Delia	104
6.2	Experiences of learning: Phyllis	109
6.3	Experiences of learning: Hester	115
8.1	Inclusion and exclusion: Susan and Francis	146
8.2	Community action: Carol	151
8.3	Community action: Declan	155
9.1	The take-up of adult learning	163
9.2	Average number of courses taken of each type	164
9.3	Estimated effects of different levels of participation	170

Tables

9.1	Changes in outcomes between ages 33 and 42	165
9.2	Interpretation of the estimated effects of taking one or two courses	167

Contributors

Angela Brassett-Grundy is a Research Officer within the Centre for Longitudinal Studies at the Institute of Education, University of London. She has a background in clinical psychology, is completing a part-time MA in Integrative Psychotherapy and provides weekly therapy to adults with disordered eating at Guy's Hospital for South London and Maudsley NHS Trust. She has carried out research into mental ill-health, both in the NHS and in higher education. Recent publications include *Family Learning: What Parents Think* (Institute of Education, 2003, with Cathie Hammond) and *Researching Households and Families Using the Longitudinal Study* (Office for National Statistics, 2003).

John Bynner is currently Professor of Social Sciences in Education at the Institute of Education and Executive Director of the Wider Benefits of Learning Research Centre, and past Director of the Centre for Longitudinal Studies, the Joint Centre for Longitudinal Research and the National Research and Development Centre for Adult Literacy and Numeracy. His previous posts include Dean of the School of Education at the Open University and Director of the Social Statistics Research Unit at City University. He has published widely on youth transitions, education and social exclusion, including *Young People's Changing Routes to Independence* (Joseph Rowntree Trust, with Peter Elias, Abigail McKnight and others), and *Changing Lives* (Institute of Education, 2003, with Elsa Ferri and Michael Wadsworth).

Cathie Hammond is a Research Officer at the Centre for Research on the Wider Benefits of Learning at the Institute of Education, University of London. Before developing her interest in social research, she worked as a social worker, teacher of English as a foreign language, and computer programmer. Her publications include *The Wider Benefits of Further Education: Practitioner Views* (WBL Research Report 1, 2001, with John Preston) and *Learning to be Healthy* (Institute of Education, 2002).

John Preston is a Research Officer in the Centre for Research on the Wider Benefits of Learning at the Institute of Education, University of London.

Prior to his research activities, John worked as a lecturer in Further Education. His research interests are in social capital, social cohesion and more generally in issues of class and social exclusion. He has conducted funded research for the DfES and CEDEFOP, and his publications include *Evaluating the Benefits of Lifelong Learning: A Framework* (Institute of Education, 2001, with Ian Plewis) and *Education, Equity and Social Cohesion* (WBL Research Report 7, 2003, with Andy Green and Ricardo Sabates).

Tom Schuller was until late 2003 Professor of Lifelong Learning at Birkbeck and a founding co-director of the Research Centre on the Wider Benefits of Learning. Since then he has been Head of the Centre for Educational Research and Innovation at OECD in Paris. Recent books include *Social Capital: Critical Perspectives* (Oxford University Press, 2000, edited with Stephen Baron and John Field) and *International Perspectives on Lifelong Learning* (Open University Press/McGraw Hill, 2002, edited with David Istance and Hans Schuetze).

Acknowledgements

We would like to acknowledge the financial support of the Department for Education and Skills; the Department is not responsible for the views expressed here. We are grateful to Leon Feinstein for his help on the quantitative analysis; to Andy Green, Zoe Fowler and Martin Gough for their participation in the fieldwork; to Elaine Kitteringham for her help in preparing the manuscript; to all the respondents for their time; and to those who helped us generously in the organisation of the interviews.

Part A

Background and approach

Chapter 1

Studying benefits

Tom Schuller

Introduction: from participation to effects

This book is about how learning makes a difference to people's lives, as individuals and as members of their community. It is more than likely that anyone picking up the book – you, the reader – will be broadly predisposed to believe that learning does indeed bring benefits; we do not on the whole devote time to reading about things in which we have no belief. Whether as students (and former students), teachers or some other form of educational professional, or simply as members of a society where learning is increasingly emphasised as the sine qua non of personal or collective achievement, most people have a strong sense that without education their world would be a poorer place, economically but also intellectually, culturally, socially and even morally. Moreover, this perception derives not from abstract knowledge or political rhetoric but for the most part from direct experience. Most of us consciously owe our social and occupational position to some degree of educational achievement; we translate that knowledge into concern for the success of family and friends, and of the wider society; and we see the sad effects on others of educational failure. Stock learning-lauding phrases abound, from Aristotle ('Public education is needed in all areas of public interest', *Politics*, Book 8) to the current Prime Minister ('Education is the best economic policy we have').

But the ways in which learning actually affects our lives, individually and collectively, remain relatively unexplored in systematic empirical fashion. That people get better jobs because they have qualifications is obvious, and the relationship between education, income and occupation is well established at the individual level (Carnoy 2000; Blöndal *et al.* 2002). Better educated populations tend to prosper (OECD 1998). Even on this economic front, however, the mechanisms which translate learning into benefit are still quite poorly understood, especially at the level of the organisation or, still more, the state. For all the political rhetoric, the behaviour of many organisations shows that they do not believe that investing in people's human capital is essential to their performance (Keep *et al.* 2003).

Of course, education is not only about economic performance. If we turn to the social benefits of learning, there is a mass of anecdotal evidence about how learning can transform lives; the problem is to translate this into systematic understanding of the processes by which it occurs. In the UK, for example, Adult Learners' Week is an annual promotional event, now copied throughout the world, which celebrates the achievements of individuals who have broken out of often very difficult circumstances by means of education. Numerous small-scale studies address the benefits of particular forms of learning, for instance in relation to health or personal well-being (see for example West 1996; McGivney 2002). Such qualitative accounts – systematic or anecdotal – are important, for they can bring illumination and personal testimony. However, they are generally limited not only in scale but also in the conception of the outcomes they explore. At the other end of the scale, large datasets, containing hundreds of pieces of information on thousands of people, regularly reveal associations between levels of education and most dimensions of social prosperity: more educated people live longer, in healthier environments, hand on more physical and cultural capital to their children, and so on (McMahon 1999; Ferri et al. 2003). Statistical correlations of this kind provide an important indication of how learning is related to changes in different aspects of people's lives, but the mechanisms by which this occurs are not as directly evident as might be supposed and the analytical tools for identifying them are not sufficiently developed to provide a rounded account. Moreover, there are problems with causality in this level of work: is it education which leads to better health, or do healthier people find it easier to engage in education?

The challenge is to bring together these different kinds of evidence, in order to be able to estimate the effects of learning within a broader and coherent framework. The purpose of this book is to take a step forward along the path towards a clearer understanding of how learning affects people's lives, especially in the positive sense of generating individual and collective benefits. Our aim is to do this through the following complementary approaches:

- presenting results from in-depth interviews with 145 individuals of all ages beyond 16, exploring what learning has meant to them, and from 12 group interviews with tutors and facilitators;
- matching these findings to data from large-scale datasets containing information going back over nearly five decades;
- presenting some tools for analysis which we hope will be taken up, refined and used in further research by others as well as ourselves.

The focus of much educational research, especially in relation to adults, has been on what might be called the input and process aspects, to the neglect of outcomes other than examinations passed or qualifications gained. Far more attention has been paid to why people do or do not participate in learning, and to what happens in the classroom or other setting, than to what happens as a result of that learning. We set out here to redress this.

The natural assumption in many quarters is that the outcomes of participation are not only positive but are also more or less self-evident. If this is the case, the most important thing is to get more people into education, and to improve the quality of the education through curricular or pedagogical reform and through more resources. The expectation is that this will solve a good part of our problems, individually and societally. However, the original assumption is very rarely examined: what actually happens as a result of all these educational efforts, and how?

It appears remarkably hard for those involved in education – as providers, policy-makers or researchers – to sustain a focus on the outcomes of learning, and it is worth reflecting briefly on why this should be the case. There is a mixture of political and pragmatic reasons. Those responsible for policy naturally tend to concentrate on participation rates because these have an immediate salience. Their apparent significance can be quickly grasped, and a message deduced and broadcast. Targets can be set, and progress monitored and reported. The number of students is the most obvious single indicator of educational growth, so progress is most easily presented in terms of student enrolments, regardless of the quality of the student experience or what actually happens to the students as a result. This is not a cynical comment but a reflection of political life and, if properly constructed and managed (a significant qualification), numerical targets are a healthy means of political accountability. However, adult educators as well as politicians tend to take it for granted that participation is what counts, since adult education is self-evidently a good thing. Their livelihoods, or at least their standing and morale, depend on buoyant demand. For those in or near the classroom, their experience repeatedly brings them evidence of personal development and transformation. So practitioners also naturally tend to maintain a focus on participation, without necessarily feeling a need to look for patterns of positive or negative outcomes or to give a public account of the way education translates into change.

There are also more pragmatic and technical reasons for concentrating on participation. Estimating and analysing participation is far easier than assessing the effects of learning. At a rather basic level, its meaning is generally (though not always) clear. People are enrolled or not enrolled, whereas what counts as a beneficial outcome from learning is much harder to specify and measure. More importantly, the core data on participation are routinely collected, at least for the more formal types of education. Institutions compile enrolment figures, and reporting them is now fairly routine, if often burdensome. The availability of these kind of data naturally skews the balance of analysis towards participation rather than outcomes.

Participation in itself raises few problems of causality, other than in respect of motivation. There is a constant search for ways of improving motivation, to find the triggers which will enhance people's willingness to engage in learning and to remove the barriers which prevent or impede it. However, a focus on participation entails none of the complexities that we encounter when we try to trace out what may or may not happen as a result. It is not only a question of reverse causality (for example, that being in good health enables participation rather than resulting from it); far more difficult is disentangling the sets of inter-actions between all the different factors which shape both the decision to take part and the outcomes that result.

Finally, researchers who do wish to go into greater depth have easier access to current than to past students. Tracing the latter is difficult and expensive, and there is therefore a natural tendency to collect information on people who are studying now rather than on those who took part some time ago. Current students can of course report on benefits or effects which they have already experienced, but can only predict what further effects might ensue. They cannot tell us about effects that only emerged after the course had finished, or only became clear to them in retrospect. The effects may be quite long delayed. This is one reason why both biographical approaches (Alheit and Dausien 2001) and analyses of longitudinal data (Bynner *et al.* 2003) are so important, exploring in their different ways changes in individual lives over a considerable period of time – especially when both approaches are brought together in the same framework.

None of this is to devalue the work done on participation, which continues to demonstrate the divides that exist in our populations (Sargant *et al.* 1997, Sargant and Aldridge 2003), and nor is it to ignore individual studies done of groups of students, such as female returners (Cox and Pascall 1994). It is simply a reminder of the way our understanding is weighted towards the input rather than the outcome end of the process. Our research sets out to sketch a range of different kinds of benefit, tracing both direct and indirect effects of formal and informal learning, and capturing some of the dynamic interactions between the economic and the social.

Background and definitions

Having already used 'education' and 'learning' almost interchangeably, we need quickly to establish the boundaries of the work by offering some background to the study and definitions of the concepts used. This has political as well as ana-lytical significance. The Research Centre on the Wider Benefits of Learning (WBL) was set up in 1999 in the first term of a new Labour government, as the first of a series of research centres to be funded directly by the Department for Education and Employment (as it was then known – now the Department for Education and Skills). The Centre's brief was as follows:

1   to produce and apply methods for measuring and analysing the contribution that learning makes to wider goals including (but not limited to) social cohesion, active citizenship, active ageing and improved health;
2   to devise and apply improved methods for measuring the value and contri-bution of forms of learning including (but not limited to) community-based

adult learning where the outcomes are not necessarily standard ones such as qualifications;

3   to develop an overall framework to evaluate the impact of the lifelong learning strategy being put in place to 2002 and beyond to realise the vision set out in the former DfEE's 1998 Green Paper 'The Learning Age', covering both economic and non-economic outcomes.

The political significance of this initiative had several aspects. First, the WBL Centre was the first educational research centre to be funded directly by the Department, reflecting the position of education as the government's top manifesto priority in 1997. Second, this was part of a wider governmental commitment to basing policy on research evidence, in education and other fields. This was not quite the technocratic celebration of the 1960s Labour government, but it nevertheless signalled an intention to give policy-making a sounder technical and empirical basis. In other words, alongside the commitment to education came a desire to raise the level of rationality involved in policy, basing it to a greater extent than previously on empirical evidence gathered and analysed within explicit conceptual frameworks. Third, the Centre's title and remit demonstrated that whilst the role of education in promoting economic performance was declared to be central to the prosperity of the country in a global economy, alongside this sat the wider goal of enhancing social well-being and cohesion. The distinction was reflected in the setting up, almost simultaneously, of a Centre on the Economics of Education, whose remit deals firmly with productivity and labour market issues (http://cee.lse.ac.uk/).

Against this background, our analyses deal with 'wider benefits' in two rather different senses:

1   *non-economic benefits*, i.e. those that are not measured directly in terms of additional income or increased productivity;
2   *benefits above the level of the individual*, i.e. from family/household through community to the wider society, as well as those accruing to individuals.

In both cases, there are boundary issues. How do we mark off the economic from the non-economic, and to what extent are community level effects simply the aggregate of individual effects? Most obviously, many of the relationships which we explore between learning and other spheres are strongly mediated by income and employment, and benefits to the community often feed through the benefits to individuals. However, our starting points are as defined above.

We need here to address two closely interrelated questions. First, 'benefit' is an inherently value-laden term. What appears to one person as an unambiguously positive outcome may be rather more dubious to others. In some cases there will be near universal agreement, for instance if learning can be shown to lead directly to improvement in physical health, but in other cases there is genuine room for divergence of opinion. If education is shown to be associated with a diminution in respect for authority, is this a good or a bad thing? The answer will depend partly on the interpreter's view of the extent to which such respect is positive because it signals a degree of social order, or negative because it denotes unhealthy deference. This is largely a matter of degree: total disrespect tends to chaos, its converse approaches totalitarianism. Where the ideal point on the spectrum is to be found is very much a matter of judgement.

Second, it would be foolish, and counter-productive in the longer term, for educational enthusiasts to deny that learning can lead to mixed or negative outcomes, for the learner or for the wider social unit. Learning is a risky business. Individuals can lose their identities or their friends as a result of changes brought about by participation in learning. A clear example of the ambivalences involved is the potential impact on family life, where one family member's personal development may come at the expense of pain or loss on the part of others. There are poignant accounts of adult learning being accompanied by marital discord or even breakdown (remembering that the causal relationship between the two is often complex, so that incipient or prospective breakdown may have been the trigger for more than the result of one partner's participation in education).

Any overall evaluation of such events inevitably involves both personal judgements, on the quality of the specific relationship or at a more general level on the institution of marriage, and some kind of weighing-up of the differential impact on different parties. In Willie Russell's play/film *Educating Rita*, is Rita's climbing of the Open University ladder, from working-class routine to a more educated but unpredictable new life, an overall good? Most of us would say yes, but there are downsides, and not only in the eyes of the husband left marooned in his traditional milieu; communities too pay the price of the modernisation and social mobility to which education adds such impetus. This, broadly, is the kind of issue which contemporary discussions of a 'risk society' deal in (Beck 1992); education can act as a kind of ballast or insurance, offering people a better chance of security in a changing world or rescuing them from difficulties; but it can also dispel certainties and accentuate feelings of insecurity. In short, analysis of the kind we engage in entails value judgements; needs to recognise that there may be costs and trade-offs involved; and may on occasion reach the conclusion that the overall balance sheet is negative.

More difficult to discern, but equally significant, are the ways in which the gains achieved by some individuals or groups directly or indirectly disadvantage others. Education can serve to reinforce inequalities of power and social stratification, without those involved being aware of it. Even where an expansion of opportunity is designed to redress inequality, the result may be perverse. There is mounting evidence that the recent expansion of higher education in the UK has benefited underachieving middle-class children more than those from poorer backgrounds (Galindo-Rueda and Vignoles 2003). In short, at both the individual and the societal levels, education has very mixed outcomes which need careful unpacking and that also bring to the surface normative issues of quite fundamental kinds.

Our focus was primarily on the positive aspects, but we consciously allowed for the possibility that learning is a risky business and our evidence confirms this. The book is not a paean of praise for learning and the benefits it brings. We have tried to bring out the complexities and ambivalence of the effects of most learning experiences. We encouraged our respondents to take a broad view in what they told us, and not to concentrate only on benefits. That said, the research undeniably focused more on positive outcomes, which has two implications. First, although there are many general lessons to be learnt from our evidence, we do not claim that the experiences which we analyse are representative across the population. The aim is to investigate the complex links between education and changes in individual and social lives within a lifecourse perspective. The fieldwork respondents were all involved in education, though in very different ways, and we do not include in the sample interviewed people who had no such recent involvement. Although the stories cover education experienced throughout the lifecourse, including schooling and subsequent education, and although they are far from uniformly positive, they are not representative. They are more comprehensive at the positive than the negative end of the spectrum of possible outcomes.

The second point is rather different, and concerns theory rather than methodology. The frameworks we employ are broad in their application, but we do not take as our point of departure consideration of the overall role of education in modern society, for example in relation to social stratification or the reproduction of power (Halsey *et al.* 1997; Karabel and Halsey 1977). We make certain assumptions, for instance that increased civic engagement is broadly a good thing, without engaging in a fundamental debate over whether voluntary activity is a substitute for public services and social capital a smokescreen for reduced state expenditure. On the other hand, we do work outwards from our evidence to identify critical issues and themes, so that these wider features of social scientific discourse are not ignored, and we use our evidence to illuminate the tensions and contradictions which characterise educational policy and practice. We discuss this in more detail in the next chapter when we come to explain the triangular framework developed for the fieldwork.

Two further boundary issues concern the definition of learning. Our primary concern is with learning that takes place after completion of compulsory schooling or, more loosely, the completion of initial education. However, schooling is a major influence on both subsequent learning and the other domains, so the first spell of education cannot be excluded. Our biographical approach allows the full range of effects to be taken into account. It shows, amongst other things, how long-lasting the effects of initial schooling can be on people's motivation for learning.

Second, we are concerned with 'learning' and not only 'education' or 'education and training'. We therefore go beyond learning which takes place in formal institutions or as organised training. In order to promote comparability with other research we adopted the definitions used in the National Adult Learning

Surveys, studies initiated in 1997, which are now building a solid evidence base for changes over time in the patterns of learning in the UK. The definitions are as follows:

Taught learning:

- Any taught courses leading to a qualification, whether or not the qualification was obtained
- Any taught course designed to help develop skills which might be used in a job
- Any course, instruction or tuition in driving, playing a musical instrument, in an art or craft, in a sport or in any practical skill
- Evening classes
- Learning which involves working alone from a package of materials provided by an employer, college, commercial organisation or other training provider
- Any other taught course, instruction or tuition.

Non-taught learning:

- Studying for a qualification without taking part in a taught course
- Supervised training while actually doing a job (i.e. when a manager or experienced colleague has spent time helping a person learn or develop skills as specific tasks are done at work)
- Time spent keeping up to date with developments in the type of work done without taking part in a taught course
- Deliberately trying to improve knowledge about anything or teach oneself a skill without taking part in a taught course.

This taxonomy has its flaws, for example in the way it reinforces a distinction between the formal and informal ways people learn. However, it is reasonably functional, and it made sense for us to build on work of this kind already done. We therefore used the NALS categories as a checklist for ourselves and our respondents to define the activities in which we were interested. The central feature of the typology is that it includes only learning that is intentional, and excludes the accidental.

Conclusion and outline

What we have aimed to do throughout the book, without spending too much time on methodological issues, is to make explicit our approach to analysing different types of data, and to bringing them together to build a multi-dimensional picture. The general issue of the benefits of learning, and especially the focus on causality, make a multi-dimensional approach especially important. In some cases our analysis is based on the application of established tools and techniques. In other areas we have been more exploratory or experimental, and we have felt it useful to make this explicit so that future research can draw on and improve our approach. It is a little like traditional mathematics exercises where students are required to 'show your working' in addition to the final answer, except that here we rarely claim to have produced a right answer in the mathematical sense. We are part of a process of technical and conceptual evolution, with a particular stress on the integration of quantitative and qualitative evidence.

The next chapter lays out our approach in more detail. We first discuss the conceptual framework developed specifically for this study, a triangle which relates three types of capital. We give details of the way fieldwork was carried out. We then present a matrix which distinguishes between the transformative and sustaining effects of learning. We intend these as contributions to debates on how the effects of education should be conceptualised and investigated, and the triangle and matrix are as much an output of the research as the empirical results that follow.

Part B (Chapters 3–8) presents the results of the fieldwork, divided into the three strands on which we concentrate: health, family life and social capital. In each case we begin with an overall discussion of the theme, locating it in the wider literature. The extent of this discussion varies; the theoretical debate on social capital is less mature and more in flux than on the other themes, so we devote more space to it. We then analyse the information yielded by the full set of interviews, to identify key thematic issues. The second chapter in each set presents a small number of individual case studies, allowing us to go into depth. The individuals are contextualised as far as possible, to give an idea of how representative they are compared with the population as a whole. The cohort data available to us includes only people up to age 42, and some of our respondents are considerably younger or older, so there are limits on this contextualisation. We attach to each case study a diagram which gives a pictorial summary of the effects of learning, adding a further dimension to the presentation of results. As with the triangle and the matrix, we offer this diagrammatic approach as a potential additional tool for researchers engaging in similar investigations in future.

In Part C, Chapter 9 presents relevant results from quantitative analysis and shows how these link to our fieldwork results. This underlines the complementarity of quantitative and qualitative analysis, and outlines the ways in which the interaction between different types of evidence is crucial for a deeper level of understanding. The final chapter revisits the principal themes and draws together the main conclusions of the work; it also raises some further theoretical considerations, and offers some pointers for future work and policy implications.

We have opted to attribute single or variously joint authorships to each chapter. However, the effort has been a thoroughly collective one, with each member of the team reading and commenting on repeated drafts. We have learnt much from each other in the process.

Chapter 2

Three capitals

A framework

Tom Schuller

Our concern is with the outcomes of learning, measured not in terms of examinations passed or qualifications gained, but in relation to areas such as health, family life and social capital. Because this is a relatively new area for theoretical and empirical analysis, we started by developing our own approach to investigating these. In this chapter I lay out the conceptual framework which we fashioned for the fieldwork. This takes the form of a triangle, with three key concepts, each specified as a different form of capital, at the corners. I discuss each of these capitals – human, social and identity – in turn, first in general terms and then in their application to our concern with the benefits of learning. I then reflect on the use of the triangle as a means of coming to grips with the complexities and interactions of the issues. The aim is not to set out to provide a comprehensive account or critique of the literatures involved, but to deploy the concepts collectively as a way of capturing the multiple processes involved in an analysis of learning outcomes.

The framework

The triangle includes a number of items which are the benefits of learning, directly or indirectly, and this is the kernel of the whole book (see Figure 2.1). The simplest way to address our analysis is therefore to think of learning as a process whereby people build up – consciously or not – their assets in the shape of human, social or identity capital, and then benefit from the returns on the investment in the shape of better health, stronger social networks, enhanced family life, and so on. However, we have at the outset to make things a little more complex, for these outcomes themselves feed back to or even constitute the capitals. They enable the capital to grow, and to be mobilised. So the items listed inside the triangle can be seen also as 'capabilities', in the immensely creative sense that Amartya Sen uses the term in his analysis of poverty (Sen 1992, 1999). Capabilities represent the freedom to achieve: the combination of functionings which range from basic health to complex activities or states such as being able to take part in the life of the community. The absence of these

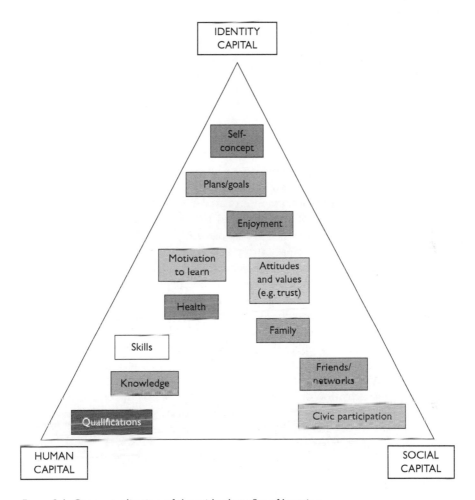

Figure 2.1 Conceptualisation of the wider benefits of learning.

capabilities deprives a person of the opportunity to accumulate the assets from which the benefits in turn flow (see also Chapter 9).

Laying out a model of this kind enables us to pursue two types of analysis. One is to specify a certain number of outcomes, and to trace the pathways which lead from various forms of learning to these various types of outcome. We do this primarily in relation to health, family lives and social capital, though the triangle includes a slightly larger range of outcomes. These pathways may be simple and direct; for example, a particular learning episode may lead directly and visibly to a change in behaviour, as when someone stops smoking as a result of a course on personal health. They are more likely to be multiple and complex, with a learning episode combining with other factors to lead to several different outcomes. Exploring these sequences is important if we are to avoid simplistic conclusions, or solutions which suggest that a single dose of education, or an additional qualification, will resolve personal or social problems. It is even more important if we take seriously the notion of lifelong learning as an integral part of people's lives, as distinct from an occasional added activity. Even in relation to children and education as an initial phase of life, it is hard to disentangle the effects of education from those of family background or local context. The further along the lifecourse people are the more their previous life experience comes into play, and learning forms part of complex patterns of cause and effect with a host of different factors interacting over time.

Second, then, the model allows us to investigate the interactions between the different outcomes. For example, we can make some assessment of how self-esteem and civic participation are interrelated as joint outcomes. Someone may take part in a course completely unrelated to the civic sphere, but through it gain sufficiently in self-confidence to take part in a local tenants' group. People's health will influence their capacity to take advantage of educational opportunity and their capacity to participate in civic life; conversely, their health will be influenced by their educational level, and by their involvement with other people in social or civic networks. The arrows of causality can point in any direction, at least hypothetically. Almost any permutation of two or more areas is a meaningful relationship to explore. We explore these at one level by drawing on large-scale longitudinal datasets (see Chapter 9). However, the interactions are so complex that we are unlikely to aspire to bring them all into a single equation with numerical values assigned to each interrelationship. Qualitative investigation of dyadic and multiple relationships is needed to illuminate the interactions between the different spheres of people's lives. Moreover, we need to do this diachronically, over time, as well as synchronically, capturing the interactions at any given point.

Human capital

I begin with the most familiar of the concepts, human capital. Human capital refers to the knowledge and skills possessed by individuals, which enable them to function effectively in economic and social life. Its origins as a concept go back to Adam Smith and beyond, but contemporary work is generally traced back to the work of American economists in the early 1960s (Schultz 1961; Becker 1964). The key insight in human capital theory was that investment in education produces returns, in more or less the same way as investment in physical capital does. The theory is used to explain variations at different levels: mainly between individuals with different levels of qualification, but also between countries with different stocks of human capital (see, for example, Lynch 2002). Coming from the economics stable the main focus of human capital analysis has been on earnings at the individual level, or on productivity or economic growth at the macro level, but it has also been used with a much broader focus, notably in relation to health (see Grossman and Kaestner 1997; Gilleskie and Harrison 1998).

One initial critique of human capital theory came from educationalists who reacted strongly against the economistic character of the theory and its perceived implications for educational policy and practice. The critique reflected the highly charged ideological climate of the 1960s and 1970s. It remains a salient strand in the debate, but the criticisms today concentrate less on the concept itself, which is broadly accepted as generating fruitful lines of enquiry and significant results, and more on its application to policy analysis. The debate over the way learning policies are dominated by an economic agenda is a live one, but no one challenges the relevance of human capital as a concept. Yet despite its acceptance into the orthodoxy of analytical thinking, human capital continues to exhibit weaknesses, some of which are highly germane to our theme.

In the first place, although the definition of human capital is generally accepted, the validity of what is used to measure it is still problematic (see OECD 1998). International comparisons tend to use duration of education – the number of years spent in school – since chronological time appears standard across countries, whereas qualification levels continue to pose problems of comparability. Within countries the comparability problem does not arise in the same form but persists nonetheless in at least three respects. First, qualification structures change over time as countries reshape their education systems.[1] In the UK, successive waves of change, many of them bringing with them new qualifications, have accentuated the difficulty of capturing changes in human capital stocks over time (to say nothing of the confusion caused in public and employers' minds). The volume of change is a source of considerable political concern, notably in the difficulty that employers, parents and indeed students themselves have in understanding the meaning of the vast range of qualifications on offer. Second, there are long-running debates about standards, and whether the same level of achievement is required in order to acquire a given qualification; this is an annual issue when A level results are published showing rising numbers of young people attaining this level. Third, changes in relative levels of human capital within a given population alter the significance attached to different types and levels of qualification. Getting a university degree today, when over one-third of the youth cohort go to university, is obviously very different from reaching the same level when only one in twenty went. Both the relative advantage of having a degree and the relative disadvantage of not having one will change, but in very different ways. The distributional issue is a major one in many respects, but is often ignored (see Green et al. 2003).

The capacity of human capital analysis has increased enormously over recent decades, with the accumulation of massive datasets and the development of sophisticated analytical techniques. Technological developments allow us to quantify and analyse information in ways which scholars even one generation ago could never have envisaged. Nationally and internationally, we can sort populations according to any number of social characteristics. Nevertheless, two questions remain. The first is the elementary one of validity: to what extent do the measures capture the actual qualities in humans which enable them to increase their productivity, enhance their labour market prospects or improve their performance in broader domains such as parenting? Everyone would accept, although to very varying degrees, that qualifications are only one measure of competence and knowledge (OECD 2000). Other factors, for example dispositional attributes such as willingness to act as a team player or contextual factors such as the level of investment in workplace technology or neighbourhood quality, intervene substantially to constrain or enhance the effects of human capital growth (see, for example, White and Hill 2003).[2]

The second issue is that of establishing clear causal relationships between investment in human capital, and outcomes. Multiple associations exist, at all levels of analysis, between qualification levels and a range of variables, including most of those in which we are interested in this study: that is not only income, but also health, well-being, criminal activity and so on. However, moving from association or correlation to cause and effect is often a giant leap, involving large assumptions. The following comes from the most sophisticated general analysis yet of the social effects of education:

> Education might generate benefits in three ways: by changing individuals' preferences, by changing the constraints individuals face, or by augmenting the knowledge of information on which individuals base their behavior. *Ascertaining the causal impact of education, as opposed to associations of education with various outcomes, is extremely difficult* because education is a process in which there are many inputs, some of which reflect choices of individuals, families and communities. These choices are made in the presence of important factors that are not observed by analysts in most data sets used to analyze the effects of education.
>
> (Berhman *et al.* 1997: 3, our emphasis)

In other words (and the authors are more wedded to rational choice vocabulary than we are), you can show over and over again that education is associated in some way or other with a whole range of other aspects of human life, but these associations will tell you little about what actually causes what; and the process of causation is unlikely to be of a neat, linear, A-leads-to-B kind. We have more to say on this later on, in Chapter 9, when we discuss the integration of quantitative and qualitative evidence but also present individual case histories.

Social capital

Social capital is much more of a newcomer on the scene, though like human capital its origins can be traced back to classic texts of political economy and sociology (Woolcock 1998; Schuller et al. 2000). However, over the last decade its presence in social scientific discourse has mushroomed, with exponential growth in application. It is less closely tied to education, but our discussion here is for obvious reasons phrased in that context.

Social capital is most generally taken to refer to the networks and norms which enable people to contribute effectively to common goals (Putnam 2000). Unlike human capital, it is not (or not only) a personal attribute or asset, but refers to the relationships that exist between individuals or groups of individuals. It is most commonly operationalised by reference to attitudinal measures, for example of expressed trust, or to behavioural ones, such as levels of participation in civic activities. It is the latter set which is more central to our use of the concept, so we are exploring what the mechanisms are that underpin the association between levels of education and participation in most forms of civic activity, but we are also interested in the way learning affects the extent to which people show tolerance and other characteristics which bind society together.

In spite of its massive growth in popularity amongst social scientists and, to a lesser extent, politicians, social capital is less securely established than human capital as a concept with a proven track record of analytical applicability (Baron et al. 2000). It is notable, however, that one of its earliest substantial empirical applications was in the field of education. James Coleman used the concept to explore why, in some cases, school students from poorer backgrounds out-performed better-off peers (Coleman 1988); he attributed it to close and mutually supportive relationships between school, home and church, with parents knowing each other and sharing values in such a way that the young people had a consistent educationally positive message from the different influential forces around them. Whether or not Coleman's results are accepted, they formed a striking use of the concept and helped to propel it into social scientific discourse.

Arguably, the trajectory of critiques of social capital resemble those of human capital in some interesting but contrasting ways. Ideologically its proponents have been attacked for providing a smokescreen for authoritarian notions of communitarianism, in the sense that they are taken to subscribe to a unitary view of society which ignores issues of power and conflict. Normative positions are, it is argued, disguised behind well-meaning but superficial notions of community and cohesion (Blaxter and Hughes 2000). This is the mirror image of the early critiques of human capital for its economistic bias, and for smuggling in assumptions about the goals of education which do not command universal support. Social capital is also accused of being a Trojan horse for neo-classical economics (Fine 2001), though ironically most pure neo-classicists reject it as a term on the basis that it does not conform to their understanding of 'capital' (Arrow 2000).

Pierre Bourdieu's discussion of social capital (Bourdieu 1986) is rooted more directly than Putnam's in issues of social class and the reproduction of power relations, but deals less with broader social domains such as civic participation. Bourdieu is better known for his use of cultural capital to explore how cultural practices explain the reproduction of social relations between classes (Bourdieu and Passeron 1977). One strand of the debate over social capital suggests that the concept is simply superfluous, since cultural capital captures most of its components but has the added merit of including issues of social class and social conflict into the analysis. However, in Chapters 7 and 8 we have drawn extensively on Bourdieu's theorising to explore issues of power and social stratification, whilst retaining the broader concerns with civic participation represented in the political science school of social capital.

Measurement is an issue in relation to social capital, as it is for human capital but with a different complexion. Here the issue is not just one of validity, but of definition. Social capital is used far more variably than human capital – so variably indeed that its critics say that it cannot be reasonably regarded as a coherent concept (Portes 1998). It is used to refer to individual expressions of attitude or value, for instance in cross-national studies such as the World Values Survey; to refer to behaviour, such as levels of civic participation – itself a term of some dispute, as it is operationalised in very different ways; or more broadly to apply to the quality of relationships between individuals or social units. One important aspect is the problem of aggregation: is it possible to use measures which operate at the individual level, such as expressed levels of trust, and aggregate them into a measure of social capital which is taken to apply to a neighbourhood, region or nation?

A final relevant problem is that of circularity. Is social capital a means to achieving a better (i.e. more prosperous, healthy or happy) society, or is it in effect a characterisation of that society? Often it appears to be used both as a means and an end, preventing good analytical purchase. For some, the uncertainty this implies is enough to suggest that social capital should be abandoned, at least on the analytical front, in favour of other more focused tools.

For all these difficulties, social capital has already shown great potential for generating new insights in debates which have sometimes become constricted and over-elaborate. It is worth noting that the OECD, probably the foremost proponent of the human capital orthodoxy in its role as promoter of economic prosperity, has recently embraced social capital as a crucial complement to human capital (OECD 2001), and the World Bank's use of it to underpin its approach to poverty and development has generated enormous interest (Dasgupta and Serageldin 2000). However, in a more academic context, with less international bureaucratic baggage, there is great heuristic value in testing out its application. There is a curious complex of factors to be handled. We need to avoid the decontextualised approach, which sees education as a wholly individualised activity and its outcomes as the responsibility either of the learner or of the provider of the learning (teacher, community or institution), whilst ignoring the social relationships within which any learning takes place. We cannot treat education as a kind of policy portmanteau into which all kinds of social issues are shovelled in the hope that they will be sorted out eventually, and we cannot wait for factors to be held constant whilst we perfect instruments of analysis or aspire to unanimity on the values that should characterise our societies.

Before we turn to the third point of the triangle, we can sum up by relating this discussion to points made in the preceding chapter. First, we need to bear in mind the breadth of the field that we are addressing – both the range of experiences that the notion of learning embraces, and the range of outcomes which can flow from those experiences, more or less directly. Precision is important, but there will always be trade-offs between precision and scope. Second, we have argued that the topic of learning benefits is highly underdeveloped. In such an immature field, it seems to us particularly appropriate to deploy a range of conceptual tools rather than rely on a single instrument. Third, we perceive there to be real value in exploring the interrelationships between different but overlapping concepts, in order to capture the dynamics of the processes involved in learning.

Identity capital

Identity capital is an even newer kid on the conceptual block. If human capital comes from the economics stable and social capital from the socio-political, identity capital draws primarily on the discipline of social psychology. The term was coined by James Côté, after reviewing and synthesising a wide range of research in an effort to analyse experience in late modern societies (see Côté 1997; Côté and Levene 2002). Côté's particular focus is on the changing patterns of transition from youth to adulthood, and what resources young people are able to draw on in managing that transition, but the concept can be applied far more widely, across the full lifespan.

The problematic nature of identity and its maintenance has of course a very long philosophical tradition (see, for example, Parfit 1984) and a slightly shorter but still very dense sociological context (Castells 1997). Next to family and occupation, education has a leading role in people's understanding of and confidence in their own identity (see, for example, De Ruyter and Conroy 2002). Obviously, in forming, maintaining or modifying identity an individual is located within a wider social context. This poses particular challenges when globalising forces operate strongly, and local or national institutions are weakened. Education can play a part in enabling individuals to sustain their individual identity within this local or national identity (see Antikainen and Harinen 2002 for an example from Finland).

Côté and Levene argue that concepts such as human and cultural capital are useful for understanding mobility and reproduction but insufficient to understand the multi-dimensional nature of transitions, when education and labour market institutions are poorly regulated and status differentiations persist on the basis of age, class, gender and race. Thus, they say:

we have seen the need for a concept representing a different type of capital associated with identity formation, namely, the varied resources deployable on an individual basis that represent how people most effectively define themselves and have others define them, in various contexts.

(Côté and Levene 2002: 142)

In their definition, identity capital refers to two types of assets:

1 tangible assets, which are socially visible. They include such things as qualifications, and memberships of networks;
2 intangible assets, which include ego strengths such as internal locus of control, self-esteem, sense of purpose in life, ability to self-actualize, and critical thinking abilities. These ego strengths give people the capacity to understand ('ego synthetic' abilities) and negotiate ('ego executive' abilities) the various social, occupational, and personal obstacles and opportunities that they are likely to encounter throughout late modern life. There is both a subjective/experiential and behavioural component.

(Côté and Levene 2002: 144)

We use identity capital in a more restricted sense than its originators, to refer only to their category of intangible assets. Côté and Levene make an understandable but ultimately unconvincing case for identity capital to be the grand concept under which other capitals are to be subsumed. We recognise the potential value of the concept, which is why we adopt it, but find it more fruitful to set it alongside other capitals without assigning overall primacy to any. The key advantage of this is that it allows us free play to look at the interaction between capitals, without predetermination of which is most significant as an asset or influential in determining outcomes.

Identity capital, then, refers to the characteristics of the individual that define his or her outlook and self-image. Our usage of it includes specific personality characteristics such as ego strength, self-esteem, or internal locus of control, but recognises that many of its components are socially shaped and not inherent personality traits. These characteristics, as we shall see, are vital factors at almost every stage of the learning process. They are major determinants of motivation, and whether or not people choose to engage in learning; they affect their performance in the classroom or other setting; and – crucially for us – they are also an outcome of learning. We deal particularly in later chapters with the interrelationship between learning and self-confidence, which pervades almost every area. The fact that identity capital is involved at all these stages makes it immediately similar to the other capitals: it is impossible to define universally whether we are dealing with a dependent or independent variable. In other words, it is both input and output, cause and effect. The measurement issues identified in relation to human and social capital – the validity of the indicators used, the danger of over-precision in the application of quantitative techniques and the problem of circularity – apply also to identity capital.

Identity capital as defined above raises one final point; whilst this too applies to the others, it has a rather different sense. There may be an assumption of 'the more the better' in respect of all three capitals. The more skills and qualifications, the more networks and social contact one has, the better one is placed as an individual. At the collective level, the more highly qualified a society is, and the more closely bound by social ties and common norms, the better – or so it might be thought. However, the inclusion of this third pole prompts an intriguing question: can one have too much capital – in this case, too strong a sense of identity (or ego) or too much self-confidence – for one's own good and in relation to others? We cannot answer this kind of question directly, but only by placing it in the context of individual cases on the one hand, and the interaction between the different capitals on the other.

Triangular relationships

As suggested above, one simple but reasonable way of looking at the triangle is to think directly in disciplinary terms. Identity capital represents the psychological pole, human capital the economic pole and social capital the political pole, each with a 'socio-' tag prefixed. Most learning experiences and outcomes can be interpreted in terms of an interplay between these three. Some will be clearly primarily economic, for example where a person undertakes vocational training with an expectation of income gain or career advancement, or primarily personal, as with a course in meditation techniques. However, there are few instances where only one of the three poles comes into play. Almost always it will be more convincing to map things against a dimension running between two poles – for instance the socio-economic as the training helps people expand their social networks, or the socio-psychological where the meditation gives them the confidence to participate more in community life. Usually it will also be more fruitful and realistic to bring in the third dimension as well, if that can be managed.

The triangle is designed to recognise the fact that these three dimensions intersect, and that many of the outcomes are a combination of two or all three of the polar concepts. Into this triangle we have placed, for the purposes of this study, a number of outcomes in which we are interested. We have given them a physical location in the triangle, though this is rarely fixed in the respective distances it represents from the different poles, or in their relation to each other. The imagery must not be taken too literally. Thus health (physical or mental) is the product of the skills individuals are able to deploy, of the sets of relationships in which they are involved and of their personal outlook on life and view of themselves; and all these factors interact. This will vary from case to case, and we have aimed in the diagram only to give an approximate modal position, where one might most commonly expect an individual set of circumstances to be found. For each outcome specified in the triangle it would be possible to locate it slightly differently than we have done, for instance closer to the identity capital apex. The function of the physical image is heuristic, to allow different possibilities to emerge.

Obviously the model is a simplification, in at least three senses. First, there are many more items that could be included in the triangle as actual or potential outcomes of learning. One example, which is relevant to our own future programme of research but is not included in the triangle as here presented, is criminal activity (or its obverse, law-abiding behaviour): how learning affects propensities to engage in different forms of illegal behaviour. Another, difficult to capture but emerging strongly from our fieldwork, is the general socialising effect of education: the mere fact of bringing together people from different backgrounds serves to extend our general understanding of each other, whatever the actual content of the education. The model is selective, not comprehensive, in its content. It is designed to serve as a framework within which other issues can be included, depending on the priorities or interests of those using it. We hope that people will be interested in using it, modified as appropriate to their own purposes.

Second, the outcomes have been given quite simple labels, but represent complex and sometimes contentious concepts. We cited crime as an example of an omitted outcome; the notion of what should be counted as criminal activity raises all kinds of hotly debated issues. Even on health, the definitions of various forms of health, or the extent to which one concentrates on one form of health (e.g. physical) more than another (e.g. mental), are not technical matters but are full of social ambiguity and significance. There are those who would argue that it is inappropriate or even dangerous to label depression as a negative state and to assume that alleviating it through education is an unambiguously positive outcome. We accept the overall contention that each concept needs to be critically examined, though we would also argue that at some point broad judgements do need to be made about whether changes in one direction or another are preferable – as in the case of reducing levels of depression.

Third, the model appears static. It presents the areas on which we are concentrating our analysis of the outcomes of learning in this particular programme of research. However, these are not necessarily final outcomes. In some cases, and some contexts, they could be regarded as intermediate outcomes. For example, participation in civic activity may be seen as a good in itself, something which is regarded as a defining feature of a flourishing and healthy society. However, it can also be regarded as a means to a further end, in the sense that civic engagement leads to greater social cohesion. In our view, it does not make sense to attempt to define a single linear sequence with discrete categories of intermediate and final outcomes which hold good in all circumstances. Items can and will be allocated to the intermediate or final category according to the particular focus of interest. Hence the model simplifies in being static as it is presented on the page, but this does not mean that our analysis will be similarly static.

Scope and methodology

The fieldwork

The fieldwork comprised two projects, originally conceived of as distinct: on Learning and Social Cohesion, and on Learning and the Management of Life-course Transitions. A total of 145 interviewees were drawn from three geographical areas chosen for their cultural and demographic diversity: an area of North London, an inner-city region of high ethnic diversity; a semi-rural area of Essex with a mainly white population of below average income; and Nottinghamshire, a county that combines urban and rural, with a spread of socio-economic lifestyles.

Selection of interviewees for both projects was based on purposive sampling, drawing on people involved in a range of different learning contexts, from informal community settings to higher education. The interviewees comprised learners drawn from a variety of contexts, spanning formal and community-based settings and almost the full range of levels. They split roughly 2:1 female: male (see below); covered an age range from 16 to over 70; and were from a variety of ethnic backgrounds. Appendix 1 contains details of the respondents' socio-economic profile.

The decision to use the same areas for both projects was deliberate, since we foresaw that there would be a good deal of overlap. The methodology used – in-depth interviews with a clear topic guide – was common to both, with sections of the interviews common to both projects. The overlap indeed materialised, with data gathered in each that are highly relevant to the other. People interviewed on the social cohesion project had things to say about managing change in response to having children, and those on the transitions project often talked about their participation in civic and voluntary activities, a principal theme of the social cohesion project. More generally, both sets of respondents had things to say about the effects of learning on their psychological health and family lives.

The transitions project was initially designed to focus on the changes in people's lives occasioned by the entry of their children into the formal school system. However, it soon became apparent from our pilot work that the changes involved, and the pathways into work, education or other activity, were too diverse for the notion of a single 'transition' to be sustained. We therefore recast this particular project somewhat more broadly, in terms of adaptation and change. The project involved interviews with parents (mainly mothers) whose youngest child was between five and eight years old (in some cases slightly older). The rationale for this sampling was that they were able to talk about the changes that occurred between childbirth and the stage of their life at which they no longer had a child below school age in the household. Respondents for both projects were identified through a variety of learning contexts, both formal educational institutions and informal initiatives.

The guides we developed contained key topics to be covered, encouraging respondents to range widely over their life stories, beginning with their experience of school. The interviews were recorded, and lasted from 45 minutes to over 2 hours. Of the 145 interviews, 120 were transcribed; we excluded a number of interviews which in our judgement yielded insufficient information to be worth transcribing. We analysed each transcript by focusing initially on the primary outcome fields identified in the triangle set out in Figure 2.1 (see p. 13); and then on other outcomes emerging from the account. Transcripts were read by a second researcher to confirm, supplement or revise the first interpretation. This cross-checking secured a level of reliability, as well as acting as a prompt for deeper interpretation and a safety net to capture information omitted by the first reader.

Quantitative datasets

The evidence from this fieldwork is complemented by evidence from large-scale datasets. These include the 1958 and 1970 British Birth Cohort Studies, known as the National Child Development Study (NCDS) and BSC70 respectively. Both these longitudinal studies have involved following up large-scale samples from birth into adult life, with data collected in NCDS at ages 7, 11, 16, 23, 33 and 42, and in BCS70 at ages 5, 10, 16 and 26. We have drawn particularly on NCDS data relating to changes in the lives of adults between the ages of 33 and 42.

These cohort studies are a remarkable source of information, providing a huge amount of information across a wide range of areas of social and political interest (see, for example, Ferri et al. 2003). Yet there are limits on how much even this level of information and expertise can tell us about the actual pathways that people follow in the various strands of their lives, and the factors which shape these strands. We have been able to place these data alongside our fieldwork results, in order to contextualise them and to complement them, as we show in Part B of this book. In our current work we have been able to develop this relationship further, into full-scale integration of quantitative and qualitative approaches. Results from this are discussed in Chapter 9.

First effects: sustaining and transforming

I turn now to results from the research, giving a general account of different outcomes of learning. As we analysed the narratives of our respondents we naturally looked for substantive outcomes, both behavioural and attitudinal. However, we became aware of how misleading it would be to focus only on the kinds of effect that mark a distinct and discrete change, though these are indeed the clearest indications of educational result. Many respondents reported on the way in which they felt taking part in learning had affected their lives, but without this marking a distinct break in what they did or how they looked at the world. Capturing these effects required an additional component in our ana-lytical toolkit.

We therefore developed a simple matrix, which is represented in Figure 2.2. One dimension represents effects of learning running from those that pertain very much to the *individual* alone, to those that benefit the wider *community*. In many cases learning has both kinds of effect, but for the purposes of this exercise this is a useful distinction. The second dimension distinguishes learning that brings about *transformation* in people's lives from learning that enables indi-viduals and communities to *sustain* what they are doing. The former type of effect is most commonly reported and celebrated, quite reasonably, for example in the accounts of individual achievement gathered during Adult Learners' Week (ALW). However, we point also to a very important conservation effect, where education prevents decay or collapse (at individual or community level) or consolidates a positive state of stability, in addition to those instances where it brings about change of a more or less dramatic kind.

By definition, the sustaining effect is less visible than the transforming. Indeed, the former is from one angle always hypothetical, since it could be understood as referring to the avoidance of a negative development that would otherwise have occurred. A further difficulty is the time lag that is often involved: if education were not available, it would in most (but by no means all) cases be some time before the consequences were really felt. For example, if all adult education services were removed from a given area, we might expect to see increased levels of depression and therefore pressure on mental health ser-vices. However, in such a situation there are likely to be many other variables at work that would affect the outcomes, and the effect might only be a gradual one, so an area level effect might not be very strongly evident.[3]

In spite of the difficulty of the counterfactual we have no problem in includ-ing such benefits, and in attributing them to learning. On the contrary: this

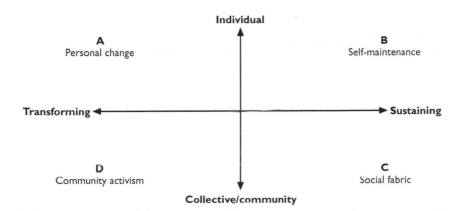

Figure 2.2 Classifying the effects of learning.

sustaining effect is a hugely important benefit of learning, which has gone largely unrecognised – partly because it is not easily visible, but also because of the taken-for-grantedness of learning. Any estimate of the benefits or general effects of learning should at least try to come to grips with the way it acts to sustain and nurture some of the most fundamental aspects of social life. But we would be very unwise to attempt some kind of natural experiment, eliminating learning opportunities in order to see if the world really collapsed.

On the other hand, we cannot simply assume that all education benefits individuals and communities by holding things together in this way – still less that it does so as well as it possibly could. So this line of argument should not be used to justify any and all educational provision, on the grounds that we have to assume there would be negative effects if it were removed or reshaped. There is ineffectual education, as in any service. However, even where there is some effect, a broad approach to estimating outcomes throws up questions about whether the benefits which derive from learning might be achieved more effect-ively by other means – either by organising our education system differently, or by strengthening other social institutions or policies which produce these results. So we need to explore as far as we can the ways in which learning insu-lates, inoculates or buffers us against personal and social threats, but also to include in this exploration the possibility that the kinds of effect pointed to might be achieved more fully through other means.

We turn now to the matrix and briefly discuss each of the four quadrants in turn; the substance is explored in more detail later on. In the top left quadrant (A) come the effects which are familiar from ALW and other accounts (though none the less stirring for their familiarity), where individuals have changed their personal or professional lives by taking part in some form of adult learning. The narrative here generally includes reference to some particular episode or course which led to transformation, and we have several such stories in the following chapters. At its most spectacular an educational light has been switched on and the individual experiences some kind of Damascene conver-sion, but there are many less wholesale transformations where only a part of the person's life is affected. Importantly, the learner may not at the time even realise the significance of the experience, but recognises it only in retrospect. This unrecognised change will be rarer in the case of transformation, which usually implies significant change over a limited period in ways that are subjec-tively acknowledged, than it will be in relation to the sustaining effect.

In the top right quadrant (B) we locate the kinds of effect that contribute to the individual's ability to sustain him- or herself in a reasonable state of well-being or health, physical or mental. We have many instances of individuals reporting to us that without their regular education class they would have lapsed into depression; or that they were already somewhat depressed, as they now realise, but were first stopped from sliding further down and then had their mental health improved (shifting them towards the left in the matrix). However, the reference here is not only to the prevention of ill health but also to the maintenance of positive forms of well-being, where learning enables people to continue to live fulfilling and useful lives. We have much more to say on this below, because it is a type of effect which rarely figures in the literature.

The more such an effect occurs amongst any given population, the more this benefit spans the vertical axis and takes us down into the third quadrant (C), as the sustaining effect on an individual contributes to the sustaining of a community's mental health. If we cannot speak exactly in those terms (i.e. of a community as such having levels of health), since communities are made up of individuals, we can certainly speak of a collective environment that is conducive to sustaining health. And healthy people are more likely to help others maintain good health, by example if nothing more. Sustaining the social fabric goes far beyond straight issues of health, obviously. It can refer, for example, to broad socialisation effects, as members of a community learn to understand each other's values and positions, and to communicate with each other as fellow citizens (embodying the skills and dispositions which Jurgen Habermas refers to as communicative competence (Habermas 1987)).

The fourth quadrant (D) refers to cases where learning has enabled or stimulated social change. This may be through the agency of a single individual, or through collective learning. The action may be focused on a specific issue, such as the improvement of local schooling, or it may be more general. It is the transformation of the collective environment, or features of it, that counts here. Our evidence includes a variety of instances of activism, for example in relation to women's health or to local council issues, where learning prompted or enabled people to come together in order to try to bring about change. We need, though, to bear in mind that the term 'community activist' has connotations that many of those whom we might place in this category for the purposes of this analysis would reject. We are dealing not only with people who think of themselves as activists but also with those who are engaged in bringing about change in a more gradualist, less publicly prominent way.

All the categories identified through this matrix can contain negative effects, though in some cases this is harder to imagine than in others. Thus learning may unhealthily inhibit individuals from change, confirming them in their current unsatisfactory roles as opposed to beneficially enabling them to maintain their stability, or leading to deterioration. It exposes people to risk and stress. Or it may bring about social transformation, but of a kind that is damaging.

Here we need also to distinguish between effects on the learner and effects on others. There are in the broader literature examples of education's modernising role bringing severe costs to traditional communities. First generations of working-class university students have sometimes come into conflict with traditional ties and affiliations in the family and outside, where the values and aspirations associated with this level of education are not appreciated. The friction can be extremely painful on both sides. Similar problems arise in relation to some minority ethnic groups, where the effect of education on the younger generation is to drive a wedge between them and their elders. Because our fieldwork evidence comes only from those engaged in learning and not from their family members or colleagues, there is no way of cross-checking on these kinds of effects (though we shall be doing so in future research); even so, we have some illustrations of how the benefits to a learner can be accompanied by negative effects on others – an externalisation of costs which is not often brought into the equation.

We also reiterate that the whole discussion is saturated with value judgements. Not all outcomes are universally welcome. As noted, we acknowledge that there may be negative outcomes, for some or indeed all of those affected. However, this does not dissolve the question of on what basis we are to judge whether outcomes are beneficial or not. The question can be applied at all levels, from nation to household to individual. When we cite in Chapter 4 a woman who learns to play an active role to improve women's health in her neighbourhood, the 'benefit' can be criticised if one adopts the perspective that such voluntary activity lets the state off the hook – and, in fact, the person in question described in some detail how she had to counter perceptions that she was moving away from her working-class roots by engaging in middle-class 'volunteering'. So almost any outcome – beyond very basic physical health – can be looked at askance. Several of our case studies provide examples of just such ambivalent effects.

The causal relationships implied in this use of the matrix can refer either to specific learning *episodes*, where people describe the effects of a particular course or other learning experience, or more loosely as a function of their overall learning *careers*. The former are the most easily recognisable types of 'effect'. Thus individuals may report how participation enabled them to change their behaviour in particular ways, for instance in the way they relate to their children, or in stopping smoking. The effect may be an intended one, but need not be – for example, where a computing course designed to give IT skills incidentally but importantly improves a parent's interaction with his or her children. This is a direct effect, even though the designers of the course may not have had anything of the kind in mind. A career is by definition extended in time, and therefore very likely to be somewhat more diffuse in its effects. In its more extended forms, indeed, it may be virtually co-terminous with the full lifespan of the individual, so that one is faced with the prospect of attempting to encompass within the analysis all the changes that occur over decades.

All four quadrants are meaningful categories represented in the experiences of our respondents, and we believe could be helpful more generally in classifying the experiences of other learners. Moreover, such a typology enables us to stress, crucially, the sustaining role of education, which we argue is often neglected. However, the poles of the axes are to some extent in artificial opposition, especially when the analysis is applied dynamically. Thus a sustaining effect is rarely if ever a matter of static conservation, as if individuals are enabled to preserve themselves in some kind of learning-generated aspic. As with riding a bicycle, neither people nor relationships can easily stand still. Education can, though, enable the individual or the community to grow and develop. Without some kind of momentum, and therefore change, most personal identities or sets of social relationships cannot flourish or even survive. We acknowledge that distinguishing this from transformation is then a matter of judgement. As so often, it depends on the timescale involved. By and large, transformation entails some kind of relatively sharp break with the past, whereas sustaining suggests continuity and evolution.

Similarly, the effects on individuals will almost always have some kind of wider social effect, however small. If someone stops smoking, the main benefit will be to his or her own health, but it may also help that of family and friends, directly by removing the effects of passive smoking but also by reinforcing a non-smoking norm which makes it easier for others to stop, or never start, so there is a collective gain. It also, in a marginal way, releases resources within the health service (though it may increase pension expenditure because of increased longevity). Likewise, enabling someone to be a more effective parent benefits the children, both directly in day-to-day interactions and because more educated parents generally give their children a better start in life. It also has a social effect. If growing up with book-reading parents is generally beneficial, then the more book-reading parents there are around the stronger the norm will be. Evidently, the gains are not always positive in sum, with everyone gaining; raising parental aspirations for their children's education is likely to be broadly beneficial, but can in a competitive world displace others in the queue for university places or good jobs. At its worst it can turn into a destructively competitive environment where even the winners are harmed.[4] However, the overall point is that the individual/collective dimension, like the sustaining/transforming dimension, cannot be treated definitively as a linear axis along which individual cases can be plotted. This means that both dimensions of the matrix are to be understood as heuristic rather than definitively reporting devices. It prompts us to think about the dynamic interaction between on the one hand continuity and change, and on the other hand individual and collective effects.

Collective agency

Let us explore these arguments in more detail, drawing on the data but without giving individual examples; these figure in the following chapters. First, a major conclusion from our work is that learning plays a vital role in enabling people to carry on their lives in the face of a whole range of competing and often stressful demands, public and private. We have heard many people, especially women, say that taking part in education enabled them to maintain a sense of personal identity whilst bringing up small children. They had previously experienced the feeling of being completely submerged in the demands of the children and of the tasks associated with childcare. Typical comments refer to the physical relief of getting out of the house, the provision of a temporal structure to days and weeks which otherwise risked going past in an undifferentiated blur, and access to adult conversation to punctuate potentially infantilising exchanges with and about their toddlers. All these effects are largely independent of what the parents were actually learning, but nevertheless a function of their participation. The remarks about their previous lives were by no means always negative, but they recognised that beyond a certain point they would start to lose their adult identities, and the social costs of child-rearing would rise. Taking part in some organised learning avoided this, or where it had already started to occur it turned the process round.

In some cases, the effect was to enable people to carry on more or less as before, but with renewed commitment and enjoyment. They would have managed, though the experience of parenting would have been much less positive for them, and consequently their children would probably have gained less. In other cases, there was a stronger sense of rescue. If they had not had the access to learning opportunities, there would have been some qualitative change in their lives, almost certainly for the worse. There was an implicit apprehension in many of the remarks. Neither we nor they can tell what these changes would have been with any degree of confidence, but this was the sense of what they reported. There was little melodrama; none of our respondents seriously reported that they would have collapsed, or abandoned their roles completely. However, there is no doubting the significance of the effect.

Looked at from one angle, the sustaining effect can be seen as the prevention of negative transformation. Education is beneficial because it stops people from experiencing unfortunate changes. This is indeed the case, prosaic as it may seem. But in the first place this casts things in too negative a light; many of our respondents were distinctly positive about their lives, but doubtful whether this would have carried on at the same level. Second, however, this ignores the wider dynamic. Education is not a shield that protects people from experience, but is a means of managing the experience in some more or less purposive fashion. It gives a sense of purpose and direction, even if not necessarily in any conscious or explicit sense, and in so doing converts experiences into something more positive than they would otherwise have been.

The sense of dynamic is crucial to understanding this, as people's outlooks and circumstances change. The sustaining effect of education may be fully *preventative*, so that in the case of parenting the mother or father never actually has significant problems with child-rearing. However, the problems may already be occurring before the parent starts to participate, whether or not this is the actual motivation for participation. Education may have a *restorative* effect, re-establishing equilibrium, or a *curative* effect, if the problems have become somewhat more severe. So there is a rough spectrum, and how an individual case is located along the spectrum often depends on how large a chunk of the lifecourse is brought into focus.

This kind of language smacks too much of medical problem-solving, of education as a kind of vaccine or treatment for individuals, which is all very well – see the very successful *Prescribing Learning* initiative (James 2001) – but needs balancing. This is where the individual–collective axis comes into play. Education empowers people, but not only as solvers of their own problems. Often it gives them a sense of agency which is inseparable from their interaction with others. Evidence from one of the group interviews, with family learning tutors in London, illustrates this well. The group consisted of nine women who worked with mothers from ethnically diverse backgrounds, on a variety of family learning initiatives. The tutors, to be clear, were reporting on their impressions of the benefits to learners; so these were perceptions only, but from a group of experienced tutors who were free to challenge or confirm each other's accounts.

First, learners benefit from understanding that other experience similar problems. In the case of parents, learning that other parents cannot always control their irritation or anger with their children, or do not understand the school curriculum, or have children who engage in antisocial behaviour such as biting, can come as a huge relief, and restore self-confidence. This benefit may accrue even if the individual does not actually contribute but simply listens to others recounting their experiences; but the articulation of problems – simply being able to speak about them to a sympathetic audience, without this necessarily being cast in any therapeutic mould – can be enormously helpful. It is important to note that the effect here is not merely one of resolving a specific problem, pressing though that may be. It is a wider one, of feeling part of a broader community with common challenges and difficulties. Education ropes people together experientially, so that they are less likely to take a tumble down the mountain.

Second, there is often a natural further step in the pooling of solutions to these problems, ranging from practical tips to broader approaches. This is the building of collective knowledge. Even if solutions are not pooled, ideas about access to relevant knowledge may be, so that individuals can follow these up themselves. Third, though, learners come also to realise that there may be no single best way, and different approaches are valid. They can hear that others do things differently without being preached at, and this offers them alternative patterns to their own behaviour which they can choose to adopt or not. This in turn enhances their sense of agency and responsibility; they have choices to make. Education enhances the solutional gene pool, whilst partially shortcutting the lengthy and painful process of evolutionary trial and error.

The point is not only that the learning is a collective experience, but also that the benefits which flow from it cannot be interpreted only in terms of the individuals. What the tutors were describing was a loose form of socialisation – loose because it was to a large extent non-prescriptive, but nevertheless enabled participants to have a clearer sense of their own practice and norms, against a wider background. The process is important in building up trust relationships between the learners and a whole range of social institutions – most notably schools, but also health and social services – with which they have often had uneasy relationships. Where family learning works well trust levels go up, to mutual advantage. This of course cannot be guaranteed, since the statutory agencies' norms and behaviour may not be seen as helpful or sympathetic, but it raises the chances of it occurring.

This group interview also threw up a good example of the tensions or conflict which can occur as a result of learning. This drives home the point that learning can be ambiguous or double-edged in its effects; and that evaluation of these depends on norms that may not be universally shared. The example encapsulates the tensions of modernisation and cultural change. The moderator of the interview asked whether the learning involved had effects on wider family relationships, going beyond parent–child. There was a collective intake of breath on the part of the group members, and then a burst of laughter from several members. One said: 'I'll need another biscuit to get the blood-sugar level up . . .'. They then talked about the marital stresses which had resulted from wives' participation and personal development. The stresses included (predictably) a gender dimension, as husbands responded to changes, but also a generational one which was if anything more acute, since many of the tutors engaged largely with members of the Bengali community: more than one member of the group recounted having hostile communication, directly or indirectly, from mothers (or mothers-in-law) who profoundly resented the changes in their daughters' behaviour inspired by their participation in family learning. Raised aspirations, for example in wishing to set up home as a nuclear family independent of the extended family, were a common source of friction.

Yet conflict of this kind can be seen as broadly inevitable, and education can help people to manage it. The group also reported on how Bengali immigrants wished both to absorb some British practices and to retain practices and values from their country of origin. Some of the younger generation are learning Bangla, and this helps them to remain in touch with older generations without necessarily subscribing to all their values.

We explore many of these issues in greater depth under the three main themes of health, family and social capital in Part B. The purpose of this section has been to develop the thinking underlying the notions of sustaining and transformative effects, interpreted at individual and collective levels. We have argued for a dual use of the matrix generated by these two dimensions: on the one hand as a device for locating individual cases within a rough typology and reflecting on their distribution across the different types, and on the other as a means of exploring the interactions which occur along the axes, to avoid unrealistic dichotomies.

The key conclusion, bearing in mind the reservations about definitive allocation of cases to specific locations on the matrix, is that the sustaining effects of learning are very powerful and should not be allowed to be overshadowed by more dramatic instances of transformation. The latter are impressive and welcome (even though transformation at any level may be accompanied by significant costs to others), not least because they can provide positive and empowering models for others. We have personally found the examples of education-induced transformation provided by a number of our respondents striking and even inspiring. However, the visibility and profile of such examples (whether for researchers or the media) can push to the margins the persistent unspectacular role of learning in enabling people to cope better with daily challenges and to turn these challenges to good effect. This conclusion risks sounding fully functionalist: education is to be seen as a good merely because it enables society to keep ticking along. It should already be clear that this is hardly our perspective. The importance of the sustaining effect reflects more the stressful and turbulent nature of contemporary society.

Notes

1 Despite the previous sentence, there has always been considerable variation of educational structure within the UK (see, for example, Paterson 1994), increasingly so in a devolved political structure.
2 There is a fascinating, but highly challenging, debate to be had over the extent to which the sophistication of current analytical techniques is matched by the validity of the measures used (Schuller 2000). Imposing towers of quantitative analysis are erected on foundations which may, on closer inspection, be less than fully secure.
3 However, area effects may be critical in respect of other aspects. Measuring the impact of education on social cohesion, for example, is arguably best focused on the community or area level, though ideally we should also try to capture the differences between these and national level effects. See Sampson et al. 1999 for detailed work on this.
4 This is why social capital and distributional issues are intimately connected; Putnam's work especially shows a link between social solidarity through redistributive policies, typical of Scandinavian countries and some states in the US, and levels of civic engagement (Putnam 2000: Ch. 17).

Part B

Themes and case studies

Part B comprises three pairs of chapters. The first chapter in each pair discusses one of the main themes in our work, relating it to wider research; we begin with health, and follow on with family life and social capital. The second chapter presents three or four individual case studies selected from our interviews to give particular illustration to the issues raised in the thematic discussion.

For most of the case studies we provide a box which contextualises the individual in a wider population of similar cases, drawing on data from the cohort studies (see Chapters 1 and 9). This gives a sense of how the person compares to others on a number of issues and measures. This is not possible where the individual is too far away in age from the cohort population.

To accompany each case we also present a diagrammatic summary of the evidence. In these diagrams the thicker lines represent the particularly strong relationships as perceived by the author. Only those relationships that are discussed in the text are shown, as opposed to all of the relationships elicited from each interview.

Chapter 3

The impacts of learning on well-being, mental health and effective coping

Cathie Hammond

This chapter presents findings that link experiences of learning with health outcomes. Analyses of the fieldwork data suggest that learning can develop psychosocial qualities – namely self-esteem and self-efficacy, a sense of identity, purpose and future, communication and other competences, and social integration – which promote well-being, mental health and the ability to cope effectively with change and adversity, including ill-health. Respondents' accounts also indicate which aspects of the learning experience may be important in relation to the promotion of positive health outcomes. A basic guideline for those wishing to maximise wider benefits is that the pedagogy, curriculum, student mix and institutional context should match the strengths, interests and needs of the learner.

Introduction: policy, practice and evidence

Reviews of the relevant evidence converge on the conclusion that education, as measured by years spent in education or highest qualification gained, leads to better health. These findings apply to measures of physiological, mental and psychological health. Although effects are on average positive, they vary depending on the health outcome and the learner's gender, age and previous level of education (see, for example, Feinstein 2002a; Hammond 2002a; for reviews of the relevant studies, see Grossman and Kaestner 1997; Hartog and Oosterbeek 1998; Ross and Mirowsky 1999; Hammond 2000b).

I have previously suggested a typology of intermediate factors linking education and health as a first step towards understanding the processes through which education affects health (Hammond 2003). The factors described below can be categorised as economic, access to services, emotional resilience and social capital. In real life, these factors are related to one another as well as to education and health in complex ways. They are presented separately for conceptual simplicity.

Each additional year spent in education has positive returns in terms of *income and socio-economic status* in countries the world over (see, for example, Asplund and Pereira 1999 for a review of European evidence, and Johnes 1993 for a review covering developing as well as developed countries). Generally, health inequality means that individuals of higher socio-economic status are relatively healthy both physically and psychologically (Black *et al.* 1982; Acheson 1998). Education benefits individuals' health by enabling them to move up the socio-economic ladder. This does not necessarily improve the situation of those who are left behind.

Effects of education upon health outcomes are mediated also by ability to *access appropriate health and health-related services*. The 'inverse care law' (Hart 1981) refers to the finding that areas characterised by deprivation and high levels of health needs also exhibit low take-up of health services. Educational success (or the lack of it) may affect individuals' abilities to communicate effectively with health professionals and to understand and evaluate the health-related messages that they are given. These abilities benefit more educated individuals, but not the communities in which they live.

Emotional resilience refers to the dimension of individual difference that spans the ways we deal with adversity and stressful conditions and how they affect us (Garmezy 1971; Anthony 1974; Rutter 1990). Almost by definition, resilience contributes to better health: mental, psychological and physical. The relationship is perhaps most obvious in relation to depression since rates of depression are correlated with levels of self-esteem and self-efficacy, which are themselves central to resilience (e.g. Battle 1978; Burnette and Mui 1994; Turner and Turner 1999). However, in relation to depression, the directions of causality are unclear because loss of self-confidence and self-efficacy are symptoms as well as possible causes of depression. It is possible to imagine a vicious circle whereby individuals whose levels of resilience are low initially respond to adverse conditions by developing symptoms of depression, which themselves undermine their personal resilience to further adverse conditions. Education may play a part in breaking this cycle.

Resilience contributes to physical health, first through the promotion of positive health practices, and second through reducing chronic (as opposed to acute) levels of stress. Reliance upon nicotine, alcohol and other addictive substances, as well as certain patterns of eating, are sometimes responses to adversity and stressful conditions (Allison *et al.* 1999). Individuals who (through their education and learning) feel independent and confident, who are good at solving problems, who possess a sense of purpose and future, and who mix with peers who share these characteristics and live healthy lifestyles may respond to stressful conditions in ways which are less damaging to their health and possibly more effective in reducing levels of experienced stress in the longer term. Whereas short-term stress responses may be essential for survival, long-lasting stress exacts a cost that can promote both the onset of illness and its progression (see Wilkinson 1996: 179–181 on studies demonstrating that stress erodes physical health).

Social capital 'refers to features of social organisation, such as trust, norms, and networks, that can improve the efficiency of society by facilitating coordinated actions' (Putnam 1993: 167). It is discussed in detail in Chapters 7 and 8; here I concentrate on the link between social capital and health. A review of the evidence suggests that the number of years spent in education is positively correlated with individual-level characteristics of social capital (Glaeser 1999) and that greater social capital leads to better health outcomes (Kawachi et al. 1997; Lomas 1998). Putnam (2000) suggests that social capital has a positive effect upon physical health because healthy behaviours are reinforced, chronic levels of stress are reduced, and access to medical services is improved. Within health promotion, there has been a 'paradigm drift' away from the provision of health-related information for individuals towards a community development perspective (Beeker et al. 1998), with an understanding of health-related behaviours as being shaped by collectively negotiated social identities (Stockdale 1995). Health promotion initiatives in Britain now emphasise whole community approaches to tackling health inequalities. For example, Health Action Zones explicitly link health to regeneration, employment, housing, education and social cohesion.

The discussion above draws on numerous studies that investigate either the outcomes of education (on the one hand) or determinants of health (on the other) and provide a basis for the typology of intermediate factors. The findings presented in this chapter similarly concern the factors linking learning with health, but no piecing together is necessary as the data are biographical in nature. The fieldwork research involved in-depth interviews with 124 respondents, plus 12 group interviews with practitioners. Interviewing a large number of respondents does not in itself add much to a qualitative study of this kind, but interviewing respondents with a wide range of life experiences – especially learning experiences – does. We have been able to investigate complex processes that are not easily disentangled using quantitative approaches across a very wide range of learning experienced by individuals from a variety of social backgrounds and encompassing a diversity of life experiences.

Obtaining a full contextual understanding of respondents' learning and life experiences was necessary in order to disentangle effects of learning from other factors that influence people's lives throughout the life course. Whitty and colleagues refer to 'the cumulative effects of low social class of origin, poor educational achievement, reduced employment prospects, [and] low levels of psychosocial well-being [upon] poor physical and mental health' (Whitty et al. 1998: 642). Systematic analysis of case studies enabled us to investigate the ways in which economic, political and social structures constrain people's lives and limit or maximise the effects of learning. The biographical nature of the interviews also meant that both immediate and longer-term outcomes of learning could be investigated.

The design of the research was based on an understanding of health as encompassing not only physiological states but also mental and psychological ones. The interest was in both positive health and ill-health. Reflecting the typology of mediating factors outlined above, I assume that health may be influenced by a combination of social and psychological factors, as well as biological ones (Nettleton 1995; Crossley 2000).

Findings concerning mediators that link learning to health are summarised in Figure 3.1. The health effects of learning described by respondents fell into three categories: subjective well-being (SWB); effective coping, including coping with physical ill-health; and protection and recovery from mental health difficulties. In Chapter 2, we suggested that learning both sustains and transforms lives. Here we exemplify this more general finding: effects of learning that protect mental health are sustaining, and learning that leads to recovery of mental health is transforming. The processes involved encompass the maintenance and development of SWB and effective coping.

SWB refers to 'how people evaluate their lives, and includes variables such as life satisfaction and marital satisfaction, lack of depression and anxiety, and positive moods and emotions' (Diener et al. 1997). There is debate as to whether SWB is set at an early age, such that changes in income, health, family status and so on affect levels of SWB during adulthood for short periods only (e.g. Costa et al. 1987). Based on secondary analysis of a national US longitudinal survey (the General Social Survey), Easterlin (2003) presents a convincing argument that SWB is affected for periods of ten years or more by changes in health and family status, but not by changes in income. Although our respondents described educational impacts on well-being, it is not clear from their accounts to what extent education per se had long-lasting effects. However, learning effects on well-being interacted with other impacts of learning and led to changes in life circumstances, which appeared to have cumulative and lasting impacts on well-being.

Effective coping is a consequence of emotional resilience, described above as the ways in which we deal with adversity and stressful conditions. Lazarus and

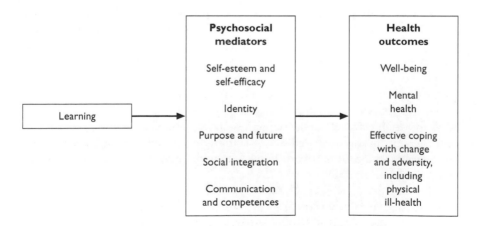

Figure 3.1 Mediators between learning and health outcomes.

Folkman (1984) suggest that coping strategies that are effective in one context may be ineffective in another, which implies that learning may lead to effective coping in some but not all areas of a learner's life. Howard *et al.* (1999) reviewed the literature concerning effective coping amongst children and concluded that the internal assets that consistently describe the resilient child are autonomy, a sense of purpose and future, problem-solving skills, and social competence. These internal assets match the psychosocial outcomes of learning described by respondents.

Thematic analysis of the case study evidence revealed five groups of psychosocial outcomes of learning that led to these health outcomes. They are closely related to the groupings of intermediate factors presented at the beginning of this section. Economic factors did not emerge strongly as mediators between education and health, probably because respondents were not encouraged to talk about them. Nevertheless, respondents' accounts demonstrate the ways in which economic conditions shaped the impacts of education.

The following sections present evidence relating to the five groups of psychosocial resources that emerged as intermediate factors linking learning to health outcomes: self-esteem and self-efficacy; identity; purpose and future; communication and competences; and social integration. The final section discusses conclusions.

Self-esteem and self-efficacy

Self-esteem and self-efficacy are related but distinct constructs, and the literature on each is substantial. They are dynamic personal attributes that are both experienced internally and expressed through behaviour, what Mruk (1999) refers to as aspects of one's 'lived status'. Learners' accounts exemplify changes in 'lived status' because they describe changes in self-esteem and self-efficacy in terms of both feeling and behaving differently.

Increased self-esteem is probably the most universal and widely documented 'soft' outcome of learning, and our findings bear this out. Every practitioner group and many individual respondents talked about self-esteem as an outcome of learning that was of central importance to them. Self-esteem refers here to 'a generalised feeling about oneself that is more or less positive' (Emler 2001). It includes the conviction that one is competent, and that one's competences are worthy (Rosenberg 1965; Branden 1969).

Self-esteem is built when convictions about competence match up to or exceed aspirations (James 1890). Doris had left school without qualifications and returned to learning in later life, where she acquired competence in literacy.

> Before, I thought I couldn't do it. I got the idea I couldn't do it, but of course I could. It just showed me that it can be done [...] It boosts your confidence loads.

As aspirations were fulfilled through learning, respondents developed new ambitions, reflecting the interplay between self-esteem, aspirations and a sense of purpose and future. I return briefly to this interrelationship in the section below on purpose and future.

Increased self-esteem was experienced as specific to certain abilities, feeling better about oneself generally, and feeling better about oneself in relation to others – students, contemporaries and friends, members of the family, and others in a general sense. However, some respondents described negative experiences within the education system during which they had failed to learn and which had undermined their self-esteem in each of these areas. Naomi describes the lasting impact of her failure to achieve at school:

> We had a school reunion last year. [. . .] When I walked in that room I still felt like I was perhaps not as good as them. [. . .] I always [. . .] feel as though I'm not [. . .] quite on the same level as everybody else [. . .] Not finding it quite so easy to talk about things that are going on in the world [. . .], intellectual type things. And I sort of feel a bit scared and a bit inferior.

Bandura (1997) defined *self-efficacy* as an individual's confidence in his or her ability to organise and execute a course of action to solve a problem or accomplish a task. Some respondents described this sort of confidence as an outcome of learning:

> It [college] has given me the opportunity to do what I want to do. [. . .] more able to make your own choices yourself, like running life.
>
> (Declan)

Respondents of all ages, ethnic backgrounds, occupations and educational backgrounds mentioned increased self-esteem and self-efficacy as outcomes of their learning. This applied regardless of the respondent's initial level of confidence. Those who had previously failed in educational settings appeared to gain confidence particularly from successful learning experiences. This echoes findings from a recent survey of practitioners in further education (FE) in England: practitioners believe that those students who particularly benefit in terms of self-esteem are those who have failed in education previously and for whom FE offers a 'second chance' (Preston and Hammond 2003).

In contrast to findings from a review of research about effects of self-esteem (Emler 2001), we found no negative effects of increased self-esteem on health. Emler reports that high levels of self-esteem are associated with holding racist attitudes, rejection of social influences, and risk-taking behaviours such as driving too fast or under the influence of alcohol. One explanation why we did not find these effects is that risk-taking behaviours was not in the topic guide, although attitudes and behaviours contributing to social capital were. Another is that self-esteem developed through adult learning as opposed to other processes is often accompanied by the promotion of other qualities such as acceptance of one's limitations and the need to learn, openness to new ideas, and future orientation, which counterbalance some of the reported negative effects of high levels of self-esteem.

Self-esteem and self-efficacy developed through learning can have positive effects upon psychological health. These relationships are sometimes reciprocal, the enjoyment derived from courses seeming to have positive effects upon confidence. Carol is a mother with small children who had been caring for her sick mother:

> I'd really come down and the confidence and the buzz I'd got from working had totally gone within a matter of nine months I would say, so when I came to this course it took me a few weeks to get back in the rhythm of learning again. I really took off, back in a sort of learning situation, doing my homework, etc., and I really enjoyed it. I thoroughly enjoyed it, and my confidence came back up.

Many respondents described how learning had given them the confidence to take more control of their lives. They felt empowered to take advantage of opportunities and to tackle an issue 'instead of just brushing it under the carpet'. They were more relaxed with strangers, said what they thought, and took more active roles in their communities. A high proportion of respondents and every practitioner group talked about how experiences of learning built up confidence to progress to further courses, or apply for new jobs. Some mentioned that learning had led them to visit places that they would not otherwise have visited, such as art galleries, museums and libraries, and to travel in other countries.

In contrast, other's accounts illustrate how education can undermine confidence and thereby raise barriers to progression. Nadine left school without qualifications and worked in an office until she married at the age of 21. She had two children, and when they started school she enrolled on an Open University course in Arts Foundation. She had to wait for a year to start, and when she did the course was above her level without sufficient support to meet her needs. She left after the first few classes. She says:

> I felt really, really dim [. . .] like a failure. [. . .] It was a real letdown. [. . .] It did put me off for a long time.

Increased self-efficacy and self-esteem positively affect individuals' abilities to cope with potentially difficult situations. Participation in adult education courses gave Elsa confidence that she would be able to cope after her husband left her with three small children, and the confidence that Denise developed through a course in ICT helped her to face the fact that there was something seriously wrong with her son and seek appropriate help.

Other respondents mention how confidence gained through education protected their mental health (a sustaining effect) and contributed to recovery of mental health (a transforming effect). Marjorie had recurrent mental health difficulties and consequently took early retirement. At the time of interview she was attending courses at a centre used by people who had mental health difficulties, which she felt had sustained her mental health because they bolstered her confidence. Gareth had recently recovered from a period of dependency on amphetamines, ecstasy and crack, and enrolled at an FE college. The educational experience rebuilt his self-esteem and efficacy, which had a transforming effect on his psychological health.

Effects of learning upon confidence also contributed to how people dealt with physical ill-health. Greater self-esteem and self-efficacy, acquired through learning experiences, can lead to more positive attitudes in relation to health:

> It (further education) has made me more determined to beat the doctors. [. . .] You control your own fate. Fate does not control you.
>
> (Declan)

and empower individuals to seek new lifestyles better suited to changing health status:

> Helen [name has been changed] is currently off work on long-term sick with a back injury, and has gone from somebody with absolutely zero confidence the first time I saw her [. . .] and now she's bursting with confidence. She's fantastic! She can't wait to go on to another course. She wanted to go and get another job.
>
> (Tutor group interview)

Several parents had learnt about health and safety and this knowledge combated their fears of ill-health and its consequences.

We have seen that educational experiences can have negative as well as positive effects upon self-esteem and self-efficacy. This raises questions about which aspects of learning experiences are important in developing these outcomes, and the processes involved. The answers have implications for policies designed to provide education in such a form that wider benefits such as self-esteem and the health benefits to which these psychosocial resources lead are maximised for all participants.

Success in learning appears to be crucial to developing confidence, and this applied not only to those respondents with few qualifications and low confidence to start with. Violet is an example of a highly qualified respondent whose success in adult education increased her self-esteem. Now retired, she worked in the civil service, and has a post-graduate degree and five children. She described taking a pottery course and remarked with great pride that she had actually managed to make stuff that looked 'almost decent'. On the other hand, failure to succeed undermined confidence. In many instances the effects were long lasting and not confined to the specific area of failure. Naomi's poor achievement in maths at secondary school undermined her social confidence for many years. Clearly, feelings of social inferiority as an adult (in her thirties) cannot be wholly attributed to failure in maths at school, but her account clearly connects this school-time failure with a more general lack of social confidence in her adult life.

If success in learning is central to the effects of learning on self-esteem, then we need to examine what helps people to succeed in education. Respondents mentioned that support and encouragement from teachers, support and encouragement from classmates, and the right level of challenge were important aspects that contributed not only to educational success (and thereby self-esteem), but also to self-esteem directly (see below).

Although success in itself appears to breed confidence, several respondents mentioned that recognition of their achievements by others was also important to them. Doris compares the sense of achievement she feels from college work, which is recognised by her tutors, to the lack of achievement she feels from cleaning the kitchen floor, which goes unrecognised at home. Perry, who has moderate learning difficulties, made ceramic animals, and the fact that fellow students liked them enough to buy them gave him great satisfaction.

Education also promotes self-esteem by enabling successful learners to help others. Social confidence was further built up through being required to participate in a group, something which many respondents found difficult at first, but which they appreciated because it empowered them to manage and enjoy social interactions. The mix of students in the class appears to be important in relation to building confidence. For more confident individuals, a heterogeneous mix provides greater opportunities to develop social attitudes, skills and confidence. However, individuals who have specific difficulties and lack confidence in general or in specific areas seem to fare better in groups of students who share similar difficulties. Angela, who has dyslexia, found college easier than school because she was in a class with other students who also had difficulties reading. Individuals with mental health difficulties benefit from learning in centres designed for them as clients. Presumably, like Angela, they find learning with others who have experienced similar difficulties to themselves less threatening than learning in a more mixed group. Through these experiences of learning, individuals develop confidence and may move on to learning in a more heterogeneous group.

The ethos of a class or educational establishment can also contribute to individuals' self-esteem. Although Penny had no qualifications, she felt that school had built her self-esteem because the school ethos made pupils feel that they were valued equally and had something to contribute. Support and encouragement from teachers not only contributes to educational success, it also develops self-esteem directly. This was mentioned more often, although by no means exclusively, by students who lacked basic qualifications and by tutors teaching courses at relatively low levels. Students with lower levels of confidence may benefit initially from smaller classes with flexible curricula, in which teachers have the freedom to provide the support required.

Identity

Aspects of identity that emerged from analysis of the case studies were self-understanding and the capacity for independent thought. The capacity for independent thought maps onto one of the two dimensions of identity recognised by Marcia (1966): exploration, which is the development of personal values and beliefs as opposed to unquestioning adoption of those that one grew up with; and commitment to goals, values and beliefs presumably involving loyalty, perseverance, and also some elements of self-understanding. Effects of learning on self-understanding and independent thinking were described by respondents in terms of personal development. This resonates with Waterman and Archer's (1990) emphasis on identity formation as a lifelong process that is reflected by age and changes in life circumstances.

Respondents of all ages, occupations and levels of education, and of all varieties of family structure, talked about gaining a clearer sense of identity, self-understanding and independent thought as outcomes of learning. Practitioners also described self-understanding and growing independence as outcomes of the courses that they taught. The exceptions were respondents who described their ethnic background as Indian, Pakistani or Bangladeshi, who did not mention these as outcomes of learning. Perhaps this reflects the small numbers of respondents from these backgrounds; another explanation is that discourses about identity are affected by cultures, and because of their cultural backgrounds these respondents tended not to talk to interviewers about changes in identity – or, if they did so, expressed these effects of learning in terms that were not understood by the interviewers.

Mary had obtained 'Highers' in Latin and German as a young woman, and she studied German in her retirement. This gave her a sense of reconnection with her youth. For younger respondents, moving from school to college provided an opportunity to explore one's identity. This effect was highlighted by Phillippa, who had attended school with her identical twin, but moved to college without her twin at the age of 16: 'It's like making a fresh start, I think. I think I needed it.' In contrast, Declan did not find his further education college conducive to exploring his identity as a gay man:

> There were no avenues. There was no way of exploring how I was feeling at the time. You couldn't go and talk to anybody because if you tried, they were all like, 'No, no, no! That's a big taboo. I don't want to talk about it [. . .] No, don't want to know. Go away. I've got questions to mark and things like that.'

Doris' experience of rediscovering her identity through adult education after a period of intensive childcare was shared by many mothers with small children:

I'm just a person. I'm not somebody's mum. And that's what I've learnt. I was just there for everybody else. Then it's like, 'You've got a name'

Education had given some a sense of independence and the ability to think things through for themselves:

You learn from your family what's right and what's wrong and what you should do and what you shouldn't do. And then [...] as you get more educated, you understand why what they said might be right. [...] Education tells you a bit about all the aspects of it, so you can pick out to go your own way.

(Edgar)

Edgar's comment illustrates the way in which different influences are compared and evaluated against one another as an individual develops his or her own opinions, ideas and identity. However, some educational experiences, mostly at school, had discouraged independent thought.

Greater self-understanding and independence of thought feed into other positive outcomes, for example personal growth, the formation of less discriminatory attitudes, and a better understanding of society and one's place within it. These have positive implications for health, efficacy and fulfilment, applying both at individual and collective levels.

However, personal development can lead to conflict and difficulty because it challenges the status quo. The level of difficulty that this poses depends upon the rest of one's life outside the learning environment. The learner's personal development and increasing independence can lead to conflicts within the family, and to repression of one's 'new self', as illustrated by the account of Aayla, a woman who was born and educated in Algeria:

At university you can discuss and you can do something, you can be involved in activities, you can be in associations. But when you finish your studies, you have to be the girl you were when you left home to go to university. That means [...] you don't discuss, and you don't think, and you don't change your mind, and you don't – that means you have to accept again. [...] It was difficult. It was really difficult.

Greater self-understanding feeds into effective coping because it leads to the recognition that issues need tackling. Better understanding of one's situation in its wider context can put personal difficulties into a perspective that makes them easier to cope with. Regaining a sense of identity through education helped respondents to deal with situations they found difficult, such as caring for small children, and making changes as children developed independence. It protects and promotes mental health. Elsbeth's pottery classes enabled her to express tension in positive ways. In fact, venting her emotions by bashing air out of clay could be fun and productive, and ultimately the process helped her to regain her old self.

Skills in independent critical thinking developed through education enable individuals to understand and evaluate the plethora of messages that emanate from a variety of sources relating to health:

> It [the master's course] helped in finding things out and questioning them [. . .] Because I've done the MSc, I can reject some of the things because they're scientifically based and I've done the Sciences [. . .] 'Where's your evidence?' It's this way of thinking, isn't it, in a science-based way.
>
> (Denise)

What aspects of education and learning are important in developing identity, self-understanding and independence? One is that participation in education is one of the few things in many people's lives that concerns themselves, and themselves alone. This is especially true where individuals have made a positive choice to enrol and when learning is self-directed. It is separate – emotionally and physically – from the spheres of life that encompass relationships and responsibilities:

> It gives me that little bit of life that is mine. Not my kids', not my husband's. And this little bit is here for me and only me.
>
> (Hermione)

The element of compulsion to attend classes regularly encourages and validates the attempts of individuals to continue with their studies, and also gives individuals an element of structure to their lives. On the other hand, there is greater flexibility than is usually associated with paid employment.

Subjects that encourage reflection were cited as particularly valuable in terms of generating self-understanding and personal growth – Counselling, Access Planning, Anthropology and, as an informal learning experience, travel. However, some respondents had found the reflective aspect of classes too challenging for them. For example, family history was a means through which respondents had learned about their families, which contextualised their identities, but practitioners reported that students studying family history who were adopted tended to drop out because 'they find it very difficult to cope with'. Learning is valuable when it provides challenges that individuals are able to meet, but can be damaging when the challenges are beyond the individual's capabilities.

Many respondents who had studied the creative and performing arts talked about the value of these subjects in enabling them to question and re-evaluate and consequently grow as people. These subjects were also valued because they allowed self-expression:

> The messier [the class] the better. That's why I used to like clay. You could squish it through your hands and get it all over you kind of thing, but you

still make something at the end of it. Yes, there's nowt like it when you've
had a row and you've got to get the air out of the clay.

(Elsbeth)

Ede had attended a primary school in Nigeria where she had been taught how
to grow food, how to hunt, and other basic survival techniques. This learning
led to a very basic sense of independence, 'like being able to tie your shoelaces'.

Purpose and future

A sense of purpose and future is closely linked with self-esteem, self-efficacy and
identity. As noted in the discussion about self-esteem above, we found that
when respondents met aspirations, this led to both increased self-esteem and
the formation of new aspirations, which contributed to a sense of purpose and
future and also the opportunity to increase self-esteem further, as higher aspirations were met. Pulkkinen and Rönkä (1994) note that commitment (in the
sense of perseverance) is integral to both identity and future orientation, which
is the term that psychologists often use to refer to a sense of purpose and future.
I suggest that commitment is also a component of self-efficacy.

Trommsdorff (1983) conceptualises future orientation as a quality that is
both affective (i.e. affects one's emotions) and cognitive. It develops through a
process of exploring, goal-setting and commitment (Nurmi 1989, 1991). These
features of future orientation are reflected in the accounts.

Respondents from a wide range of backgrounds mentioned a sense of purpose
or future as an outcome of learning, mostly in relation to progression to better
jobs or further education. Interestingly, no one under 25 talked about this
outcome. Older people, on the other hand, referred to initial education as a
time when their aspirations had been raised or crushed. Most of those who
talked about purpose and future as outcomes of learning had suffered setbacks in
their lives. Some simply felt that through education their futures looked
brighter, that they had more opportunities and were doing something worth-
while with their lives. Others talked more specifically about how educational
experiences had helped them to discover the direction they wanted to pursue in
their working lives. This was mentioned particularly by students from other
countries whose first course was in English as a second language, and who,
through college, formed realistic goals and found ways of pursuing their objectives.

Education, especially obtaining qualifications, was seen as a means to progression. In contrast, some experiences of early education had narrowed
opportunities, either through explicit 'advice' or implicit expectations. Assumptions that only girls in the top stream of grammar school or from middle-class
families would go to university had narrowed the occupational choices of
several older respondents. Younger women had received gendered careers
advice:

> It was all Child Development, sewing, needlework, and stuff like that [. . .] I would have liked to do something that wasn't so girlie [. . .] It was just geared up towards becoming secretaries.
>
> (Mandisa)

Schools with an academic emphasis tended to lead young adults to underestimate their interests and undervalue their talents in the creative arts. As a result, several had embarked on academic courses and careers, and later changed direction to pursue more creative activities.

Clearly, a sense of purpose and future contributes to positive psychological health, and Howard et al. (1999) suggest that it helps people to cope effectively. Many parents of small children mentioned this outcome of learning as particularly relevant in helping them to cope with managing lives dominated by relentless childcare and domestic chores. Participation in education gave these parents an alternative focus, which was often seen as a first step in readjusting their lives as their children gained independence. In similar ways, purpose and future were important in terms of protecting mental health.

For those forced to take early retirement as a result of physical disabilities, education contributed to the formation of a positive attitude towards the future and a means through which alternative occupations could be explored and achieved. Nina is retired due to industrial injuries. Her recent learning has:

> given me purpose. It's given me a goal to go for. [. . .] Computers is my way forward. [. . .] I think it's opened a new world for me.

In addition, education offers an alternative lifestyle and direction to individuals who have adopted lifestyles perceived as destructive to themselves and to the communities they live in. Grace was expelled from school and became involved in fraud, but after having a child she turned to training and access courses as an alternative way of life. Daisy comes from a background dominated by exclusion and dependence upon drugs. Her sister had died recently from an alcohol-related illness. She sees education as 'a way out' of self-destruction.

When education raises aspirations that cannot be met, the consequences may be difficult to deal with. Jason is a qualified accountant in his own country, and fled to London as a refugee. Because his labour market qualifications were not accepted in England, he had to start his career again from scratch. He and his wife both cite the crushing of aspirations, raised originally through educational success, as contributing to the onset and progression of his depression. Jason's story illustrates the importance of context on the effects of education. If he had lived in a different context (for example, his own country in a time of peace), then the effects of his education would have been very different. Similarly, the effects of Aayla's university experiences were shaped by the family home she moved back to.

What aspects of learning generate a sense of purpose and future? As with so many outcomes, confidence in one's abilities is fundamental. Stacey describes how loss of confidence in her ability to draw discouraged her from pursuing her interest in art, which at the time of her interview had become an extremely important and fulfilling part of her life:

> This was in a primary school and [. . .] I drew this picture that was labelled 'Watt Tyler – dead'. It was this person lying in a pool of blood. And I got something like A minus for the writing and D for the picture. And it was such a clear comment that you are rubbish at drawing but you're not bad at writing. Those sorts of little tiny things stay with you and make you think.

Teachers who face difficulties similar to those faced by students (or their family members) can be important role models, giving students hope for their own futures. Faith learned sign language because her son was profoundly deaf. The teacher was also profoundly deaf, but had a successful and fulfilling life. Faith remarks, 'It gives you hope.' Closely related to a sense of purpose are the structure, routine and focus that learning imposes. These can provide distraction from cares and anxieties, which is important in promoting well-being, mental health and positive coping. This is particularly relevant to life situations otherwise lacking structure or meaning, or that are otherwise experienced as difficult.

An aspect of focus mentioned as important in relation to all health outcomes (well-being, coping and mental health) is that it provides mental stimulation, stops one 'vegetating'. For some parents with small children, participation in learning enabled the parent to 'get away from the Postman Pat mentality' and 'use [their] brain' again. The stimulation provided by education was particularly important also for those with physical health problems, who felt that the rest of their body was 'shutting down'.

Some respondents had experienced difficulties coping with the demands of their courses in the context of lives that were already very busy. Enthusiasm about their learning contributed to the problem because they were highly motivated to spend as much time as they could afford (and often more) on their studies. These individuals felt 'split up into bits', 'a terrible sense of guilt'. They can become exhausted, irritable, and 'snappy'.

Communication and competences

The development of knowledge, understanding and competences are explicit aims of education and learning. Competence in verbal and written articulation and understanding is necessary for communication to be effective. In addition, communication assumes shared codes of behaviour and understanding – when to articulate and when to refrain from articulation, which turns of phrases to use in particular situations, and at what level of formality and friendliness – which demands knowledge and understanding of discourses based on cultural capital rather than pure competence.

A basic level of competence and communication is obviously required to develop and pursue interests, which in turn contribute to well-being. Beyond this, people had little to say about the effects of knowledge and skills acquired through learning upon their well-being or mental health. On the other hand, competences and communication appear to be important in helping individuals to cope more effectively with a whole range of difficulties, many of them health-related. Findings from other research (see Howard *et al.* 1999) suggest that problem solving and communication skills contribute to resilience, and this is borne out by our accounts. Education appears to promote a positive approach to problems through teaching patience and a logical approach, coupled with the certainty that problems can be fixed in the end. Education also enables individuals to see their difficulties within a broader perspective that may encompass more than one way of tackling a problem and more than one solution. In emotionally charged situations, this approach helps some individuals to take 'a deep breath' and consequently a more rational and effective approach.

Communication skills developed through education contribute to the social integration of immigrants (most basically, through learning English), and to people's ability to deal with systems – in this context, health systems. Communication skills in this instance involve knowledge and understanding of different types of discourse and their appropriate use, and can be seen as a form of cultural capital. Communication skills enable individuals to deal diplomatically and rationally with professionals who wield power over them – for example, controlling access to services. In addition, education can give individuals the technical jargon and accepted phraseology that makes it more likely that they will be understood and taken seriously:

> Because I went to grammar school and then I worked in a hospital laboratory for 20 years – but because I've come from that background, you're able to talk to people at the same level. You know what to say, when to keep quiet [. . .] It's the same with teachers and everyone [. . .] You're educated to their level.
>
> (Denise)

Written communication skills, developed through education, can also be useful in accessing health services.

Knowledge and understanding of health-related issues often helps individuals to deal with their own ill-health or the ill-health of somebody close to them. When Maisie's husband was diagnosed with depression, she went to the library and found out about the condition, which she found tremendously helpful. Similarly, Ahmed used local libraries to find out about his wife's condition (schizophrenia), and this helped him to deal with the situation he found himself in. Ede used her knowledge and skills therapeutically through giving her daughter aromatherapy massages. Denise, whose son was diagnosed with Asperger's syndrome, suggests that education may be necessary to understand

and evaluate health information, and consequently to understand a condition and access appropriate treatments.

If education enables individuals to access limited health services, where does this leave those with low levels of education, who may have equal or greater health needs? This outcome of education benefits the individual, but it may do so at the expense of somebody else, and consequently compounds existing inequalities by enabling the better off individual or family to gain priority. This is an example of what is already well established in social policy circles – that it is on the whole the middle classes who benefit from much welfare expenditure.

Social integration

Learning experiences have impacts upon social integration, which can be positive – 'like you're a little bit more worthy – You're a part of society' – or negative:

> It broke down my confidence completely, I think, and it was not necessarily confidence in myself, but confidence in my ability to communicate and make friends and just to think that people are going to be friendly.
>
> (Ingrid)

Chapters 7 and 8 discuss theories concerning social and cultural capital, and present evidence that social integration is an outcome of learning. Here, I examine how social integration, developed through learning, affects health outcomes.

Putnam (2000) argues that social capital has a positive effect upon physical health because healthy behaviours are reinforced, chronic levels of stress are reduced, and access to medical services is improved. Schlossberg et al. (1995) suggests that social resources and social competences contribute to personal resilience. Our evidence is that social outcomes of learning protect mental health and contribute to well-being, effective coping and the adoption of health behaviours.

Respondents enjoyed the social aspects of their classes, and these sentiments were echoed in the practitioner groups. For some, simply being forced to mix with other students protected them from isolation. Some courses provided opportunities to visit public places (e.g. museums, galleries, the public records office), which had positive effects on well-being and built confidence to visit other venues in less formal groups. This finding illustrates the close inter-relationship between positive psychological health and civic participation.

Meeting people in educational settings helped students to deal with difficult situations. For example, contact with other students reminded mothers caring for small children of the adult world they had been involved with before having children, and distracted them from their anxieties. One tutor suggested that meeting others helped students to put their problems into perspective because they recognised that other people face similar difficulties. Another reported that re-integration, distraction, and gaining perspective through education was particularly relevant to recently widowed men.

Mixing with students in a context that promotes learning may be particularly effective in developing supportive relationships. Students are forced to mix with others whose life experiences may be different, in contexts that feel safe and encourage openness and co-operation. This facilitates the sharing of opinions and sometimes personal difficulties. Several people reported feeling particularly close to their classmates.

Some overseas students attended English classes which put them in contact for the first time with others with whom they could share experiences and knowledge, and with whom they became friends. This helped them to cope with the difficulties they encountered upon arriving in a strange country. Classes can also act as a forum for the exchange of health-related information. The examples given by respondents were not spectacular, but they were nevertheless significant to the individuals concerned. Respondents were not asked about effects of learning upon health behaviours, but some commented that through making friends with fellow students they had joined a gym or changed their diet. By contrast, some college friendships led to experimentation and dependency on illegal drugs.

Conclusions

Based on thematic analyses of the case study evidence, five groups of psychosocial attributes emerge which are developed through learning and education, and which contribute to the range of health outcomes mentioned by respondents. These psychosocial attributes are self-esteem and self-efficacy, identity, purpose and future, communication and competences, and social integration, and the health outcomes are well-being, mental health and effective coping. These findings are summarised in Figure 3.1 (see p. 40).

The introduction to this chapter set out a typology of mediating factors that link education and learning with health outcomes. The factors were economic, access to health-related services, emotional resilience and social integration. There is little evidence from the case studies about the economic outcomes of learning because this was not a focus for the study. Although there is some evidence concerning take up of services, this was not explicitly addressed. The groups of psychosocial mediators that emerged from analysis of the case study evidence are all attributes of emotional resilience, which appears also as a health outcome (effective coping).

The aim of our research was not to build a new or comprehensive model, but to develop a fuller understanding of those processes linking learning with health outcomes which respondents talked about. Respondents' accounts were shaped by the topic guide, and by their inclination to talk about issues that felt positive and familiar. The ways in which immediate psychosocial outcomes (or mediators) impact upon psychological and mental health outcomes appear similar across the whole span of psychological health, from despair and depression at one end to positive psychological health, fulfilment and personal growth at the other. This implies that learning can benefit the health of all individuals, regardless of their initial levels of psychological and mental health.

All five groups of psychosocial mediators impact on subjective well-being, mental health and effective coping. However, communication and competences primarily affect emotional resilience and consequently contribute indirectly to psychological and mental health. Effective coping could be positioned in the model as a psychosocial mediator as well as a health outcome in its own right. The lack of evidence for a direct link between competences and psychological and mental health reported here resonates with the finding from the quantitative analyses reported in Chapter 9 that taking courses leading to vocational qualifications, which are by and large competence-based, led to few health and social capital benefits. The case study evidence indicates that competences developed through learning do affect health, but indirectly, and the complexity of relationships between learning, competences and health outcomes may mean that it is particularly difficult to identify positive health impacts for competence-based education.

We have reported both positive and negative impacts of adult learning. These were found also in the quantitative analyses. Negative outcomes are attributed to educational experiences, but if we examine the processes involved, it becomes evident that it is failure to learn as opposed to learning itself that has negative effects. Negative outcomes appear to result from individuals being placed in a situation where they expect and are expected to learn (and this includes learning to socialise), but for a combination of reasons fail to do so.

Because education presents challenges, it provides opportunities for development at individual and community levels, but simultaneously carries an element of risk. The evidence presented here suggests that providing challenges that students can meet is central to building self-esteem. If challenges are not met, the consequences can be damaging and long-lasting. The provision of adequate support by the teacher is therefore crucial, but the ethos of the institution appears to be important also, and so does the attitude of fellow students. For students whose levels of confidence are low initially, the most supportive learning environment may be a class with a high teacher to student ratio so that the teacher is able to give plenty of time to each individual, and which contains a group of students who face similar difficulties in relation to returning to learning. Subjects and teaching styles that encourage reflection, creativity and self-expression are particularly important in relation to developing self-understanding and independent thinking. Wider curricula are more likely to offer opportunities for all individuals to discover their strengths and interests and so develop aspirations and plans for the future.

The wide scope of this research highlights the unsurprising finding that different types of learning provision suit learners with different characteristics. It provides evidence of a new kind for the importance of student-centred learning. A basic guideline for those wishing to promote wider benefits that emerges clearly from this research is that the pedagogy, curriculum, student mix and institutional context should match the strengths, interests and needs of the learner. Also important, but perhaps more difficult to influence, is the need to align the objectives of education with social, political and economic values that are dominant in some sphere of the learner's context. The effects of mis-matches between personal and educational objectives on the one hand and the economic, political and cultural context of the learner on the other are exem-plified in the accounts of Aayla, Fraser and Jason. Mis-matches could be recti-fied through changing either educational objectives or social, political and economic values, or both. The cases mentioned are examples where education led to personal and social benefits, which were limited by social, economic and political pressures. For these people, the first questions raised concern these pressures rather than the objectives of the education.

An over-arching finding from this chapter is that education enhances all health outcomes through enabling individuals to see their lives in a broader context. This is achieved through raising self-esteem and feelings of efficacy, broadening people's knowledge, understanding and attitudes, providing alternatives and opportunities, giving people new and different interests and focuses, generating a sense of purpose and future, and through greater social integration. There is an expansion from looking inwards to looking outwards, which has positive effects upon health along the whole of the mental health continuum and enables individuals to cope more effectively with ill-health and other types of adversity. We see this as a progression in (or from) education that is enmeshed with personal and social development. Perhaps this conclusion is what one would expect, because learning must always be about questioning and extending boundaries. Nevertheless, it is an important one because it is a crucial aspect of learning in relation to the generation of wider benefits, and one that distinguishes it from other activities that might also be beneficial to health, such as participation in work or leisure activities that involve minimal learning.

Chapter 4

Mental health and well-being throughout the life course

Cathie Hammond

In Chapter 3 we saw how the immediate psychosocial outcomes of learning contribute to a variety of health outcomes. For conceptual simplicity, the processes involved were examined separately in relation to each psychosocial outcome. Clearly, human experience is more complicated than this analysis implies. Learning outcomes combine dynamically with one another and with the other factors that impact upon an individual's experience throughout his or her life course. In this chapter, we capture this complexity and demonstrate the ways in which learning can lead to health outcomes, through the in-depth analysis of case studies.

The case studies were selected in order to illustrate effects of learning in relation to the range of health outcomes that people talked about, which emerged from the analyses reported in the previous chapter: well-being and fulfilment, recovery and protection of mental health, and coping with potentially difficult situations, including physical ill-health. They also represent diversity of experience in terms of gender, ethnic identity, social background, previous education and life events.

The chapter begins with a description of how Gareth copes with unresolved emotions, first through drugs and then through rehabilitation and counselling. The second case study is the story of Beryl, who retired at 51 as a result of ill-health. Denise is a mother of primary school age children, who has coped with the ill-health of her mother and father-in-law, and with her son's learning disability (Beryl and Denise are outside the age range which would allow us to compare them with the cohort profiles). Consuela experienced enormous difficulties when she emigrated from Venezuela to live in London at the age of 14, but nevertheless has retained a positive attitude. The final section is a discussion of comparisons and conclusions.

Chapter 3 concludes that health outcomes are maximised when the learning provided matches the learner's strengths, interests and needs. We extend this conclusion by observing how these interests, strengths and needs are shaped by the individual's biography and stage in the life course. The transforming and sustaining effects of learning are best understood within a life-course context, characterised as it is by periods of continuity and discontinuity. Learning experienced at times of continuity tends to be sustaining or consolidating, whilst learning experienced at times of discontinuity tends to be transforming.

In Chapter 2, the transforming and sustaining effects of learning are represented as two ends of a continuum. Similarly, the distinction between periods of continuity and discontinuity is blurred. Periods of (relative) discontinuity are referred to as life events, milestones, turning points, psychological turning points and transitions, reflecting different emphases in definition. In contrast to earlier descriptions (e.g. Parkes 1971 and Schlossberg 1981), my use of the term does not necessarily imply external triggers (events or non-events) or limited duration, although it does imply internal reassessment. It is captured by Clausen's (1993) description of psychological turning points:

> perceived long-lasting re-directions in the path of a person's life accompanied by self-reflective awareness of or insight into the significance of the change in the person's life.

Nevertheless, the periods of discontinuity identified in the case studies are on the most part triggered by changes in life circumstances.

Gareth

> I'm no longer the junkie that skulks about. I can go out and hold my head up high.

Gareth is 43, white, male, with no qualifications, and is single without dependent children. On the basis of his previous occupation he is middle class, but currently he is a student. A formative aspect of Gareth's background is that he spent his childhood in care. We therefore compare Gareth with members of the NCDS, who were all aged 42 in 2000, who spent time in care during their childhoods.

Amongst 42-year-olds in Britain in 2000, about 71 in every 10,000 were white males with qualifications below five GCSE passes who had spent some of their childhood in care. Amongst this group, a relatively low percentage had participated in learning during the previous 9 years (38 per cent as opposed to 61 per cent for all 42-year-olds), and of these learners, almost all had gained no qualifications (95 per cent). The proportion of courses that led to qualifications for this group was well below the average, at 4 per cent. This finding is worth noting because those who, like Gareth, lack qualifications would probably benefit from acquiring them, but are instead participating in non-accredited learning.

People sharing Gareth's characteristics are much more likely to be clinically depressed than other 42-year-olds. They feel less in control of their lives, and are less likely to report high levels of life satisfaction. A relatively low percentage of people 'like' Gareth belong to any organisation (7 per cent as opposed to 18 per cent of 42-year-olds overall), and a lower percentage report an interest in politics (30 per cent as opposed to 43 per cent of 42-year-olds overall).

Gareth is fairly representative of people who share his demographic characteristics. His most unusual feature is that he has participated in adult learning (only 38 per cent of people like him do so). But like others who share his characteristics, Gareth has gained no qualifications over the past 9 years, he is not clinically depressed (any more), appears to have quite positive efficacy and life satisfaction, and he does not belong to any organisation. It is unclear from his account whether he would describe himself as interested in politics or not.

Gareth is white, British, middle class by previous occupation (he was studying full-time when he was interviewed), and aged 43. He was abandoned by his mother and as a teenager had a sexual relationship with a foster sister (no blood relationship), who became pregnant. The baby was adopted, which left Gareth with confused emotions that he was unable to resolve. He pursued a successful career as a high-earning advertising photographer, which supported his habitual dependency on drugs. Following rehabilitation two years before the interview, he had embarked on an access course in Psychology and Sociology. He describes himself as 'a middle-aged, white, heterosexual, cross-dressing [laughs] male'.

Gareth's secondary schools (he went to two) were outside the area he lived in. They failed to address his difficulties with reading, or to recognise his abilities in mathematics:

> I went to secondary school out of the area, I never – From then on, I never really felt, yeah, part of a community [. . .] I felt the school had me down as a dunce. And if you do that, you take people's confidence away.

Gareth rebelled by drinking and smoking, and mostly by 'just not going'. All in all, his school experiences compounded the insecurities and alienation that developed during his early life.

In order to tackle his slow reading his foster parents engaged a private tutor, who sexually abused him. After leaving school at 15, he attended stage school, dropped out, and enrolled at a further education college to re-sit his O levels. It was there that what he calls his 'drug career' began:

> That's where I first got introduced to drugs, and acid was really big at that time. And acid and education don't mix and I preferred acid to education, so that's what – it became a drug experience more than an educational experience. So I left that and carried on my drug career [. . .] a progress path from mild drugs, through speed, through acid, through cocaine, to crack.

It was through college that Gareth started to use the drugs that later had negative effects upon his psychological, mental and physical health. However, an introduction to illegal drugs at college is not uncommon amongst young adults, and does not lead to long-lasting health-damaging behaviours amongst the majority of students. Although college provided the opportunity to experiment with drugs, it was not the reason why Gareth became dependent on them. Instead, his dependency probably resulted from the unresolved difficulties, insecurity and alienation that he had grown up with. Unfortunately, these had been increased rather than addressed or counterbalanced by his educational experiences.

After leaving college, Gareth worked as a photographer's assistant. He enjoyed the work and was good at it. Informal learning outside an institutional setting played to his strengths. The effects upon psychological health and social integration are not discussed, possibly because at this stage his life was dominated by drugs. Economically, he benefited. He was earning up to £1,000 per day, working hours that suited him, and this supported his clubbing and drug-taking lifestyle.

However, this lifestyle was not sustainable. Perhaps as his tolerance to the drugs increased, Gareth was no longer able and perhaps no longer entirely wished to avoid the unresolved difficulties that had led to his dependency upon them in the first place. He describes how life lacked reality and meaning, at least in relation to his clubbing community:

> The trouble with a community based on drugs is that if you take the drugs away, there's no community there. The community is the shared experience, rather than an actual community, you know. You were all living in the same drug experience, but that's not a real community.

As time passed Gareth 'gave up photography and just concentrated on being a drug addict', and his life became increasingly alienated and pointless:

> I had drugs on hand all the time [he was storing them for a dealer] so I didn't have to go out and buy or anything. And I hardly ever left my flat, and when I did it was like walking out into an alien world.
>
> For a long time, I didn't feel like I was doing anything – that I was literally waiting to die. And on several occasions, I nearly did die – through ODing

His desire to break out of this lifestyle was a turning point. He entered a rehabilitation programme and joined a self-help group. Gareth describes this process of rehabilitation and counselling as a learning experience that led to personal liberation and growth. It helped him to feel that he could control his life and act independently.

Gareth stopped taking illegal drugs, but still needed to rebuild his life, for photography was 'drug-ridden'. Fortunately, peer counselling had led him to discover an interest and talent in counselling. He saw FE as a means to pursuing this as an alternative career. Thus, learning through therapeutic counselling and FE provided Gareth with a lifestyle and purpose not related to drugs, which was probably crucial to his continuing rehabilitation:

> The most important thing [about FE] was that it got me out of the flat. It got me into a social situation and stopped me isolating.

Despite 'being liked' at college, he explains:

> Having been isolated for six years, I still do find building relationships quite difficult. Casual acquaintances I can cope with – but strong – strong relationships I find still difficult.

Nevertheless, through college Gareth has become integrated into a new community. Contact with students from other backgrounds together with the content of the sociology course has also prompted him to re-examine his views, resulting in greater openness towards a wider range of people:

> When I came here, I was very dogmatic about my beliefs. I didn't approve of single mothers because of my own life experiences. I didn't think they could give a proper – raise a child properly, that is. Having been surrounded by a lot of single mothers, I realised [that] isn't the case. Learning sociology and looking at issues more intently, I found really difficult at first. But obviously, when you look into these things deeper, you know, yeah, you do have to take other things into perspective.

College also represents the means to tackling deep-seated feelings of alienation and inferiority:

> When I went to secondary school out of the area, I never – from then on I never really felt – yeah – part of a community. I mean a small select circle of close friends. When I got into photography, I didn't do any training, I became a photographer's assistant and learned the trade that way. And I always felt like a cheat. All my life, I felt like a cheat. [. . .] I could go and train to be a counsellor, which is a two-year course, but I want to, for once, get a firm grounding so that, you know – so I do my psychology and counselling degree and then do my counselling training. So that I've finally got a firm base. I know I'm good enough, you know, as opposed to always thinking that I'm not good enough.

Gareth's account reflects a wish to feel fully integrated into a system, and also secure in his knowledge and abilities. College has built his confidence through providing him with realistic challenges, with clear recognition that he has met these challenges ('getting good results'), and through giving him a role in which he is liked and respected. This leads to an enthusiasm to continue learning, coupled with greater openness and participation. Gareth cites taking part in the interview and speaking openly in class as examples. Participation is rewarded by positive feedback and the respect of others. He describes a virtuous cycle whereby confidence leads to risk-taking, which is rewarded and further strengthens confidence. Increased confidence feeds into well-being, sense of purpose and optimism. The account illustrates how integral the development of social attitudes, behaviours and identity can be in relation to the promotion and maintenance of positive psychological health.

Gareth's experience of FE was not the therapeutic intervention that enabled him to tackle deep-rooted psychological difficulties and overcome despair, depression and dependency on drugs. However, as a follow-up to the therapeutic interventions of rehabilitation and counselling, education provided the opportunities and support he needed to consolidate and build up his psychological health and well-being. He went to college during a period of relative discontinuity, and the effects were transforming at a personal level.

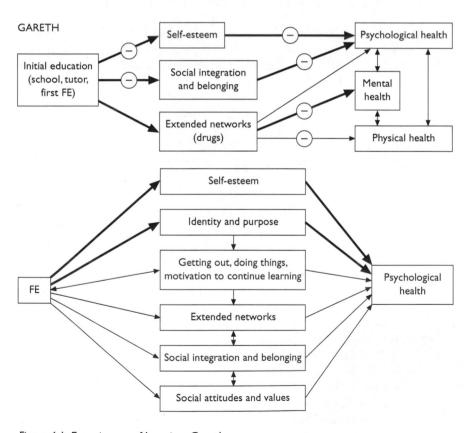

Figure 4.1 Experiences of learning: Gareth.

At the end of the interview, he is asked if he has anything to add about his experiences of FE:

> It's been really, really good. It's – It was the right thing, in the right place at the right time.

Thus, learning generates wider benefits when it meets the interests, strengths and needs of the learner. These are determined by the learner's social context – their gender, ethnicity, class, sexuality, locality, history, financial resources, and the stage in the life course when the learner experiences learning. Whether learning meets these interests, strengths and needs depends upon the nature of provision in terms of content, level, pedagogy, student mix and setting. Gareth's final experience of FE provided a good match for his interests, strengths and needs, but his earlier school experiences did not, and the effects upon his health and social integration of these two episodes of learning were dramatically different (see Figure 4.1).

Beryl

> Once upon a time, I daren't even go anywhere, I'd be frightened. But now I dare do anything.

Beryl is 58, white, British, working class by family background and previous occupations, and has lived all her life in Nottingham. She is married with a daughter and son in their thirties, who both live nearby.

Beryl describes herself as having been a 'nervous kiddy' who stayed within her immediate family unit, and 'never went far'. She did not enjoy activities outside the family, including school. She remembers the teacher hitting her on the head, and that she was no good at writing or spelling. The 'best thing' about school was the two subjects that she was 'good at' – needlework and cookery. When she left school Beryl worked in a factory as a sewing machinist, and years later joined a sewing club. This is an example of a 'sleeper' effect – that is, an outcome of education that lasts over years (in this case, an interest and confidence in sewing) which is only expressed in activity later, when the time is right.

· Beryl got married and had two children. She stopped working in the factory and started cleaning, because she could fit this around her domestic responsibilities. Later she worked as a cleaner in an old people's home, which resembled her mother's employment as a Home Help. Beryl likes and enjoys the company of older people. She took early retirement at the age of 51:

> [I] went to see the doctors and things, and they just said you know, like, 'You can't go to work.' So that was it.

Beryl was sorry to stop working. Her description of how she came to take early retirement implies that she was not involved in making the decision and that she did not negotiate or even discuss the situation. However, the choice had an enormous impact upon her life. One wonders whether she might have taken a more active role in deciding whether to continue with her work if she had been more confident, believed that she should have more control over her life, felt more on a par with the doctor – if, possibly, she had experienced more education. Even if the outcome had been the same in the end, feeling that this had come of her own choice might have helped her to deal with its consequences.

The combination of symptoms (she had Menière's Disease and tinnitus, which are characterised by ringing, vertigo and nausea) and losing her job made Beryl 'really low':

> I sat in the house and I didn't do nothing and I got really depressed, and I'd got to get myself out.

A friend encouraged Beryl to enrol at college, and enrolled with her. This transformed her life. As with Gareth, the timing of participation was right because it came at a time when she needed help in adapting to change. In addition, she has found the level of support that she needed: 'She [the teacher] makes you feel welcome. She's always got time for you.'

Beryl describes herself prior to taking any courses as 'very shy', a 'very depressed, very nervous person':

> It's only since I've been to college that I've come out of myself [. . .] It's changed my personality a lot [. . .] More confident. I can do things what I've never dreamed of doing. Like I go to the gym.

Her increasing confidence must in part be due to her mastery of basic skills. She gained what she refers to as 'word power': competence to write a letter and use a dictionary, and she must also be more confident in her use of numbers and ICT, for she learned to use databases, spreadsheets and the internet. She says 'It's nice to know new things', and is clearly proud of her achievements. In addition, going to college has brought Beryl 'out of myself'. She emphasises 'company' and 'chatting', and that she has made 'loads' of friends through college. As her self-belief has grown, she demands, and probably commands, more respect from those she comes into contact with. She answers back if someone upsets or frightens her, whereas before she would have 'backed away' and cried.

The process of learning 'takes my mind off my ears'. Similarly, new social interactions and, as we see below, greater family involvement and civic participation provide a structured and enjoyable way forward that provides distraction and helps Beryl to cope with symptoms that are potentially very disabling. She sees participation in college as pivotal in her own re-alignment from isolation, depression and ill-health, to social participation and positive health. 'I've been ever so healthy and well since I've come here [to college].'

Skills acquired at college have enabled Beryl to contribute to her grandchildren's education. She often takes her two young grandchildren to school, and stays to help them with reading or writing at the beginning of the school day. This is rewarding in itself, and positively affects her family relationships. 'It's nice to tell your children things, your grandchildren, and they get proud of you because "Nanny can do that".' Beryl is referring here not only to her input at school, but also to the things she makes at her sewing club, which she gives to her family. Her interest in sewing is shared by her daughter, and they attend the sewing club together.

The sewing club is but one of the activities that college has led to. At the beginning of the interview, Beryl describes with self-satisfaction her busy life and varied activities, which clearly contribute to her identity and self-esteem. A relatively private new activity is that of writing her own Christmas cards. She also plans to start writing letters. She goes to the gym and keep fit, which she would 'never have dreamed of doing' were it not for college, and almost by definition these courses have positive impacts upon physical health as well as identity and esteem. Through college, the gym and the sewing club her social networks have been extended, and the confidence and enjoyment derived from these networks have led to additional civic participation of a more explicitly

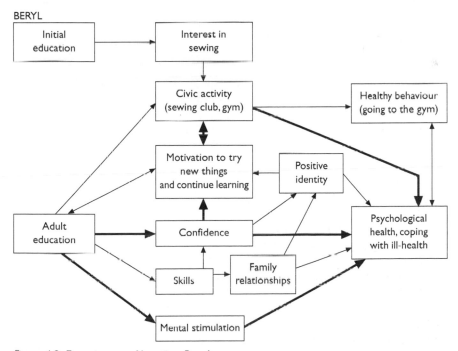

Figure 4.2 Experiences of learning: Beryl.

altruistic nature. Beryl is 'confident' to ask her neighbours if they want help, and to help them out. She also visits the local Church Hall (where the sewing club is held) to socialise with elderly people and encourage them to go to college.

Beryl's story is of a positive spiral in health, well-being, identity, family functioning, civic engagement and motivation to continue learning. Learning in her late fifties has had positive and transforming effects on Beryl's health and quality of life, and on her roles in the family and community. Her account illustrates the interrelatedness of these outcomes, and demonstrates that after a lifetime in which active learning appears to have played a minor role, involvement in quite basic education at the right time can have dramatic effects (see Figure 4.2).

Denise

> [Adult learning] helped me cope with the situations I was in and it's given me a break from it.

At the time of the interview, Denise was in her fifties. She is white, British, grew up on a council estate in Nottingham and attended the local grammar school. She was not happy there. The school may have had problems, but what is clear from Denise's account is the alienation she experienced as a result of a mismatch between the cultures of home and school:

> The grammar school didn't give me any confidence. It took what little confidence I'd got away because I came from a council estate and [the school . . .] tried to be like the private schools and it was very hard for me when I was there to fit in because you didn't fit in. There was one world at school, one world at home and it was completely alien. They were reading books, going to the theatre. I'd never been to the theatre in my life.

Although Denise was capable, she was not encouraged to go to university. The implicit assumption (there was 'no career guidance at all') was that she would be a teacher, nurse or secretary. Consequently, her description of how she came to work in a medical laboratory for two decades comes across as a passive process. We cannot know whether her occupational life would have been more fulfilling if school had promoted in her a more proactive attitude towards her career; however, she does comment somewhat wistfully that it would have been easier to obtain a degree at university straight after school than through day release whilst working.

Day release was hard work, but Denise hoped that additional qualifications would lead to promotion and she enjoyed the change of scene that day release gave her. Moreover:

I've always done study and I've enjoyed it. I realise now, it's like my hobby.

So this phase of education added pressure to her life, but it also made a positive contribution and sustained her well-being.

Denise married, divorced and re-married. She started a Master's course, but when she became pregnant gave up her studies and job. She and her husband had waited before having children, and she wanted to stay at home with them. However, when the time came, she found herself also looking after her sick father-in-law and her sick mother, which 'spoilt it [time at home with the children] for me'. Denise explains why she took the responsibility of caring for her father-in-law and her mother, as well as the two children:

> I went to this grammar school that made me feel bad about myself and got rid of my confidence, so I never considered myself, to say, 'No, I can't cope.'

This is a remarkably strong, lasting and negative effect of early education upon her confidence and assertiveness, and consequently upon her ability to feel in control of decision-making. It resonates with the rather passive way in which she appears to have followed her career in the medical laboratory.

We can infer that if her grammar school experiences had not undermined her confidence, she would have been less inhibited about saying, 'No, I can't cope.' What we cannot infer is what she would have decided to do. The situation was tough, however she dealt with it. But as with Beryl's decision about taking early retirement, feeling that she had made the choice about her role may have put a different spin on her experience, impacting upon her psychological health.

Having pre-school children was more difficult than Denise had imagined. It was not that childcare was unexpectedly demanding, but that she was not able to get on with doing anything else:

> You're at home with the children, so you can't do anything [. . .] If you don't do anything, nothing's going to happen.

For the first time in Denise's account, she describes taking positive action to change the course of events. She joined the Playgroup committee and took courses, which fitted around her chosen responsibility to care full-time for her sons.

The first course, in Child Development, was too basic for her, given her level of scientific knowledge, but she found the Learning through Play course useful and enjoyable. The pedagogy and content were 'totally different from what I'd done before' and relevant to her interests. This highlights the need to understand progression – educational and occupational – within a life course context. Moving from a Master's course to a basic level Learning through Play course might not be considered progression from a conventional standpoint, but Denise's interests and needs had moved on and so for her the Learning through

Play course represented a progression in learning content that matched the progression in her life from childless employee to full-time parent.

The Learning through Play course heightened Denise's awareness that her son Ben had developmental problems. Although it was not diagnosed until Ben was eight years old, he had a form of learning disability called Asperger's syndrome. This placed extra demands on his care, which was hard enough for Denise. However, what made the situation particularly distressing was that the condition was not diagnosed, and so his difficulties were not understood by the professionals whom she called upon for help. For example, the speech therapist advised Denise to talk to him more, which made her feel confused and inadequate. Eventually the co-ordinator for special educational needs at Ben's primary school referred him to a paediatrician, who diagnosed Asperger's syndrome. Thus, it was through the school education system that Denise eventually obtained a diagnosis for Ben.

Before the condition was diagnosed, Denise blamed herself for Ben's problems:

I thought it was me [. . .] You think to yourself, 'I'm doing wrong.'

Influenced by her earlier education, Denise read childcare books, and as she became increasingly concerned about Ben's development she read more. But the books described the development of children without developmental difficulties, who were not like Ben. Her education had taught her to take things on authority. It had not developed her abilities to think independently or to question, and it had undermined her self-confidence. Consequently, her knowledge of Ben's development compared to that described in the books reinforced her feelings of confusion and self-blame:

Because it's written down, it must be true sort of thing. This person's an expert. [. . .] When I was at school, you sat there [laughs] and were taught and you kept quiet. 'This is how it is. Don't question it.' Since I wasn't used to [childcare], you would just accept. It was the same at college I think to a certain degree.

Denise needed a break from domestic responsibilities and worries. The courses provided respite, and made her feel that she was getting on with her life.

Denise took a course in counselling when her sons were three and four. This was another new subject for her. She enjoyed it, gained confidence from participating in group discussions, and learned to value and reflect upon her feelings, which contributed to self-efficacy. The course also provided access to counselling for herself, which was useful at the time. The effects of the counselling course contrast with the effects of her school education, and this probably reflects differences in institutional ethos, pedagogy, content and student mix. In addition Denise chose to take the counselling course, and so it matched her interests and needs.

The following year, she studied Information Technology and Resource Management. Gaining familiarity with computers made her feel 'more part of the modern world', and learning how to prepare her *curriculum vitae* and prepare for job interviews increased her confidence to apply for higher-level jobs. She obtained a distinction, which was an enormous boost to her confidence, even though she was already aware of her capabilities.

Although Denise did not find employment easily, she remained confident and puts her lack of success down to prejudice on the part of prospective employers. She is much more independent and assertive. Her role as carer forced her to take control and make things happen – 'If you don't do anything, nothing's going to happen'. The course in counselling encouraged her to think reflectively and independently, and the course in ICT developed her occupational confidence. She could see that as the children grew less dependent, alternatives would be available to her. She decided not to return to her previous occupation, and was thinking about a new career.

Throughout this period, Denise continued to seek recognition of Ben's difficulties, without success. She describes how her previous education disabled her and her more recent education helped her to communicate with professionals, even though they did not always give her appropriate help:

> Because I went to grammar school and then I worked in a hospital laboratory for 20 years – but because I've come from that background, you're able to talk to people at the same level. You know what to say, when to keep quiet [. . .] It's the same with teachers and everyone [. . .] You're educated to their level Because I've had the education, I've got the language.

Her more recent studies in counselling and IT increased her confidence to ask for professional help.

Once Denise had obtained a diagnosis for Ben, she researched Asperger's syndrome, using the internet, leaflets and self-help groups. However, the syndrome is wide ranging in its symptoms and severity, and so it was difficult to make sense of the information. Her scientific education, especially at Master's level, helped her to understand and critically evaluate this information:

> All the books, they're not particularly written for parents. It's written for other professionals – psychologists and it [the Master's] has helped me read the books [. . .] and understand. And strangely enough, because I've done the MSc, I can reject some of the things because they're scientifically based and I've done the Sciences [. . .] 'Where's your evidence?' It's this way of thinking, isn't it? In a Science-based way. I'd been used to reading scientific papers and extracting the information from them. That helped. [. . .] I can cope with [. . .] the scientific jargon.

When Denise was interviewed, she was working as a parent support worker in schools. She enjoyed the work, and it fitted around the needs of her children. She had discovered her interest in communicating with others through her counselling course, and had developed the confidence to attempt a change of career through the course in IT and Resource Management. So her recent education contributed to her choice of employment, her success in it, and consequently to her fulfilment and the enrichment of the school communities where she worked.

Denise's account represents a curious mix in outcomes of education. She has acquired knowledge, skills and professional status, which have helped her to negotiate health messages and health systems. But she lacked confidence in her intuitions, and independence.

A number of studies have found a class gradient in the diagnosis of difficult-to-diagnose conditions, such as chronic fatigue syndrome and allergies amongst children (see Heinrich et al. 1998; Wessely, Hotoph and Sharpe 1998). These conditions are diagnosed more often amongst individuals of higher socio-economic status than they are amongst individuals of lower socio-economic status. However, the class gradients are not found when the prevalence rates of the defining symptoms of the conditions are measured. This implies that the association between higher socio-economic status and higher rates of the diagnosed conditions reflects an association between class and rates of accurate diagnosis rather than an association between class and the prevalence rates of the conditions themselves. One explanation for this finding is that middle-class patients, who tend to be more educated, share cultural capital with health professionals, and consequently communication about symptoms and needs is more effective.

On this basis, one might imagine that Denise's education and subsequent occupational status would have enabled her to obtain an early diagnosis of her son's condition. However, her account suggests otherwise. Maybe this is because the impacts of her education were shaped by the working-class background that she comes from. Denise felt alienated and inferior in her grammar school because the school culture was incongruent with her own, and although she obtained a degree and started a Master's course, she did it the hard way. Day release would not offer the same range of opportunities, new experiences and time to explore them as three years spent in full-time study in a college or university setting. Her experience is not unique and resonates with literature concerning the experiences of working-class children attending grammar schools published in the 1970s (e.g. Jackson and Marsden 1962).

The last few years have been important because Denise has gained more control of her life and the direction it is taking. Initially, her caring roles forced her to 'make things happen', and life has opened out as she experienced new roles – for example, as the organiser of her children's activities, and as an employee in a job that is challenging and fulfilling. Learning which matched her interests, strengths and needs was integral to each of these roles, and consequently to the expansion of her life. It contributed to personal transformation and to the enrichment of her family and community (see Figure 4.3).

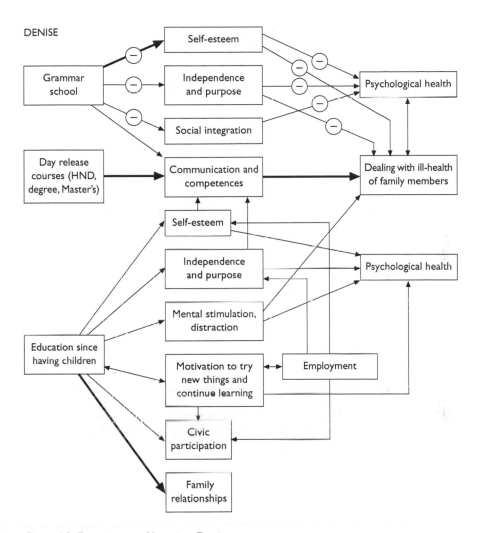

Figure 4.3 Experiences of learning: Denise.

Consuela

You're more than able to do it if you just keep focusing.

Consuela is white and was born in Venezuela. She came to England with her parents when she was 14, and still lives with them. At the time of the interview she was studying on an access course in an FE college. In Venezuela, Consuela attended a private convent school staffed by nuns. She enjoyed school and

Consuela is 26 years old. She is white, female, has no qualifications, and is single without dependent children. Her family background is middle class. Currently she is a student. Since Consuela is under 30 years of age, we compare her with individuals from the BCS70 dataset, who were all aged 30 in 2000.

Amongst 30-year-olds in Britain in 2000, about 127 people in every 10,000 were white, female, middle class, single with no dependants, with qualifications up to but not including degree level. Amongst this group, a relatively low percentage had obtained any qualifications during the previous seven years (27 per cent as opposed to 35 per cent of all 30-year-olds). This possibly reflects findings from other studies that women tend to acquire fewer qualifications than men in adulthood (see Jenkins et al. 2002).

People 'like' Consuela are similar to other 30-year-olds in terms of the proportions of individuals who are clinically depressed, who have positive self-efficacy, and who report high levels of life satisfaction. The percentage of people sharing Consuela's characteristics who belong to at least one organisation is close to that for all 30-year-olds (9 per cent), but the percentage of this group who report an interest in politics is low when compared to other 30-year-olds (25 per cent as opposed to 34 per cent). This reflects an over-representation of individuals who are interested in politics and who are not like Consuela, possibly focused on those with degree-level qualifications and above, and those who have children in education.

Consuela is unusual compared to others with her demographic characteristics in that she has acquired qualifications during the past seven years, and because she belongs to an organisation (she is actively involved in the youth group at her church). Fewer than one in ten people sharing Consuela's demographic characteristics belong to an organisation. Consuela is closer to the average in that she is not depressed and has positive efficacy and life satisfaction. She does not mention interest in politics.

gained a good grounding in self-esteem, self-efficacy and feeling part of a community. She describes this school as 'very strict but very good'. She was aware that she was a good student because she passed tests with an A+, she always did her homework, she was punctual and polite, and she received positive feedback from her teachers. Consuela was made a prefect, which was a great privilege.

The school developed amongst its students respect for others, especially adults, and a positive sense of community and social responsibility:

[We were taught] not to feel that we were there to study by ourselves, but that the school was a community. And the teachers [...] were part of that community. We were part of that community. And we were all working together to always improve it ourselves, and improving society. That was the main idea.

Her teachers were her role models. They took care to check that every student was happy in every aspect of their learning, and if there were problems they would ask parents in to discuss the difficulties. Consuela thinks that this has 'definitely, definitely' had an effect upon her positive attitude towards helping other people.

Education was highly valued within the school because it enables individuals to maximise their contributions to society. Consequently, the children at the school, Consuela included, worked very hard. At this time, she saw herself as having a 'brilliant future'. Her attitude towards learning has been central to her sense of identity and purpose throughout her life. She describes herself as 'crazy about knowledge. I really like to learn and to study, and that's just my nature.' She thinks that besides school, her family background – 'a long history of professionals' – has affected her attitude towards learning. Within her family:

There is a culture to educate ourselves, to learn as much as we can about as many topics as we can.

Similarly, Consuela's sense of community responsibility was affected by her wider family and community as well as by her school.

It was an attitude of the school, that although we were individuals, we were all part of a community. And of the country [...] We could all put a little bit of dust on the cap of the mountain [this is a common saying in Venezuela].

Thus during her early years in Venezuela she developed strong senses of self-esteem, self-efficacy and social responsibility, and hope for the future. In contrast to Denise's experience, school had a strong and positive impact that was entirely congruent with the expectations and culture of Consuela's family and home community.

Consuela left Venezuela when she was 14 years old. She and her parents came to join her sister in London, but there was an argument and she and her parents were left to fend for themselves. None of them spoke English, and Consuela's parents were preoccupied with finding housing and employment. When Consuela started school she had very little English, and even less knowledge of English society and its education system. She attended the local comprehensive secondary school, where:

> The teachers totally ignor[ed] me like I'm invisible. I felt sometimes like I was invisible. I had to pinch myself because I felt like I was invisible [...] In school, the kids, the teachers would look at me like an ant or a horrible thing.

Consuela describes how devastating this experience was for her, how it undermined her sense of efficacy and purpose, made her feel alienated from other people, and undermined her self-esteem and her psychological health:

> I remember going to – crying – home, every day. Every day. I was bullied. I was – I felt like in the – It was terrible. And because I was at that age – 14 to 15, [...] everybody is going through those biological changes. It was terrible really, a horrible time. [...] For a time, it depressed me. I was so depressed. I was absolutely depressed. Because when I was in Venezuela, I had a brilliant future. I had a brilliant future, and once being here and having all these experiences, I felt like a failure, like perhaps I wasn't good enough. Perhaps I didn't have the potential or the intelligence to do something, or – I just felt really horrible in myself.

Consuela describes how she coped with these experiences:

> I saw it for what it was – an experience. But within myself I had this strength. I had the strength that I knew that if I believed in myself, if I had faith, if I tried my best, if I was responsible, then one day it was going to be noticed or recognised or some door was going to be opened. [...] So I did feel, obviously, because I'm human, I felt sad and depressed. And at times there came this feeling or thought that maybe I wasn't good enough. Maybe that's why I wasn't being noticed. But then again something within myself would say, you know, 'That's rubbish. That's ridiculous. You know you're very good', and, you know – like sort of motivate myself, try to encourage myself to carry on, to continue.

Consuela accepted that she had no control over her situation (she spoke no English and lacked the knowledge needed to change what was happening to her), but dealt with it emotionally as best she could. In other words, she accepted what she could not change, and took control of the only aspect that she could – her emotional response. Thus, she managed to retain some element of efficacy throughout this period, which helped her to cope with the experience.

Consuela's resilience came in part from her family background, which was supportive and professional. It also came from her schooling in Venezuela, which had contributed to her positive self-esteem, self-efficacy and her belief in social justice:

> Those memories [of school in Venezuela] helped me to be able to say, 'You can do it, of course you can. You're more than able to do it if you just keep

focusing, move on, carry on and you will make it. One day you will make it.'

Consuela left school at 16 without qualifications. She studied leisure and tourism at a sixth form college, but was not given additional support despite her continuing difficulties with English as a second language. Nevertheless, she worked extremely hard, going to the library every day and sometimes studying until 3 o'clock in the morning. As a result of an administrative error, she was not awarded the diploma that she should have achieved. Her continued failure to achieve success caused her disappointment and put her off formal study for the next few years.

At the sixth form college, Consuela heard about a Latin American Youth Organisation, and for 18 months she became very involved in its activities. The aim of the organisation was to support young asylum seekers from Latin America. Classes were provided in a range of subjects including folkloric dance (Latin American folk dancing), Maths, Spanish Literature and English as a Second Language. Consuela helped 'really in every way I could', which was mostly in an administrative capacity. Later, she became involved in campaigning and fundraising so that the organisation could continue. After 12 months, she was elected president.

The interview skips over these and the following years of Consuela's life. However, one would imagine that her role in this organisation contributed to her sense of well-being and fulfilment. For she says:

> I cannot separate myself from society or from where I live. I just cannot. I might try, but I cannot. So it's important for me to be able to offer something good, positive [. . .] It's a more positive attitude.

During these years, learning remained a central part of Consuela's life:

> I never stopped studying. I was always reading, you know [. . .] literature, law, everything I could get my hands on really.

At 21, Consuela decided to re-enter education with a view to going to university. However, her educational experiences in London had not helped her to make an informed choice about how she should proceed:

> Because my education was so disorganised, I didn't know what to do next. So I tried different things. [. . .] For example, I did an Access to Law, I started an Access to Humanities and Social Sciences, which I left halfway and now I'm completing. I did a BTEC in Business and Finance. I did a GNVQ Advanced Leisure and Tourism. I did an Access to Drama. I did other courses on the side. So now I'm 26, and finally I'm doing an Access course which [. . .] I like.

This process of tasting different subjects is an example of what one practitioner teaching access courses referred to as a 'voyage of discovery' that he felt was the experience of a number of his students. It is an example of the extending nature of education through the provision of new experiences, understandings and opportunities.

Consuela's college experiences had been very positive, and this confirmed her belief in at least one aspect of the education system in Britain and in her ability to operate effectively within it:

> Before, I felt like – what's the word? – I felt like a victim. I'm a victim, you know. I can't do anything. I can't say, I can't speak, you know. And now it's very different. I'm not a victim. I'm just – I'm not more or less than anybody else.

Her educational experiences throughout her life, both the positive and negative ones, have contributed to a process of maturation in relation to her own independence and her dependence upon other people. Her school in Venezuela was formative in developing a basic belief in herself and in society, and optimism for her future. Her experience in secondary school made her aware that she could not rely on other people, that she had to do things for herself. Her recent experience of college has reaffirmed her belief that she can achieve her goals herself, but that there are many people who are willing to help her:

> Before, when I was at school [in Venezuela], I was relying on people. I thought people were like-minded, like me. I thought – you know – I had this utopian view of life, and people too. But now I realise that it's not like that. That you have to make it for yourself, and you have to make a stand, and you have to demand. You have all the right to demand. And now my experience here is so positive, because I can go to a teacher and say, 'I'm sorry, I wasn't here last week. Can you tell me what we did?' And I know that they will.

Her recent education has also been a means to achieving her goal of going to university. At the time of the interview, she had conditional offers at three universities.

Consuela's story ends on a positive note, despite her very difficult experiences as a teenager. What carried her through this period may be described in terms of 'inner strength' or resilience – a strong belief in herself, in her ability to control her experiences, and in justice, plus a strong sense of purpose and future. The positive influence of her initial education was to sustain and protect her through times of difficulty. In contrast, she hopes that her current education will contribute to positive transformations in the occupational domain of her life. Both these effects apply primarily at an individual as opposed to a community level, although her initial education contributed to her motivation and ability to trans-

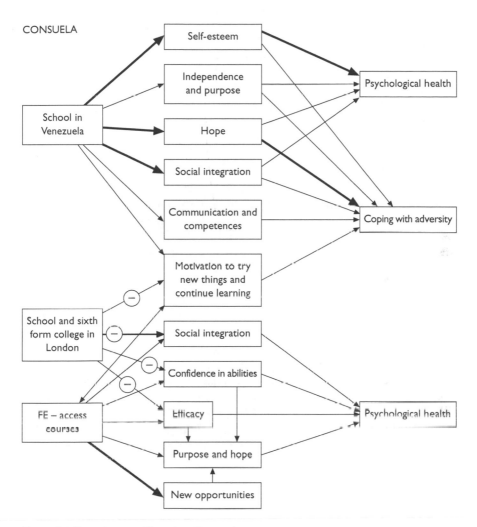

Figure 4.4 Experiences of learning: Consuela.

form the Latin American Youth Organisation, which constituted an effect at the community level. Consuela's account illustrates how difficult it is to disentangle the effects of family, culture, previous education and life events, but that congruent positive influences have profound and lasting impacts (see Figure 4.4).

Comparisons and conclusions

Each of these case studies has illustrated the complexity and dynamism inherent to the processes through which learning impacts upon people's lives, and the impossibility of understanding a learning experience and its impact upon an individual's life without reference to all aspects of the individual's life course and wider context. Each illustrates the processes through which positive experiences of learning develop psychosocial qualities that lead to both improved health outcomes and the motivation and opportunity to continue learning – through formal education, work, or other less formal channels. Learning provides wider opportunities, the means to progression, and new experiences, understandings and social contacts. This aspect of learning is described in the last paragraph of Chapter 3 as an expansion of the individual as he or she moves from looking inwards to looking outwards, and is enabled to see his or her own life in a broader context. We noted that this distinguishes learning from other activities, such as work and leisure pursuits that do not involve learning.

As in the previous chapter, we see that education can have positive and negative effects. If learning involves expansion, then inevitably it involves risks to the individual, the teacher and the institution. Thus we see failure as well as success, with its consequent costs. We concluded that the health benefits of learning are maximised and the risks minimised if the pedagogy, curriculum, student mix and institutional context match the learner's strengths, interests and needs. In this chapter, we see that individuals' strengths, interests and needs are contingent on their history, the social, political and economic context in which they have lived, and their current circumstances.

Early school experiences have lasting effects on confidence and attitudes towards learning. Sadly, school had undermined the confidence of Beryl, Gareth and Denise and resulted in feelings of alienation. Difficulties were accentuated by mismatches between the educational culture and family background. School differs from adult education in that students cannot choose to opt out of it. If the experience is unpleasant, pointless and psychologically damaging, the student has no choice but to stick with it. Negative experiences, it appears, can have profound and long-lasting effects upon people's lives. However, as Consuela's account illustrates, schooling can have equally profound and long-lasting positive effects. By their nature, children are open to new ideas, enthusiastic about learning, and malleable in the development of their personal identity, social skills and values. Their education inevitably exploits this openness and malleability – with positive and negative effects. Clearly, there is a responsibility on providers to maximise the positive and minimise the negative outcomes.

Gareth remarks that his current education is beneficial because it came 'at the right time'. This was a period of re-orientation or discontinuity. Similarly, learning helped Beryl to adapt to the onset of chronic illness and early retirement, and Denise to the changing demands of parenthood. In contrast, Consuela's psychological health and social participation were sustained in times of difficulty partly through her earlier school experiences, and Denise's life before having children was enriched but not transformed by her almost continual participation in learning.

The distinction between the transforming and sustaining effects of learning is therefore best understood within a wider life-course perspective. Other research suggests that the potential of education to impact on people's lives is great at times of change (Antikainen 1998). We see from the case studies that wider benefits are particularly visible when people take courses at such times. In contrast, learning during periods of stability is more likely to have sustaining effects that are less visible, but may nevertheless have value for the individual and the community. During periods of chronic stress or adversity these effects are protective, and during periods of more positive stability they are enriching.

Gareth's account illustrates the distinction between education and therapy. If learning has positive effects upon health, then, almost by definition, it is therapeutic. However, learning should be thought of as distinct from therapy. Therapy usually refers to interventions that specifically and directly tackle ill-health such as depression and physical diseases. Gareth received counselling and rehabilitation as therapeutic interventions to tackle his depression and dependency upon drugs, and Denise's father-in-law and mother probably received drug therapies to tackle their physical health conditions and the symptoms of these conditions. Learning is therapeutic not because it tackles ill-health directly, but because it helps individuals to deal with its consequences. It also consolidates, protects and builds up psychological health, and promotes healthy lifestyles.

In this chapter we have seen that the impacts of education can only be understood in a life-course context. They depend on social and cultural factors that shape individuals as well as on the stage during the life course when education is experienced. I suggest that learning experienced at times of relative discontinuity tends to be transforming, whilst learning at times of relative stability tends to be sustaining.

Chapter 5

Family life and learning

Emergent themes

Angela Brassett-Grundy

This chapter introduces readers to the themes relating to families and learning, which were apparent from the interviews we conducted with adult learners. It begins with an overview of the way in which families have changed over recent decades; this may help us better understand the way in which learning and education impinges on what is now a very dynamic and fluid concept. Following this, I summarise some of the quantitative research findings of the effects of learning on the family, which will set the scene for a rather lengthier presentation of the specific family-related themes found in our own qualitative research.

Family trends

The family of the new millennium is very different to that which was common-place at the start of the last century. Amongst the myriad of changing family and living patterns seen in recent decades are an overall fall in fertility; an increase in extra-marital fertility; older ages at child-bearing; smaller households and family sizes; an increase in lone parenthood; an increase in divorce rates; an increase in cohabitation; an increase in living alone; falling numbers of first marriages; and a decline in extended families and multi-family households (Fox and Pearce 2000; Haskey 1987, 1998; McRae 1999). These trends are set to continue, along with increasing numbers of stable non-marital unions, including same-sex couples; 'living apart together' relationships; never-married motherhood as choice; co-parenting; and reconstituted families built around remarriage or cohabitation. The changes have meant that family and household structures have become more diverse, and that individuals are more likely to experience living in a greater variety of families and households during their lifetime. According to Haskey (1996), the trend towards a variety of norms is perhaps the most significant aspect of post-war social change.

Current debates rage over the decline of the traditional family (i.e. two married parents, where mother is the home-maker and caregiver, father is the 'breadwinner' and children are the passive recipients of socialisation). If the traditional family unit is seen as both a norm and an ideal, then recent trends undoubtedly place this under threat. Some argue that this results in irresponsible behaviour, social fragmentation and disorder, seeing the family as in need of protection through state intervention, e.g. welfare benefits, reassertion of traditional values. New families do not conform to the long-standing gender and generational order that underpins stable, social capital-rich society, but are seen to change them negatively. Others argue that the traditional family unit is divisive and oppressive, and maintains inequalities of power. For them, contemporary family life enables individualisation, fluidity and variety, more complexity and choice, and freedom from definitive gender and generational obligations and relationships. If learning affects the traditional family unit, it depends on which side of the debate you sit as to whether you perceive the effects as positive or negative. The first case study in Chapter 6 (Delia) is a good example of how one can perceive the effects of learning differentially in this sense.

These trends have implications for the definition of a family in terms of gender, generation, age, class and ethnicity. Whilst we might be more certain of the definition of a traditional family, we are less sure of what constitutes a contemporary family. Morgan (1996) argues that families are not static concrete structures or forms; they are created through everyday, ongoing and fluid 'practices', which overlap and interact with other practices related to gender, generation, social class and ethnicity. This is similar to the ideas of Bourdieu (1977, 1986), in which social capital (of which the family is one source) is interrelated with other forms of capital (see Chapters 7 and 8).

What is certain, however, is that the family continues to be one of our earliest sources of learning. As Goleman states: 'Family life is our first school for emotional learning; in this intimate cauldron we learn how to feel about ourselves and how others will react to our feeling (Goleman 1996: 189–190). Indeed, long-term learning identities are formed within families (Gorard et al. 1998), and families are publicly recognised as potentially both rich and supportive learning environments for all members (DfES 1999). This chapter now discusses how families and learning interact with each other, taking a brief look first at findings from quantitative research.

Families and learning – quantitative findings

The effect of education on the formation and dissolution of the family is discussed by Blackwell and Bynner (2002). They highlight the fact that the relationship is a complex one, with numerous paths that individuals might follow. This makes it unhelpful to group people together according to, for example, their domestic status in order to draw conclusions about the effect of education and learning on that status. However, education is a significant mediator of social, economic and demographic influences which produce life-course changes, and is a marker for the establishment of families.

Levels of parental education have an effect on when partnerships are formed. For example, youthful marriage occurs most commonly among women with the poorest education (Ferri and Smith 1997), and those with higher educational attainment tend to be the least likely to marry – although single, childless males are found at both ends of the educational spectrum (Dale and Egerton 1997). Levels of parental education also affect when children are conceived and the numbers of children that are conceived. Highly educated women with children under five years old are more likely to be in employment and to have delayed childbearing (Dale and Egerton 1997). Teenage parenting has been found to be both a cause and a consequence of educational under-achievement (Kiernan 1997, 1999), and the most poorly educated are more likely to become younger parents and to have the most children (Ekinsmyth and Bynner 1994; Bynner and Parsons 1998; Hobcraft 2000).

Research has also shown that parental education affects children's attainment, for example in cognitive development of children from as early as 12 months (Roberts et al. 1999) and in later school achievement (Bynner and Steedman 1995; Bynner et al. 1999). Klebanov et al. (1994) found that mother's education predicted maternal warmth, which itself is linked to children's educational attainment (see, for example, Barocas et al. 1991; Diaz et al. 1991). Family functioning, as seen in affective relationships and interaction between parents and children, has also been shown to impact on children's attainment (see, for example, Hess and Holloway 1984; Ramey and Ramey 1992, 1999). Parsons and Bynner (1998) found that particular parental attributes are associated with children's educational success, such as sharing parenting responsibilities and reading to children. Indeed, there is a whole developmental psychological literature related to these issues concerning attachment theory, as espoused by Bowlby (1953, 1969, 1988) and elaborated upon by countless others, showing that securely attached infants have better cognitive development through childhood and become less anxious and better adjusted adults (see, for example, Bretherton 1985; Masten and Coatsworth 1998; Stams et al. 2002).

Parental interest in children is also associated with children's propensity to form families. Hobcraft (2000) found that those with mothers who were less interested in their education were more likely to become mothers, and Manlove (1997) found that those who become teenage mothers are less interested in their daughter's education. Parental interest in children can also directly affect children's educational attainment, for example through the relationship parents develop with their children's schools (Tizard et al. 1988; Bynner and Steedman 1995; Mortimore 1998). Coleman (1988) talks of parental interest in children as enabling children to increase human capital in the form of educational achievement (as exemplified by two of the case studies which are explored in Chapter 6 – Delia and Hester).

An extensive literature exists on family social class and children's academic attainment, in which robust international associations are found (Unicef 2002). A number of factors are related to social class which no doubt influence this association, such as geographical location, family income, parenting style and, as discussed above, parental education. Thus, quantitative findings show that learning and education affect the family in a variety of ways, including the propensity to form partnerships, the likelihood of remaining in the work force (and thus delaying childbearing), the timing of childbirth, and the interest shown in children's education. The direction of causality is far from clear and there is a plethora of mediating factors. The relationship between the family and learning is therefore a complex one, which we have begun to unpack through the qualitative analysis of in-depth interviews with adult learners. The findings from this analysis are now discussed.

Fieldwork findings

This section presents the results of the qualitative analysis of what adult learners reported themselves, focusing upon the effects of their engagement in learning on their families, and *vice versa*. These issues were not questions which were explicitly and specifically probed by the interviewers; they merely represent one of the themes which arose naturally out of the discussions concerning the effect that episodes of learning had on individuals throughout their lives.

Family themes were particularly evident in about 60 of the interviews conducted. Of these, 50 interviewees were female and 22 were white British. Ages ranged from 17 to 70-something, and were concentrated in the 35–50 age-group. As a group they possessed a wide range of educational attainment, from no qualifications to Master's degrees. The same was true of employment status: a third of those for whom this information was known were in some form of paid employment, a quarter were studying, 1 in 10 was unemployed and/or seeking work, and the remainder described themselves as voluntary workers, housewives, retired or disabled.

The main strands which unfolded in relation to family themes are presented below. In each instance the themes are illustrated, where relevant, with quotes directly from the interviewees.

Describing and defining families

The interviewees were living in a range of family configurations, including: single-generation families (5 per cent with spouse after children had left home, 3 per cent widowed, 2 per cent with partner, 5 per cent single); two-generation families (48 per cent with spouse/partner and children, 33 per cent single/separated/divorced with children); and three-generation families (2 per cent with partner, children and step grandchild, 2 per cent with mother, brothers, niece and nephew). This is in keeping with the complex and diverse household compositions identified by research quoted earlier. However, household composition does not equate to family, and no doubt different answers would have been elicited from asking interviewees the direct question, 'What does family mean to you?' Although this question was not asked, the definition of the word 'family' was touched upon by one interviewee, Evan, who referred to an elderly couple he had become fond of, referring to them as his 'adopted' parents. He also referred to his girlfriend's daughter as his 'adopted' daughter, although he did not live with either of them and had not adopted his girlfriend's daughter legally. These are relationships which are not automatically considered as sitting neatly within preconceived ideas of what a family is, and it is worth highlighting the fact that people's own sense of family does not necessarily include only those people to whom they are blood-related and/or with whom they share a living space. It goes beyond the non-blood relationships present in reconstituted/step-families, to include those people to whom we feel close and with whom we have a surrogate parent/child or adoptive-type relationship, such as the elderly couple to whom Evan referred. This links neatly with the definition of family implicated in the earlier part of this chapter, and Morgan's (1996) notion of the family as ever-changing. In reading the themes which now follow, one should have in mind the broadest definition of the term 'family'.

Motivation to learn

In some instances, individuals' families had been the direct motivation for them to participate in education and learning. On the whole, this was as the result of a positive experience discussed in terms of interviewees' early education. Angus' parents encouraged him to go to college after school. He far preferred this experience to school, which had been populated by badly-behaved pupils and bullies. Dosumu's parents, although strict, seemed to prepare her for her experience of schooling in England after emigrating here from Nigeria. They instilled in her the attitude to life which enabled her both to adapt easily to the UK education system and to make the most of her learning experiences here:

> My father was a teacher, but he retired, and my mum was a full-time mother that had other things doing by the side you know, so I had a strict background when I was growing up [. . .] I had all of these attitudes to life because of the way they exposed me to things so when I came over here I easily adapted into the system here. Maybe for another family it could be different.

Some interviewees spoke of their recent participation in learning as having been motivated directly by a family member. Rita, a black British female lone parent in her mid-thirties, stated that after finding out that she had not passed her nursing exams she decided not to bother going back to find out why, or to re-sit them. One of her sisters suggested that she would have wasted two years' work for the sake of only another three months' study in order to re-sit the exams and give herself the opportunity of passing. Rita followed her sister's advice and passed her exams on the second attempt, which she says was a valuable experience.

Several described being motivated by their children to learn in order to keep up with them, especially in relation to information technology. It was because of his daughter that Alisdair was motivated to apply to a computer course, after he'd watched her using PowerPoint on the library computer. He describes the powerful effect that this had on him, which transpired to be a life-changing (and thus transforming, to refer to the learning matrix conceptualisation discussed earlier in this book – see Chapter 2) event:

> ... she said, 'Oh it's easy Dad, you click onto that and then you get the picture and then you can type', and I said to her, I said, 'That is the last time you ever show me how to use a computer' and she said to me, 'Am I in trouble?' I said, 'No you've just changed my life.' And I thought, sod it – nervous or not nervous I will go for this, and I decided that by the time I was 40 I would give myself the opportunity to have a career.

Catherine, a middle-aged woman with two children, felt conscious that as an older mother she may be losing touch, whereas an IT course would enable her to feel more a part of the 'modern world'. She also said: 'I'm doing an English course because I'm not up to the standard that my children are, amazing as it can be.' Similarly, Hermione said that she had taken up a computer course because she felt embarrassed that her children knew more than she did.

Thus for some their families had been the primary motivating force behind their participation in learning. This ranged from their experiences of education in childhood to their more recent involvement in learning as adults. In some cases it was because they had been raised within a family culture that valued learning and education, which was then carried through to their adult lives, whereas in others it was because, as an adult, they realised that their own children were advancing beyond the point they themselves had reached.

Interactions between parental and children's learning

A set of themes emerged relating to interactions between parental and children's learning, which can be categorised as follows:

> *Valuing* – as a result of their own participation in learning, parents came to give more value to their children's educational achievement
> *Supporting* – parents were more able to offer support to their children, directly in their studies or indirectly by involvement in their school
> *Role-modelling* – parents became model learners for their children
> *Reciprocating* – children helped their parents, giving them motivation for or support in their learning
> *Enjoying* – children and parents learnt together as a highly enjoyable joint activity.

Valuing

We start with a somewhat perverse effect. Some respondents have reacted to their own negative experiences of school, and are doing things differently in order that their own children will have a different and more positive experience. Evelyn's negative experiences of school have affected how she has approached her son's schooling.

> I was picked on by the teachers for being different and for being independent and for standing up and speaking for myself, and that is what I will not tolerate ... My attitude is I don't want him disrupting the class, I do want him doing his work, but I want it recognised that he's independent, that he's got a personality.

A more predictable positive effect occurs when, as a result of their own learning, a parent is able to show interest in their child's learning and pride in their achievements. Faith's younger son, from her second marriage, is interested in history and asked her to bring home any treasure that she finds from her archaeology course dig. She has lots of books at home on castles, which her younger son wants to take to school for project work, and he has benefited from her knowledge and books on ancient Egypt that have helped with the costumes for his end-of-term play. The pride interviewees spoke about with regard to their children's attainment echoes some of the quantitative findings, and links with one of the seven psychosocial developmental priming mechanisms identified by Ramey and Ramey (1992, 1999): that of celebrating developmental advances. Such parent–child interaction, they claim, leads to better psychosocial development, which in turn enhances educational attainment.

Supporting

Some interviewees reported that through their participation in learning they had become more able to offer direct support to their children in their studies. This is seen in the example above, where Faith supplies books for her son to use at school in his own project work. Other parents felt participation in learning had resulted in them becoming more supportive of their children's learning by becoming more involved in their schools. In some cases this was because the courses the parents were attending were being run at their children's schools, and thus they became a familiar sight. Elsa, a divorced woman from a white working-class background with three children, expressed this when she spoke of how much her children enjoyed seeing her attend their school for her family learning course: 'They think it's lovely, especially because it's to do within school.' This reminds us of the research already quoted reporting the benefits of parental involvement in children's schools (Tizard et al. 1988; Bynner and Steedman 1995; Mortimore 1998).

Taking part in an IT course led to Catherine purchasing a home computer to enhance the learning of the whole family, which she says she would not have otherwise owned. She spoke of how her husband and her children use the computer, playing educational games and using CD-Rom dictionaries and encyclopaedias. The children also work on the computer together with Catherine (she says, 'If they hit a problem, I feel more confident about what to do'), and in this scenario not only is Catherine there to support and educate her children, passing on the knowledge she has acquired through her IT course, but the family is also engaged in a joint, fun activity.

Role-modelling

By taking learning seriously, adults offer a good 'learner' role model for their children. Cliff, a black African male asylum seeker, stated that his three children are proud that he and his wife are 'going to school'; he feels as though he is setting them a good example and said: 'We told them we passed our exams; they were so happy for us and it was kind of a motivation for them also to do the same.' Cliff's wife, Annabel, described the impressive manner in which the whole family learns together from the computer and CD-Roms:

> ... when they see me seated and reading it makes them concentrate more ... the atmosphere looks easier for you to learn. That's what we've trained them to do. At least when, because my learning time starts at 6 o'clock to 8 o'clock so from 6 o'clock to 8 o'clock everyone is quiet, there is no noise, all the doors are closed, everyone is seated so it makes it easier for them as well as us.

For Kashani, an Indian woman, her own studying enables her to act as a role model for her daughter, in good family learning style. She tells her daughter that she has an assignment to do for her homework, which encourages her daughter to get on with her own homework assignments: 'It's a positive effect – it's like a role model as well because she sees her mum doing it.'

Naomi has not only become a good learner role model; she has also become a good citizen role model. A white woman with two children, training to become a primary school teacher, she says her participation in learning has made her more open-minded. She believes she has become a better example to her children of someone who is aware, responsible, tolerant and respectful. She would like her children to grow up with open minds, and says that this change has come about purely as a result of her recent learning: 'It's having done my course that's taught me that, that you don't judge people.'

Ede is a white 'European' divorced woman in her mid-twenties, with three children, from a middle-class background. Her 'parent pack' courses have helped her in terms of teaching her children to be responsible, which she believes has enhanced their self-esteem:

... what I'm doing is teaching my children to be responsible adults at the end of the day, and I mean I actually turn round to them now, and like my eight-year-old son will, when he takes his clothes off, put them in the washing machine and turn the washing machine on. And I bet there aren't that many eight-year-old boys who'd do that. I just, I think that's good for him, because it boosts his self-esteem.

This effect is reminiscent of another of Ramey and Ramey's (1992, 1999) psychosocial developmental priming mechanisms which enhance children's attainment: that of guiding and limiting behaviour. Given that just over two-thirds of 12- to 16-year-olds rate their parents as the strongest learning influence in their lives (Campaign for Learning et al. 2000), it is preferable that parents become good/positive (learning) role models, like the parents interviewed here.

Reciprocating

In a similar vein, there are pleasing examples where the support from the parent is reciprocated by the child, as with Gloria. She is a white British woman in her early thirties, and as a single parent with six children she has a lot of responsibilities. This has not stopped her studying a number of courses, culminating in her pursuit of a place on a nursing course. Her children have been very supportive:

> When I first went to college the children were great. They gave me loads of back-up and said 'Yes, come on, Mum'. I've always said to the kids, 'No TV 'til you've done your homework', or 'You can't have this 'til you've done your homework, get your work, you've got to read your books', or something like that. That's what they did to me last year when I first started: 'Come on Mum, do your homework and then you can watch TV.'

Kashani is very involved with her daughter. There is a lot of two-way learning, as she accompanies her daughter on visits to museums, the Bank of England, galleries and plays. She has occasionally sat listening to her daughter conversing with her house guests and thought: 'Wow, I didn't know that; I'm learning from my daughter.' Here, it is not support for learning that is being reciprocated, but the actual act of learning: Kashani educates her daughter, and is educated by her. This echoes the findings of other qualitative research with parents on family learning courses (Brassett-Grundy 2002; Brassett-Grundy and Hammond 2003), reminding us that adults can learn from children as much as children can learn from adults.

There were also examples of intergenerational reciprocity of learning, where something taught by an interviewee's parent was then passed on to the interviewee's own children. Elsbeth, a married white woman in her fifties (now wheelchair-bound), with three adult children, spoke of how her mother had taught her cooking, cleaning and sewing, and her father had taught her woodwork; these were all things she'd passed on to her own children.

Enjoying

That learning between parent and child was an enjoyable joint activity was alluded to by many interviewees and spoken about directly by some. Beryl, a white woman in her fifties from a working-class background, mentioned that she had attended a sewing club at the local church hall with her daughter. Dale, a young white man who had experienced a very troubled childhood, with spells in care and a string of school exclusions, was taught archery at the last school he attended (a place which he says turned his life around). He has since then transferred this skill to shooting, which is a pastime he now enjoys with his father. This, he implies, has brought them closer together.

These examples demonstrate the real, tangible family enjoyment experienced by some of the interviewees through their learning. The importance of shared educational tasks between parent and child, for example shared reading, as a predictor of educational achievement has been found elsewhere (Tizard *et al.* 1988; Mortimore 1998). However, a point often overlooked in relation to shared educational tasks is that learning can be fun, and it can be the reason for bringing different family members together.

Parenting ability

Many interviewees reported a variety of ways in which their participation in courses has helped them do a better job as a parent, whether or not the courses had any overt link to parenting. The benefits included: more *confidence* in their own ability as a parent; an improved capacity to *communicate* with their children; greater understanding or *patience*; more *practical skills*, for example in devising good games; understanding more about how *others approach* parenting; and enhanced capacity to see things from a *child's view*, and to understand the child as a member of a peer group.

Unsurprisingly, this effect is most clearly expressed by those who have been on courses designed to improve parenting, or similar topics. Once again, the example of Ede can be used; her 'parent pack' courses have helped her in terms of teaching her children to be responsible and have enhanced their self-esteem. Similarly, Heidi, who has done a child-care course, has become more adept at interacting with her child. She says:

> I know how to treat him now [...] I have more patience with him [...] I know how to do some things, how to play with him more, to read him books, to do things with paper, to play, too. We enjoy the time more now, I think.

Mandisa, a black British lone parent in her late thirties, stated that her family learning group involved making toys to play with her son. She felt especially good about herself as she watched him play with the toys, whilst he was delighted that his mum had made them for him. Mandisa has also learnt about children of her son's age through her work at the school, which has taught her greater tolerance. Before she had high expectations of him that she now realises were unrealistic for a four-year-old:

> I wasn't aware that I was doing that until I came into the school and I became a little more relaxed and not so bothered about, to a certain extent, about the things that he did.

However, similar effects come from studying which is not explicitly geared to parenting or family life. Naomi says:

> I've got more patience ... I think I got a lot of that from my tutor, actually, because the way she's sat with me and helped me. I learnt from her to sit and help [my daughter].

A similar story is told by Faith, a white British woman in her mid-thirties with two children from two marriages, who thinks she has become a better mum because she has other interests – specifically an archaeology course:

> I mean, there's nothing wrong with people who stay at home all the time; that's up to them, but I know I couldn't do it and I think because I'm happier, because I've got my own interest and own little life, that I'm a better mum to them ... I think I can deal with them better because I've got other things that fulfil my life and what I need to do. The time I spend with them, I suppose, is more precious to me, you know, I can make more of it.

Not only is she a more relaxed person but she is also making more of the time she spends with the children, which has necessarily reduced by virtue of her attendance on the course. This was also a strong theme in qualitative research with parents on family learning courses. (Brassett-Grundy 2002; Brassett-Grundy and Hammond 2003)

Candice, a trainee care assistant, said that her previous literacy and numeracy courses have given her a lot of ideas about children's games and activities. Her children have learned social skills, for example, issues surrounding bullying, and her courses on disability have helped her to teach them about disability issues, bringing them into contact with 'handicapped' people. They ask her questions about the stigma of disabilities and types of disabilities, which she could not answer before doing the course.

This kind of benefit goes beyond the nuclear family and over more than one generation. Catherine, Janice and Elsbeth all provide examples of this. Catherine uses her education to help her teach her nephew to read. She considers that her learning has benefited her family and her friends, and that she has been able to pass her knowledge down to others. Janice also talked of multi-generational learning within her family, and can now help her grandchildren with their reading and writing. The confidence this has given her has transformed her relations with her children, and helped her sustain herself in her role as carer for her housebound husband. Attending creative craft classes enabled Elsbeth to make a fairy outfit for her granddaughter. She has also made furniture for her children during woodwork classes, as well as clothes, toys and ornaments. The woodwork class taught her skills which she put into practice in her daughter's fitted kitchen, and her reasons for making things for her children and grandchildren are no longer principally to save money; it is for the sense of pride she experiences, as well as to give her grandchildren something special:

> It's not to save money. It's an achievement making it. It's something new, it's something different when you make it for the kids and nobody else has got it.

One indirect benefit to the children of the interviewees is a correlate of the 'getting me out of the house' adult benefit that is often reported. Those we spoke to stated that their participation in learning enabled their children to broaden their range of social relationships through access to a college crèche or other facilities. Thus Mandisa's going to college to do maths GCSE when her son was 18 months old was a good opportunity for him to go to the crèche, where she was close by and could be reached easily:

> He was integrating himself into his own little world with his own friends and he was being a little bit more independent because he was without me, which was good.

Similarly, getting involved in education had positive effects on Patricia's children, since they were left in the college nursery to mix with other children and receive stimulation from a source other than the home:

> . . . they enjoyed the time because they knew that on certain days they'd do other things as opposed to just being with mum all the time. So they've enjoyed the different areas that they've gone into.

Once again, very similar comments were made by parents interviewed as part of a family learning research project (Brassett-Grundy 2002; Brassett-Grundy and Hammond 2003).

Parents talked about college as a flexible opportunity to spend time away from their children, and as preparation for the separation that would be necessitated by their return to work. For Celia, a young white British lone parent with two children, attending college was an opportunity for her not to worry about her children. It helped her to relax and get back into the outside world slowly, '. . . so when the time came and I went to work, I was already used to leaving my children.' She also found that the course was more flexible than work and offered her the opportunity to experiment with childcare, again, in preparation for her return to work.

Parenting is a hard and challenging job, especially in a society where traditional family life is changing. The sources of support once found in the extended family may not necessarily exist in contemporary Britain, and formal courses of learning at educational establishments may provide one alternative source of such support. In addition, if adult learning can enhance communication between parents and their children, this has implications for improved educational attainment of the children, as found elsewhere (e.g. Hess and Holloway 1984; Ramey and Ramey 1992, 1999; Hubbs-Tait et al. 2002).

Attitude of family to recent learning

Returning to the world of learning as an adult may not necessarily be considered 'normal', and the transition may not necessarily be an easy one. As mentioned earlier, family members can provide the impetus for an individual to engage in learning, but they, or the presence of a family unit, can also be a hindrance. Thus, it was interesting to extract a theme from the interviews which related to the attitude of other family members towards the interviewee's recent engagement in learning.

On the whole, families appear to have been very supportive. This was true not only of the interviewees' partners and children, but also of members of their extended family. Enid, a married mother of two in her mid-thirties, spoke of her improved self-concept which she felt was partly due to her husband's support and that this was crucial to her learning: it was only through his support that she felt able to pursue a Higher Education Access course.

The example of Gloria is worth mentioning again. She found her six children to be very supportive during her attendance at a number of courses (Access to Nursing, GCSE English, AS-Level Human Biology):

> When I first went to college the children were great. They gave me loads of back-up and said 'Yes, come on, Mum'.

In other cases, interviewees experienced a general feeling of support from their wider family. Madeline's sister-in-law and uncle, as well as her husband, were pleased that she is at college because she is getting out of the house and is no longer so depressed.

Cliff's children were supportive of his return to college, communicating this through their humour: 'They crack a joke. They say, "Father is also going to school".' Indeed, this could be perceived as harmless fun and, in a way, supportive, but it could also be perceived as a jibe and serve to reinforce the possible negative feelings an adult learner might have about their ability and competence. This brings us to the flip-side of families' attitudes to learning, where they are found to be rather less supportive, and even in some cases discouraging, belittling and suspicious (see 'Families and learning – the negative picture', p. 94). Nadine, a married white British woman, spoke of the vulnerability and embarrassment she had experienced from learning 'baby stuff'. Although her three children were largely supportive of her college attendance, one of her daughters had laughed at her, which had mixed results:

> It depends what mood I'm in. If I'm feeling pretty vulnerable about it, or embarrassed about what I'm doing – because I can, I think this is baby stuff – sometimes I laugh, but if I'm feeling [. . .] I'll say 'Don't, it's not funny' and she'll go 'Sorry, Mum'.

Although there were less positive attitudes reported of some families to interviewees' learning, these stories were few in number; the more common message was one of admiration, support, respect and pride.

Impact on family relationships

Many interviewees spoke of the positive effects that their learning had had on relationships within the family, whether with their children, their partners their parents, or more widely. These effects can enable people to sustain the fabric of family life, and on occasion also to transform it. Faith reports that her history studies have changed her children's perception of her: 'I think they're quite impressed sometimes that I know what I know It takes a lot to impress my children!' She feels that she is a better mum because she has an outside interest, which has led to an improved relationship with her children.

Education led to Kali, a woman from a Pakistani family, feeling happier, and this has improved her relationship with her husband, to the extent that he has started taking a share of the domestic responsibilities:

> More of the weight's come back onto him because I've got a job now, so, you know, he's had to kind of get up and pull his socks up a bit more, and push his weight around the house a bit as well [. . .] With me moving up in my work [as a result of recent learning], he's kind of got more proud of me and he's accepted it, and, you know, he really does help now, you know. He'll pick the children up, whereas before I used to pick them up from the school.

Enid did not do as well as expected at school, which she attributes to problems at home and a lack of support from her parents, so she had some reservations about returning to learning. However, support from her husband helped her to persevere with her studies and this in turn has helped to improve her self-concept. She jokes about the impact this has had on her improved relationship with her husband: 'I think my husband has benefited [laughs] from perhaps the more contented wife.'

A number of interviewees reported that communication with their partner and other family members had improved. For some the very subject of their learning became a regular topic for conversation, whilst for others general communication skills were enhanced. Nadine spoke of her elderly parents, with whom she had previously found it hard to maintain substantive communication because of their inactivity. Now her mother is becoming interested in the family history that Nadine is studying, and has helped to dig out some old family records. Nadine says they now have something else to talk about.

As noted elsewhere (see Chapters 3 and 4), a major health benefit to parents of young children is that education takes them out of the home and their daily routines. This in turn can improve wider family relationships. As previously mentioned, Madeline's husband, sister-in-law and uncle are pleased that she is at college because she is getting out of the house, which has lifted her depression, which must have implications for the way in which she now relates to those around her. In Lydia's case, she feels she has become more tolerant and understanding of other's positions, which has had an impact on her family relationships. She talks particularly of her relationship with her sister's family and the degree to which she is now more able to compromise when involved in joint extended family activities because she has become more tolerant.

On a different level, Gloria had suffered domestic violence at the hands of her children's father, and she feels that her involvement in a formal course of learning helped her to find the strength to leave him. Following this, he has stopped drinking, regained his driving licence, and they are now in communication again:

> It [the course] turned my life around a lot. I've seen a lot from the children's father, a lot of hassles that he's given me. I used to just sit and take it, but I don't anymore. I've seen a different side to him as well. It's like somebody has switched the light on.

This metaphor puts the effect of Gloria's learning well towards the transforming end of the sustaining–transforming spectrum, a position echoed by interviewees who stated that their learning experiences had helped them support their families through difficult times. It is clear, however, from the other examples mentioned here and the interviews in general, how much covert influence education has in sustaining, gradually strengthening and improving family relationships.

Families and learning – the negative picture

The themes which emerged in relation to families and learning were not wholly positive, and it is worth devoting some space to the stories told by some interviewees who presented a more negative picture of the interface between their family and their learning.

types of learners
obstacles —
Family life and learning **93**

Obstacle to learning

Some interviewees regarded their family as an obstacle to their learning and spoke in terms of their family of origin, referring back to a childhood in which their parents had neither been supportive nor encouraging. Evan spoke of a disrupted childhood in which his 'strict family existence' resulted in his mother periodically leaving his father and taking Evan and his siblings with her to another part of the country, only to return a couple of months later. This had a very unsettling effect on his schooling, which he believes affected his academic achievement:

> ... obviously when you move to a new area you have to start a new school for instance, make new friends; you know, you've got a different accent, you know, you have to fit in somehow as best you can, and it does affect your school work as well, I'm sure it does. Probably, looking at it in one respect, that's one reason why I didn't get any qualifications at school. It could have a knock-on effect; something I've never really thought about before.

One young interviewee, Angela, was still living at home with her parents, and spoke of her mother and brother as obstacles to her learning. In the case of her mother it was caring for her during bouts of ill-health that resulted in Angela missing lessons, and in the case of her brother it was his disruptive behaviour late at night, which often resulted in her oversleeping and missing college commitments.

Others spoke about the families they had formed themselves, and in some instances the very formation of their family had put a stop to their education. For example, Enid spoke of enjoying her City and Guilds dry-cleaning technology course, which she had to stop attending because 'then I met my husband and had the children so that was that'. This echoes the themes which emerged in some of the research reviewed by Blackwell and Bynner (2002), and is exemplified in all of the case studies in Chapter 6. In some circumstances, a move away from their extended family had resulted in the loss of a support system that had supplied the childcare which had enabled the interviewee to participate previously in learning. In Gamal's case this had had a particularly strong effect, not only because he had left his family behind in Morocco but also because he had become a single parent. He felt totally unsupported in this country, something which he felt was common amongst lone parents from ethnic minorities.

In short, families are encountered as obstacles to learning when negative attitudes towards learning are held by one's own family; when one's family and/or living circumstance are unstable; when one is faced with forming a family; and when one is subsequently juggling family life with that of work and education.

Drain on family time

Some interviewees reported negative effects on their families as a result of learning where their involvement took them away from their families. This was having an impact on the time they had available to spend with their children and partners, and the time they had available to spend on household chores. Kali complained that '. . . in the evenings I don't manage to spend much time with my children because I'm doing assignments'. In Gloria's case, the negative impact was on her domestic tidiness: 'The house fell apart. [Laughs.] The house is always a tip and washing was always sky-high and dishes and things like that.' Similarly, Naomi described how her housework became neglected for about a year when she began her childcare diploma. She described the frustration experienced by her children when she could not give them the time she used to, and in an effort to keep them from complaining and asking to be taken out she would placate them with sweets and sit them in front of a video (with possible negative effects on their health and social/cognitive development).

Negative effects on relationships

Some negative effects of learning on family relationships were reported. Again they were few in number, but are worth recounting to balance the picture that has so far developed. In some cases, participation in learning placed a strain on relationships between the learner and their immediate family members. Naomi's coursework caused her stress, which led to frequent snappy moods that her husband complained about: 'He used to say, "I'll be glad when this is finished."' Sylvia was a white British woman in her seventies from a working-class background with six children from two marriages. She said that her husband, who was suffering from Parkinson's disease, resented her studying an Open University arts foundation course, believing that she should be caring for him instead. The case study of Hester in Chapter 6 is also a good example of someone whose husband viewed learning rather negatively.

Perhaps more seriously, learning was recognised by a couple of interviewees as changing the family dynamic to the extent that a split or dissolution might result. Enid voiced her concerns on this issue, stating that she hopes she doesn't change too much through her learning, 'because you hear all these things about people splitting up and families you know, because of the pressure and that'. She is adamant that her family and her marriage are her primary aim. Once again, a case study in the following chapter (Delia) discusses in more detail the impact of learning on dissolving families.

Thus, learning can alter family dynamics. It may place strain on family relationships and, in extreme cases, result in family dissolution. As mentioned in the early part of this chapter, this may be perceived negatively by those for whom nuclear family units are sacred, and yet positively by those who perceive them as divisive and disempowering (particularly for women). Obviously each case is different, and learning will have differential impacts depending on which family member you question; again, this is a theme which is further explored in Chapter 6.

Conclusion

As notions of what constitutes a family broaden and become more fluid, the trend towards a variety of family norms continues. The relationship between learning and the family is a complex one, but learning has been found to affect the propensity to form partnerships and families, as well as the timing with which these occur. We have also seen the relationship between parental learning and children's attainment, and parental interest in and interactions with children and children's attainment. These associations were highlighted early on in this chapter from quantitative research, and have been seen again throughout the findings from our qualitative research.

Interviews with adult learners have uncovered a number of themes relating to families and learning. Interviewees spoke of the manner in which their families of origin had affected their learning and vice versa. They also spoke of how these interactions were played out in the families they had themselves formed in adulthood. The effects reported were both positive and negative; for example, families can both be the motivation to learn and present obstacles to learning. A number of themes emerged relating specifically to the interaction between parental and children's learning. These embraced issues such as increased valuing of educational achievement; ability of parents to teach and support children's learning and vice versa (very widely reported); becoming a good role model; and bringing family members together in a mutually enjoyable activity.

On the whole other family members are very supportive of learning, but in some circumstances a return to the world of study and education can provoke vulnerability in the adult learner and prompt comments of suspicion and criticism from partners and children. Occasionally learning is perceived as threatening, and family dynamics can alter to the extent that families and partnerships are split or dissolved. A stronger theme to emerge from the interviews, however, was that learning enhances parenting ability and can strengthen family relationships through the acquisition of improved communication skills. There were also reports of changed identity and confidence, which affected the interviewees' position or status within the family.

The findings from our interviews have brought into sharp focus the more subtle ways in which families and learning are associated, suggesting one or two mechanisms by which this occurs, and highlight the powerful effect that these two things can have upon each other. We are reminded of just how influential that 'intimate cauldron' (the family) is, to borrow Goleman's (1996) phrasing again, in individuals' learning lives. Policy-makers are becoming aware of the importance of families and learning, especially in terms of the link between parental education and interaction, and children's cognitive and emotional development and educational attainment. Indeed, a number of initiatives have been put into place to promote learning within families and to encourage parental interest in their children's development and education, for example family learning courses, Bookstart, SureStart, Share, Families and Schools Together (FAST). However, these projects are often patchy, inconsistent and short term, and lack long-term funding to sustain the benefits they bring. Arguments for clear family learning policies at a national level are articulated by Brassett-Grundy and Hammond (2003), the Campaign for Learning et al. (2000), and by the inspectorate (Ofsted 2000).

Chapter 6

Family life illustrated

Transitions, responsibilities and attitudes

Angela Brassett-Grundy

This chapter presents three case studies (Delia, Phyllis and Hester) in which family and learning both interact. It demonstrates the myriad ways in which a family learns, in which a family affects one's learning, and in which learning affects one's family. It includes instances of informal and formal learning synthesised in a family setting, and the ways in which intergenerational learning can occur. It also looks at the effects of learning throughout the life course, and the part played by the family at each stage. As with the other themes of health and social capital, after each case study a diagram depicts graphically the main effects of each individual's learning, utilising the triangular conceptualisation of the effects of learning (see Figure 2.1). The chapter ends with a presentation of the mechanisms by which some of these effects are possibly elicited.

The three case studies appear very similar: they all relate to heterosexual women of white British ethnicity in their thirties, with children. However, they differ in other respects, for example in their initial schooling and the qualifications they gained, and have been selected to demonstrate that learning has had a very different effect on their families and lives, in spite of surface similarities.

Delia

Background

Delia was raised with her younger brother by her mother after her father left when she was two years old. She hated school so much that from her first day she had to be dragged through the school gates daily. Subsequently, she truanted so often that she was taken into care but still refused to attend school. However, when not at school she often spent time in the library teaching herself, demonstrating that it was not the idea of learning which she disliked, but something about the *way* that she had been learning in school.

During her last three months in care, Delia began to attend school again at a special unit catering for only four pupils. She responded differently to this style of teaching, and developed a good relationship with one educator in spite of her poor initial educational experience. Possibly, the connection she made with this

Delia is a white British woman, aged 37 at the time of the interview. A mother of five children (aged 15, 14, 12, 9 and 5), she is currently living with her partner (but without her children) and is pregnant with her sixth child. She has qualifications below five GCSE passes, and spent part of her childhood in care. Based upon her employment history, Delia is working class.

Being closest in age to the NCDS cohort, we compare her to these individuals, who were aged 42 in 2000. Amongst those aged 42 in 2000 living in Britain, 64 individuals in every 10,000 shared Delia's characteristics. Amongst this group, a relatively low percentage (including Delia) had participated in learning during the previous nine years (49 per cent as opposed to 61 per cent for all 42-year-olds), although a higher proportion of those who had participated in learning had taken courses leading to qualifications (39 per cent as opposed to 29 per cent amongst all 42-year-olds). Again, Delia falls into this category.

People 'like' Delia are more likely to be clinically depressed than other 42-year-olds, and a relatively low percentage feel in control of their lives. However, average proportions report high levels of life satisfaction. The proportions of those sharing Delia's characteristics who are members of at least one organisation and who report an interest in politics are lower than the proportions for all 42-year-olds, so Delia is unusual amongst those 'like' her in belonging to a community organisation (the Students' Union), which is a direct result of her learner status.

one special teacher enabled her to retain a positive perception of formal learning which facilitated her re-engagement with the education system later as an adult. Delia left the special education unit on her sixteenth birthday, missing virtually the whole of her final year and all of her GCE examinations. She felt failed by her initial education, and made the transition into adulthood without any qualifications.

At the age of 18 Delia moved in with a boyfriend, with whom she had five children. He rarely worked and was often in the house all day. In spite of the lack of support, she spoke about parenthood as both a life-transforming and learning experience:

> The more children I had, the more it was just fascinating watching them all at different stages and growing [...] It shows you something different about yourself because you relate to them as different people and you see bits of yourself, so to me, it was a really interesting learning experience.

Delia learnt how to become a good mother (by her own definition) vicariously from her own mother, and in becoming a parent learnt something about human development and growth, human interaction (through improved communication and social skills) and herself. She 'does' a lot of her psychology in the home, referring to the knowledge she has acquired in her current college course, and we see a synthesis of formal and informal learning where formal knowledge gained on a course is applied practically in a family setting. This is no doubt related to the subject she is studying (psychology), which teaches things of direct relevance to the family – human development. Delia very poignantly and personally relates how her personality and life-goals have changed in becoming a mother:

> I think my children are the best thing that's happened to me. They've changed me in so many ways. I've stopped being selfish, I've stopped being self-destructive. I've stopped an awful lot of things because I've had a reason to live and I put most of my energies into that effect, where I wanted to be the perfect parent.

Whilst Delia's immediate family was still in the process of forming, parts of her extended family began to dissolve, through a series of deaths. These included her mother (who died when Delia was pregnant with her fifth child) and her partner's grandmother. In addition to the agoraphobia she developed at this time, Delia began to drink heavily in her struggle to cope with her grief and lack of support from her partner. However, three years later she decided to enrol at college, which represented the beginning of her path out of depression, anxiety and alcohol misuse, towards a more peaceful time in her life: this led to a change in her identity and in her familial relationships.

Learning and adulthood

Delia had completed three courses (Creative Writing, English GCSE and Fresh Start for Women, for those returning to education) and was currently on her fourth (Pathways Psychology). Her decision to start college, two years prior to the interview, was in part motivated by her family, since her youngest child was then old enough to go to nursery school. This gave Delia free time, and the anticipated pain of an 'empty nest' was thus avoided by enrolling at college.

There were many ways in which participating in adult learning had an effect on Delia and her family. The 'Fresh Start for Women' course caused her to reappraise her position of mother/homemaker, and she began to appreciate the skills she had developed in carrying out these roles. This changed the way she valued and perceived herself – a fundamental change to her identity. She also lifted herself out of the depression and panic disorder she had developed following her mother's death:

> I think I'd hit such a low point in my life where I thought I either sink or swim and I thought I wasn't going to just drown so I got a prospectus, found out about the writing course. I was a bit anxious; I asked my daughter to

go with me and had the interview. She came along for a bit of moral support [. . .] From then on I began to build myself back up again.

Here is an example of the complex interplay between health, family and education: being at college restored Delia's mental health (although the mechanisms by which this occurred are not explicitly mentioned), with a knock-on effect on the way she was relating to her immediate family, and she was once again able to leave the house in order to walk her children to school.

Delia's return to formal education had a particularly significant impact on her family, specifically the relationships she had with her partner and children. On her current course she met a man with whom she fell in love, and for whom she left her partner (and five children). This has completely changed her life, and at the time of her interview she was pregnant with her sixth child, fathered by her new partner. She speaks of the numerous things she has in common with him, some of which are academic in nature: writing, poetry, reading similar books, old horror films. Meeting him has also had a positive impact on her mental health:

> There was a certain freedom. It was like he didn't expect me to be anything whereas everybody else did and I basically went on from that, so now I'm living with him and I haven't had a panic attack since.

Delia refers again here to the positive and liberating experience that adult learning has been for her, bringing with it positive consequences for her mental health and self-image.

Engaging in adult learning has resulted in a prospective new addition to her family, which could also be considered a positive outcome. However, Delia wonders whether being pregnant now has come at the wrong time since she is juggling so many roles at once. In spite of the fact that she is finding it difficult to focus on her studies, she has told herself to persevere since she may regret it if she drops out. This determination is motivated by her previous experiences of education which resulted in her leaving school with no qualifications.

Thus, engaging in formal learning has resulted in immense changes to Delia's family formation and although finding a new partner and rediscovering love may be considered a positive thing, it has been at the cost of her relationship with her ex-partner. She has moved out of the family home, leaving behind her five children, whom she is now having difficulty seeing because of the hostility her ex-partner feels towards her. On the face of it, the effect on Delia's family of her learning has been fairly negative, but her experience of adult learning has encouraged her to face the inadequacies of her previous existence and relationship, and take stock of what she should expect out of life. It has restored the confidence and strength she once had, enabling her to make the bold yet difficult decision to leave her children and partner for a new man and new life. In spite of the geographical distance, Delia's children may benefit from having a happier, more contented mother.

Delia's interest in history motivated her to take her first college course in creative writing, since her aim was to write a novel set in Victorian Britain, and had a significant impact on her family. First, it led to research into her own family tree through time spent in a records centre. Second, she has passed the information she has learnt on to her children, for example explaining the circumstances in which children were raised in the nineteenth century and drawing comparisons to the way in which women and children are treated now. Finally, this pastime has also served as an escape from the stresses of everyday life, which have ultimately come from having five children and an unsupportive partner.

Delia's own experience of education has affected the way she approaches the learning experiences of her own children. There was a period when her youngest two children were taken out of school due to bullying, which resulted in her teaching them at home:

> We did lots of leaf printing and Maths and things that I could deal with. I could cope with times tables and stuff at that age [. . .] When they actually went back into [a different] school the teachers actually said it was as if they had not been taken away from school and she felt they were missing out because they didn't have the individual attention that they can't have in school.

Delia provided them with the one-to-one attention that she had received when she was at the special unit for truants. Her ability to teach her children at home may also have been facilitated by her self-motivated approach to her own learning when, as a child, she spent time in the library. Delia's negative experiences of school also seem to have motivated her to take an active part in her children's schooling, as a helper on trips and at plays and parties, and she is encouraging her children not to make the same mistakes that she did.

Summary

Families and learning can affect each other in a number of ways. It is likely that the departure of Delia's father and her subsequent upbringing had an impact on her schooling which led to truanting. Forming a family can be a learning experience, and watching one's children develop can be educational. One can also use the skills and knowledge acquired through formal routes to facilitate parenting and childcare – in Delia's case, her psychology course helped her to understand human development and improved her communication skills. The information learnt formally or informally can also be passed on to family members, as Delia did by teaching her children about Victorian Britain. One can also make an effort to learn about one's family through research using historical records. Formal adult education can help people appreciate the skills they possess as a parent and homemaker, which impacts on their self-identity and the way in which they relate to their family members. It can also have a positive impact on one's psychological and mental health, which has knock-on effects for the manner in which one communicates with family members. In

Delia's case, she was lifted out of depression and anxiety disorders, causing her to engage in her role as mother more fully. However, a more challenging effect of learning is that families may be disrupted through changed partnerships brought about through exposure to a wider social network, a change in self-perception, broadened horizons, a reappraisal of values and goals, and generally altered thinking. This echoes the findings of other research by the Centre concerning parental views of family learning (see Brassett-Grundy 2002; Brassett-Grundy and Hammond 2003).

If we sought to place Delia in the matrix (see Figure 2.2), learning has been a completely transforming experience for her. It has also had an impact on a number of people beyond herself, and since her identity and self-perception

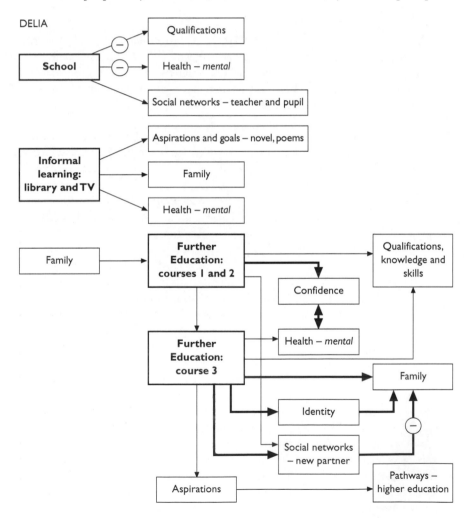

Figure 6.1 Experiences of learning: Delia.

have altered so significantly, she has become a very different person engaging in all relationships in a new way. It has thus had more of a community-level effect than an individual effect, and so Delia finds herself in the bottom-left quadrant of our matrix.

Phyllis

We turn now to the story of a woman who returned to college in order to obtain a university degree enabling her to follow her chosen career. Motivated by unfulfilled potential from school, this case study shows how a fairly happy person, who followed the normal path from school, to marriage, work and childbirth, has made a return to formal education, bringing multiple benefits to her and her family.

At the time of the interview Phyllis was aged 31. She is white, married and living with her husband and two children aged 5. Her qualifications are equivalent to NVQ level two, and she is a full-time student. On the basis of her family background she is working class.

Being closest in age to the BCS70 cohort we compare her to these individuals, who were aged 30 in 2000. Amongst 30-year-olds in Britain in 2000, about 113 people in every 10,000 shared all of Phyllis' characteristics, including those with qualifications up to but not including degree level and those who described themselves as housewives. Amongst this group of 30-year-olds 'like' Phyllis, a relatively high percentage had obtained qualifications during the previous seven years (40 per cent as opposed to 35 per cent of all 30-year-olds); Phyllis falls into this group. This contradicts findings from other studies that women tend to acquire fewer qualifications than men in adulthood (see Jenkins et al. 2002), and possibly reflects the importance of qualifications for women as they adjust their working roles to fit in with family responsibilities.

People 'like' Phyllis are more likely to be clinically depressed and less likely to have high self-efficacy than other 30-year-olds. This may be a response to the stress, hard work and restricted opportunities that arise in the adoption of childcare responsibilities within the context of a relatively poor educational background (Brown and Harris 1978). A higher percentage of people sharing Phyllis' characteristics belong to at least one organisation than do other 30-year-olds (15 per cent as opposed to 10 per cent of all 30-year-olds), which may reflect membership of organisations associated with children's education, for example the Parent Staff Association. Phyllis is one of these, in that she is involved in her daughters' school, and she pays an annual subscription to a dog welfare charity. However, the percentage of this group who report an interest in politics is low when compared to other 30-year-olds (17 per cent as opposed to 34 per cent).

Background

Phyllis has an older sister, and was born when her parents were in their forties. At the age of 19 she married and moved away from home, and seven years later had twin daughters. Phyllis went to a mixed-sex comprehensive school with a good reputation. She was a good learner and enjoyed school, and in spite of being shy she had many friends. When Phyllis was 14 her father was taken ill and two years later, just before she sat her O levels, he died. This traumatic experience affected her exam performance, and she left school at the age of 16 without having done as well as she had hoped.

Learning and adulthood

After school, Phyllis went on to a Youth Training Scheme (YTS). This included a placement in a company where she spent one day per week at college to gain further qualifications in Business English and RSA Typing stage II. The YTS, and related college courses, helped Phyllis deal with the emotional trauma of her father's death. She was looking for 'peace inside' and wanted to remain active and occupied. She could not look too far into the future because of the turmoil that her family was in at the time, and so the YTS gave her the immediate mental relief she needed. (It should be noted that the YTS benefits experienced by Phyllis seem to be in excess of those reported elsewhere (for example, see Cohen 1997).) Thus, the death of a family member prompted Phyllis to seek out peace of mind, which she achieved through participation in a training and education scheme. Phyllis' mother was pleased that she had became involved in a YTS, but felt some regret about how the family had affected Phyllis' education:

> I think she's always felt that perhaps she wasn't there for me because of what was going on in our lives. She wasn't there to support me to perhaps stop on at school. I had to more or less make the decision myself and go on. I couldn't hassle her at that time with, 'What shall I do? Shall I stop on?', or anything. She's often spoken about it and said, especially now I've gone back into education, she's said, 'If things were different, perhaps you could have stopped on at school and done it then rather than now. Now you've got all this other baggage to take with you', but that's the way life goes isn't it? I say to mum, 'It's nothing you've done. Life's what you make it.' You get things thrown at you and you deal with it and you either stick with it or you change your life. You make your own pathway don't you.

A full-time job was found for Phyllis, which meant that she had to leave the YTS. Following this she worked in Personnel until she had her children, and since then has not been employed:

> I could no way afford to go back to work because the cost of childcare would have been just too much. I wouldn't have earned any money at the end of the day, so it was having twins made the decision for me to stop at home.

This is a very real reminder that the cost of childcare can price individuals, more often women, out of the job market. Fortunately her husband was able to support the family, and her time spent at home raising her daughters has been a largely positive experience. Now that Phyllis is back in full-time education, she says that she couldn't possibly find the time to work and look after her twin daughters, which serves as another reminder that sacrifices are made in the pursuit of adult learning.

Phyllis recently took a course leading to the equivalent of a Classroom Assistant, and at the time of the interview was on a full-time HE Access course at college. Her family had a large role to play in her motivation for doing the Access course, in that her children were approaching school age and she did not want to be left indoors all day with nothing to do: '. . . it would drive me insane.' This reference to mental health reminds us of the time in Phyllis' life when the YTS came as a welcome pursuit to occupy both her mind and time, following her father's death.

Phyllis wanted to work with children and decided to go to college to work towards a NNEB qualification. Her husband helped her make this decision, and thus her family both motivated and guided her towards the pursuit of a course of formal learning: she had time on her hands because her children were at school and she needed something to occupy her mind, and her husband gave her the space and advice necessary to seek out a careers talk. She was also fortunate enough to have a partner who was able to support the family in the meantime – a luxury not afforded by all, especially lone parents.

During her Classroom Assistant course Phyllis learnt about children and how to teach and interact with them, which she has put into practice with her twins. This shows the symbiotic process of learning: the family affected Phyllis' ability to engage fully and successfully in learning, and her engagement in learning gave her skills and knowledge which could be used in a family context.

The Internet has provided a source of informal learning for Phyllis, which was the result of purchasing a home computer. This was essentially an extra resource for the children, to help them in the future with their homework, but she has found that she has been able to find a wealth of information on the Internet for herself, friends and family. She also sends e-mails, which has opened up a new way of communicating with her friends and family and is a skill she will now put to use at college.

Being involved in a college course has resulted in increased confidence:

> I think when you've had your children and you've not been in education a long time, your confidence is down here somewhere and it still seems a bit of a dream really that this is happening. I am applying to university but since I've been at college my confidence is creeping up and I'm getting more. When assignments are presented, I'm thinking, yes, yes, I know how I'm going to tackle this. In the first couple of weeks I was thinking, oh my God, how am I going to cope with this? But now I'm into that mode, my brain's sort of working again and getting onto it.

One can only surmise that a more confident Phyllis equates to a more confident mother, spouse, daughter, friend. She also sees another benefit to her family in that she will be a better role model to her children, giving them the idea that 'you can carry on and make a career for yourself' after having a family. She says, 'I think I'm giving them the right vibes.'

Phyllis' current course has also had practical effects on her family. First, it has exerted pressure on her, adding to and changing her usual daily routine, which the rest of the family have had to adapt to. At the same time, however, it has affected Phyllis and her family in a positive way, since she has developed prioritisation and time management skills. A sophisticated juggling act is required in order to fit a full-time course of study in and around a family. Second, Phyllis realises that her return to education will benefit the whole family through her increased earning potential.

Phyllis spoke about the reactions she'd had from family members to her new learner status. Her children are very positive, continually asking her how she is progressing. They are very proud of her, and her mother is also supportive. She has received mixed responses from the rest of her family, however, referring first to her father-in-law, an 'ignorant' and 'uneducated' man, who does not appreciate the value of learning and thinks that she should be 'in a job, bringing money in'. Her sister, although supportive, is slightly jealous. Phyllis attributes this partly to the fact she is pursuing a university course whereas her sister 'only' has A levels. Her sister tries to suggest that the course will be hard and questions her motivation, but at the same time praises her for her commitment and effort to achieve a higher qualification. Phyllis says that she is concerned only with what her immediate family thinks.

Family circumstances can have a detrimental affect on compulsory education in two ways: through the attainment of poor grades in exams, and through a lack of support at crucial decision-making times relating to careers and further education. Like the previous case, we see how training and learning can help individuals to cope with the emotional stress caused by family circumstances. It can also enhance one's confidence, having an impact on both the learner and all those with whom the learner interacts.

Summary

Families can act as the motivation to learn in adulthood in a variety of ways: children growing up and starting school gives caregivers the time to learn, and partners can be an important source of advice, and financial and emotional support. The benefits gained by an individual learner also have implications for their whole family: increased earning potential, better time management, better learning role model and increased confidence. Adult learners may endure mixed reactions from other family members: some are very pleased and proud of the new learner; while others feel that the learner's traditional roles (of mother and wife) are challenged, or envy a learner's ability, confidence and progress. Positive effects can spread into the long term, with informal learning with the family at home being transferred into more formal educational settings. In this example, a learner had been motivated to learn something primarily to help her children with their education, which was then transferred to her own education.

For Phyllis, we see that learning has had more of a sustaining than a transforming effect, tapping a dormant ability or unfulfilled potential. In time this may generate into a more transforming effect, as she makes her way to university and beyond. If we conceptualise the family as a community, in Phyllis' case learning was at first pursued for quite a community-level aim – to help her children. It has since changed into a more personal and individual aim and gain, with a more individual-level effect – her pursuit of a chosen career. This reminds us that individuals can move around the matrix: their position is not fixed. Thus, at the time of the interview, Phyllis occupied a position in the top-right quadrant of our matrix.

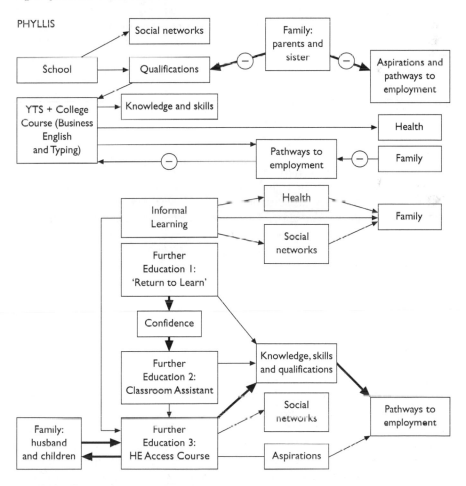

Figure 6.2 Experiences of learning: Phyllis.

Hester

Finally, we come to the case of Hester, in which we see a greater mixture of both positive and negative effects of learning on the family, and vice versa.

Hester was aged 34 at time of interview and describes herself as British from a white Irish background. She has been married for nine years and has two children: a son aged nine and a daughter aged six. She has qualifications equivalent to NVQ level three, and is a full-time student. On the basis of her family background she is working class.

Being closest in age to the BCS70 cohort, we compare Hester to these individuals, who were aged 30 in 2000. Amongst 30-year-olds in Britain in 2000, 186 people in every 10,000 shared Hester's characteristics, including those who were currently working. Amongst this group of 30-year-olds 'like' Hester, a relatively low percentage had obtained qualifications during the previous 7 years (28 per cent as opposed to 35 per cent of all 30-year-olds); Hester is one of these people. This supports findings from other studies that women tend to acquire fewer qualifications than men in adulthood (see Jenkins *et al.* 2002), and possibly the relatively low importance of qualifications for women who manage to work whilst also managing family responsibilities.

People 'like' Hester are slightly more likely to be clinically depressed than other 30-year-olds, although the proportions reporting positive self-efficacy and life satisfaction are in line with other 30-year-olds. A higher percentage of people sharing Hester's characteristics belong to at least one organisation than do other 30-year-olds (15 per cent as opposed to 10 per cent of all 30-year-olds). This may reflect membership of organisations associated with children's education, such as Hester, who is a member of the school Parent Staff Association. However, the percentage of this group who report an interest in politics is low when compared to other 30-year-olds (21 per cent as opposed to 34 per cent).

Background

Hester was raised with a younger sister, mainly by her mother since her father was often working abroad. Her parents were never involved in her education: her father was rarely at home, and her mother would invariably 'switch off' since she couldn't cope with Hester and her sister. Hester's initial schooling was disrupted in two ways: the first was the result of a geographical relocation from the South East to the North, which moved her from an all-girls' grammar school to a mixed-sex comprehensive; the second was the mental ill-health she developed due to family problems concerning her sister's physical ill-health, which resulted in Hester dropping out of her A level courses. Having been considered at one time 'Oxbridge' material, her aspiration to study law at university in order to become a barrister was not realised. Thus Hester's family had a negative effect on her learning via the mediator of ill-health, and again a lack of family support and apparent parental emotional absence affected learning in a less than positive way.

Learning and adulthood

Hester spoke about her own experience of becoming a parent in both positive and negative ways. First, she has a different perspective on life. Having children has taught her new things about herself, and she says that she has changed as her two children have matured. She described a heightened awareness relating to responsibility, safety and security, and implied that her children have given her something to live for. Second, she has acquired better parenting skills through watching how others deal with their children in the nursery playground. This was particularly important because her mother 'did not have a clue what she was doing' and so Hester 'floundered' without a 'good mother' role model. This has been of particular value in dealing with her son, who has specific special needs. Third, becoming a mum and creating her own family has affected Hester's health, although not altogether positively in the first instance. At home with her young children, her depression returned. The scenario improved when her children became involved in education themselves, and she became less depressed as her contact with other adults in the school playground increased.

Hester, like Delia, has been involved in four courses of adult learning: (1) a business course at college after leaving school; (2) a BTec in 'Women Returning to Work' after her first child was born; (3) a hairdressing course after her second child was born; and, (4) her current course, which is a one-year full-time HE Access course containing psychology and sociology options (which she hopes will lead to teacher training). Each of these has had both positive and negative effects on her and her family.

Again, simply having children can be the motivation to learn. Through witnessing her children learn, grow and develop, Hester has wanted to get involved in learning again. Like Delia and Phyllis, once her children were both old enough to be at school she was able to commit herself to a course of full-time study. Interestingly, she realises that at one time she never wanted to have a family and had ideas about a career in law, but now, having become a mother, she enjoys being with children and her learning has taken on a completely different focus, leading towards a career in teaching children.

The business course Hester began after leaving school was not a success, which she believes was due to the college perceiving her mental state negatively instead of making a realistic appraisal of her actual ability. Again her family continued having a negative effect on learning through the route of mental ill-health. The family Hester formed in adulthood also acted as a barrier when she was studying on the BTec course. Although she was able to take advantage of the college childcare for her 18-month-old son, the arrival of her second child meant that she had to drop out of the course 'through no fault of her own'. She also dropped out of the hairdressing course she started when her youngest child was 2 years old because of financial reasons. She says:

> ... the childcare was so expensive the whole family were left with about 20 pounds a week to live on and we couldn't financially do it, so I was back staying at home with the children.

Thus learning, which was sought initially to lead to work (which would fit in with family commitments), was not completed because the family became an obstacle through the prohibitive costs of childcare.

Hester described two personal practical benefits of studying on her current course. First, she has developed a better understanding of child development as result of the psychology modules, which she puts to practical use with her children. These modules enable her to understand her son's challenging behaviour, and she has developed ways of parenting that might change him. Second, the course has helped Hester manage her time better, with knock-on effects for her family since she is better able to prioritise her college and household work. The timetable she writes each week to organise her time has helped prevent her from panicking and dropping out of college due to the workload, as she did with previous courses. This has helped her children to develop their independence; they have had to 'grow up' because she cannot do everything for them anymore, which has brought the family together in a new way of relating.

Significant psychological and emotional benefits have been reaped from the course, which have had an impact on the manner she interacts socially, especially with her children. Her mental health and sense of well-being have improved:

> ... everyone's said that they see such a change in me – I'm happier, I'm working towards something I want to do and I'm using my brain for the first time in I don't know how many years and it is wonderful.

Hester's identity has undergone a significant transformation. The new-found determination she has acquired has helped her be motivated enough to continue her studies, and as a result her fellow students, who are aware of the problems she faces with an unsupportive partner and children with special needs, see her as a good role model. She intimates that she is learning in spite of her family. Her identity has also changed in another profound way:

I've started to be me whereas, I was saying before, I was a housewife and I was a mother and that was it. I'm at last becoming me and it's wonderful. It is. It's fantastic to actually go in a direction that you want to go and I think I'm a better mother because of it because I'm not frustrated so I'm not constantly nagging the kids because they're not doing what they want. I can switch off now because I've got a goal for what I want to do and they're not the reason that I can't do it. They're the reason I can do it now so it has helped an awful lot.

Formal learning has had an impact on Hester's immediate family. Through talking about her husband to fellow students, she gained a different perspective on her relationship with him and began to realise that he was a 'chauvinistic pig'. She experienced a shift in her ideology and expectations – a change which was not well received by her husband – and went from 'completely idolising' him and not being 'allowed' to say anything against him, to standing up for herself and speaking out if she was unhappy. He had told her that she was not entitled to anything but she learnt from her fellow students that this was 'a pack of lies':

> ... intellectually I'm at a very different level to my husband and I think he feels threatened if I do go and learn because he's scared that technically, if I can get the degree I want, I will be in a position to earn more money than he does and he likes to be the breadwinner. All the time I'm at home, I can be the little woman and just be a housewife. As soon as I get out and learn something, I can empower myself to do something else and I think it really scares him.

Learning can thus have serious consequences for the family, altering dynamics such that there is a shift in perceived power, the status quo (as far as traditional family gendered power relations) is changed, and one partner is left feeling threatened and inadequate. This can result in both a metaphorical and an actual split in partnerships (seen in Delia's case), a fact that Hester was warned of at college. In spite of the unknown territory ahead, she was willing to persevere with her course because the benefits it brought outweighed possible disadvantages. Her husband, however, has begun to change for the better out of fear of losing her due to the 'empowerment' she has gained. So not only has learning changed Hester and her relationship with her husband, where she now has greater autonomy: it has also changed him, highlighting the fact that learning has effects that reach far beyond the learner him- or herself.

Hester's courses have also had an effect on her children. She has learnt that you can make changes later in life 'and put things right', which she hopes they will appreciate so that 'if they make a mess to begin with' it won't be 'the end of everything'. She wants them to learn from her example. There have also been practical effects. She has a different approach to housework, and feels justified in not doing it because her studies are more important. Hester views this as a positive outcome; her husband, however, may view it differently. In addition, she no longer has the time to cook roast dinners, and instead prepares what is quickest so that she can return to her studies. This may have a negative impact on the family's physical health and the type of food her children prepare as adults in the future, yet it could also be perceived positively in terms of gendered power relations as Hester moves out of a traditional domestic role. She also now has less time to exercise, for example, through long family walks, and once again we see that in making a commitment to a formal course of learning some things get sacrificed; however, less obvious gains may result.

The interplay between family and learning is also seen in Hester's involvement in her children's education. When her children first began nursery she was pleased because she became confident that they would receive a well-rounded education. At home she didn't know what to do with them, but when they started nursery she was able to talk to the teachers and get tips from other parents in the playground. Hester has helped out in both of her children's classes, with reading, sports days, fairs and the Parent Teacher Association. Although she likes to help others, she realises that her initial motivation to carry out voluntary work at the school was that it would look good on her 'personal statement' for getting onto a teaching course. However, she acquired practical knowledge and skills that have enabled her to teach her children better and to talk to them in a language they understand. She is also more likely to organise sports events for her children and their friends when they go on outings or holidays, and has new-found confidence in her ability to put her new skills into practice.

The responsibility for dealing with her children, who have special needs, falls almost exclusively to Hester since she receives very little input or support from her husband. This reaction by one family member to another's learning, and lack of parental support, may have an impact on the children, as well as on her. Hester did not feel supported by her own absent father and her mother could not cope on her own; one wonders whether this is a pattern that is being repeated.

Summary

Not everyone has a positive parenting experience in childhood from which to draw when raising and caring for their own children. Substitute role models are an important source for learning parenting skills, and other good parents are the obvious candidates for this. The family problems Hester experienced in childhood shifted her from a path she had clearly mapped out for herself in her teens to one in which she felt aimless. Having her own family affected both her choice and timing of learning. When young, her children were perceived as obstacles to learning, yet as they grew older they facilitated Hester's return to formal education, which helped her regain some focus, feel better about herself and feel more assertive. Although the roles of parent and learner can be conflicting, educational organisations can ease this and enable those who have had children to return to learning by providing free on-site childcare. This is in part why Hester had to drop out of her first three courses, reminding us that not all courses of learning have positive outcomes: by the fourth attempt, she had found the right course for her.

Making a return to independent thought (which Hester valued whilst at grammar school), and being useful or having a goal in sight, has brought about an improvement in her psychological well-being. She is now going in

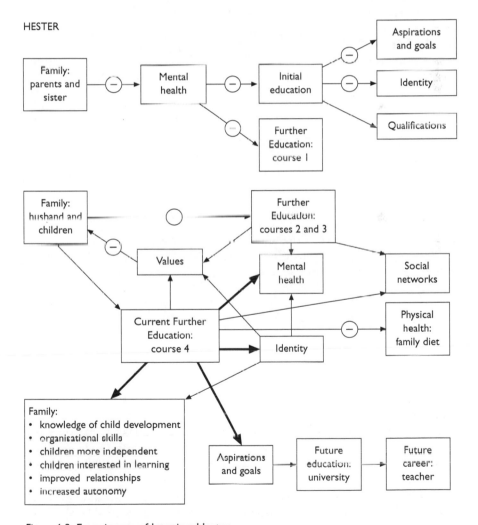

Figure 6.3 Experiences of learning: Hester.

the direction she wants to, and although these are qualities which Hester sees as positive, this case study shows that other family members may not perceive personal changes in the same way: her husband has not responded well to her increased confidence and assertiveness, and reduced focus on the housework.

One is left with the feeling that Hester is not doing quite what she wanted, and so she still carries the effects of her sister's childhood health problems well into adulthood. Her birth family and the family she has formed in adulthood have in many respects stifled her attempts to learn. Although she has regrets about not following her original path, she has tried to make the best of her situation and concludes that learning has allowed her to make changes and find a new direction in life, albeit in an unanticipated trajectory.

For Hester, we conclude that learning has had a transforming effect, completely changing her outlook and the unexpected path she found herself upon. Like Phyllis, this is a case of untapped potential, but in Hester's case learning has had a more profound effect on her identity. Her learning has had a very individual focus, pursued in order to find a suitable career. Although the family will no doubt benefit from the increased finances at their disposal, her motivation was ultimately for herself and her own gain. However, it has had quite an impact on her relationship with her husband and as such she edges towards the community end of the individual–community continuum, but not enough in the author's opinion to move her out of the top-left quadrant of the matrix (Figure 2.2).

Conclusion

These case studies demonstrate the variety of relationships between the family and learning, with both positive and negative effects, which may not necessarily be the same for the learner compared to his or her family. The positive effects of learning are often battling against other forces that exist within families, such as time constraints, responsibilities of other roles and the attitudes of other family members.

There are lessons to be learnt here pertaining to mechanisms of learning, with implications for policy-makers, yet these are conclusions drawn from three fairly similar people in terms of race, gender and age. Although learning appeared to affect them and their families in very different ways, similar conclusions might not be drawn from an in-depth study of other types of learners. That said, these cases still have important statements to make about why families affected learning in the ways that they did, and vice versa. These could be the starting points when investigating the manner in which families and learning interact in learners with different characteristics.

In looking for factors which facilitated Delia's, Phyllis' and Hester's return to learning, and mechanisms which resulted in benefits and disbenefits to accrue, we come firstly to life-course relevance. Life-course stage is important for all three cases, in that learning was enabled by virtue of the fact that these women were at specific (and similar) points in their personal histories, i.e. when their youngest child was old enough to attend school. Phyllis says that she didn't think that she could have studied for further qualifications if she had left it another 10 years; it was important for her to tackle a return to education whilst she and her children were still young, whilst Hester had been unable to make a success of her previous courses because she was looking after young children.

Secondly, for Phyllis and Hester their parent status was important in enhancing their learning in formal settings. Benefits seemed to accrue through being more mature and worldly learners, brought about through life experience. In Phyllis' case, it was something about her familiarity with employment, home-making and raising a family that made her not afraid of looking stupid and getting things wrong; being older made her more assertive and not afraid to ask questions.

The learning context also counts. Delia described characteristics of her pre-vious college courses that resulted in her experience of learning there as posit-ive, for example the teaching method. She also spoke of the atmosphere at college as conducive to learning, likening it to being at home with a group of friendly people ('. . . it was like a big family'), which again demonstrates how important the family is as a potential context for learning, as recognised by other research (Goleman 1996; Gorard et al. 1998; Buffton 1999). She contrasts the atmosphere of the college described here with the one she currently attends, which is a 'more academic' college and feels more like being at school. Delia is not so keen on this. Had she turned up at a place like this for the first time after a period spent away from education, she might have backed off and not returned, yet because she had been at the previous, more intimate college, in which she felt comfortable and encouraged, it was easier for her to attend the bigger college. This has implications for how adults can be eased back into edu-cation, and the manner in which they progress when engaged. Hester has found it easier to learn with other mums, especially those she knew before the course, who experience the same pressures outside of the course. There is something important about the fact that they are 'all in the same boat'. That other stu-dents also have immediate families is a positive factor in keeping Hester motiv-ated to persevere with her studies.

As far as Hester's HE Access course is concerned, positive effects are fostered by the flexibility of the learning provider. It has been a more enjoyable course because it is geared to mature students with outside commitments, such as families, and the teachers are more understanding when students miss a day, for example due to difficulties with childcare arrangements.

Finally, the subject being studied is also a factor that brings benefits to each learner. All three women are studying topics with relevance to children and child development (e.g. Psychology, Classroom Assistant, Teaching), and this may be why certain familial effects were seen. In addition, one of the reasons that Hester's current course of learning has been more successful than previous courses is because this time she is studying something that really interests her. This has resulted in increased motivation and commitment to the course. The conclusions of the health-related Chapters 3 and 4 are reiterated: learning is most beneficial when suited to the needs, interests and strengths of the learner.

We have seen that learning can have a powerful effect on the family (and *vice versa*), yet it can also have an impact on far wider areas of our lives; it sits in relation to and interacts with many other spheres, such as health and citizenship, as detailed elsewhere in this book. We finish with a profound quotation from Delia for whom learning is pervasive, life long and universal:

> I think everything's learning. It's not just college; it's the person you meet in the street, it's something you watch on telly. I'm a believer that you never stop learning and that you won't stop learning until I close my eyes and say goodbye to the world. Learning comes from every experience. It comes from college, and it's not *just* that. It's just the people you meet and you build things within yourself, so I would say that college is a part of it, education is a part of it, people ... everything is a part of learning and I can't really say which one does which. That's the glory of life isn't it? It's the learning.

Chapter 7

'A continuous effort of sociability'

Learning and social capital in adult life

John Preston

Previous chapters have been concerned with the influence of learning on the individual and their familial relations. The next two chapters turn our attention towards the social benefits of learning in terms of effects on social capital and wider issues of values. I begin by critically examining the notion of social capital, which has achieved a high profile both for integration into social theory and its impact upon policy-makers. Our qualitative research allows us to explore how different forms of learning influence various forms of social capital in the context of individual biographies. I show how learning has impacts on the qualitative, as well as the structural, characteristics of individuals' social networks, and how the influence of learning on social capital is contingent upon access to other forms of capital, including cultural capital. The structural components of social capital, interpreted as social networks and civic participation, are complemented by the normative components of tolerance and trust. Individual biographies reveal the complexity of processes of value formation which do not fit neatly into functionalist educational theory. The influence of learning on value formation, at least through adult education, is often transmitted through processes of value conflict and challenge as much as consensus.

Social capital in the work of Bourdieu

Social capital is a contested concept (Schuller *et al.* 2000; Green and Preston 2001). I nevertheless find it useful as a heuristic, a concept to think with and even as a concept to think against (Fine 2001). The conceptual framework developed by Bourdieu is particularly useful in understanding the dynamics and tensions apparent in the generation of civic activity through adult education. Although arguably Bourdieu did not have as finely developed theory of social capital as other theorists such as Coleman (1988) and Putnam (1993, 2000) the integration of social capital within a dynamic framework of social distinction provides a powerful analytic tool. However, this framework is tempered by both other interpretations of social capital theory and various critiques of Bourdieu's work. In particular, his theory is less applicable to the normative (attitudinal) components of social capital and social capital as a community or regional resource. Arguably too, it is less apt for examining gender, rather than class distinction and inequalities, although it has been since applied in such areas (Krais 1993; Skeggs 1997; Raey 2000a; Morrow 2003).

For Bourdieu, the concept of capital is a metaphor for the assets of individuals. However, social and cultural capital are purely symbolic in that they are of no inherent value in themselves. The value of capitals in a given 'field' of activity is both arbitrary and influenced by those who already hold power in that field. In fields of education, employment, civic and political life, an individual's access to social capital (social contacts and social knowledge), cultural capital (embodied and institutionalised cultural knowledge such as attitudes, dispositions and educational qualifications) and economic capital (financial and physical assets) will determine further capital acquisition. The theory is not deterministic: individuals adopt strategies in the exchange of capitals, the consequences of which are both dynamic and uncertain. However, neither is the acquisition of capitals meritocratic. Individuals devise strategies as a function of their existing cultural and social knowledge and practices (their habitus) according to rules structured by those who already hold capital. It is only in their symbolic forms that capitals are given value and can then be used or exchanged. Recognition of capitals as legitimate is as important as the quantity of capitals possessed. In the field of adult education, for example, those who gain knowledge through informal learning (autodidacts) cannot convert this work into social or cultural capital unless they have the class position to legitimize their knowledge (Bourdieu 2003: 328–330).

Bourdieu's location of social capital is little different from that of Putnam (2000) in that both friendships and network membership are cited as features. However, it is rather in the *dynamics* of social capital that the distinction between Bourdieu and other theories of social capital is made. For Bourdieu, the use of social capital is primarily as a resource for individual social mobility. Social capital is relevant simultaneously as a resource for individuals and families for their own gain, and for social classes (or at least class factions) in maintaining and consolidating their position:

> ... the network of relationships is the product of investment strategies, individual or collective, consciously or unconsciously aimed at establishing or reproducing social relationships that are directly useable in the short or long term.
>
> (Bourdieu 1986: 249)

Therefore social capital can be appropriated by individuals, families, groups or class factions as a source of 'material or symbolic profits'. For example, by establishing a prestigious group of connections individuals can increase their cultural, social and economic status. The 'old school tie' of those who have attended top private schools is an example of where both 'material' and 'symbolic' profits may be expected. However, others have applied Bourdieu's theories of social capital to more prosaic areas of civic activity, such as school governorships (Gamarnikow and Green 1999), children's clubs (Ball 2003a) and local politics (Nie et al. 1996).

Like forms of economic capital, the accumulation and maintenance of social capital requires work and skill:

> ... an unceasing effort of sociability, a continuous series of exchanges in which recognition is endlessly affirmed and reaffirmed.
>
> (Bourdieu 1986: 250)

As with other forms of capital, the accumulation of social capital requires direct (subscriptions, fees, gifts, displays of wealth or altruism) or indirect (time or resources) expenditure. Continuous effort is required to maintain social capital, such efforts becoming part of the individual's natural repertoire of thought and behaviour (the habitus), and to make sure that the material or symbolic profits arising from the use of social capital are not diminished. This may involve social closure through ensuring that '. . . the members of the group must regulate the conditions of access to the right to declare oneself a member' (ibid: 251).

In this chapter and the next I make use of the conceptual framework of Bourdieu to analyse the ways in which adult education impacts upon the civic lives of our interviewees. From Bourdieu, the notion that even friendship requires continuous cultural work and access to other forms of capital is examined. In doing so I refer to modalities of class, gender and race. I then discuss how the acquisition of civic skills and attitudes through adult education is embedded in social space and contingent on the identification of other forms of capital. Finally, I examine the role of adult education in the formation of values, particularly tolerance. Bourdieu's theory is less able to deal with these normative components of social capital, but I demonstrate how the development of certain forms of tolerance must be seen as related to social class as well as education.

Social capital 'fragments': networks and informal interaction

The 'fragments' of social capital, in particular informal interaction in friendship groups or neighbourhoods, was frequently featured in interviews. This often neglected feature of social capital may be the antecedent of more formal forms of participation (Parry et al. 1992; Gundelach and Torpe 1996). Empirically the influence of education on the size and maintenance of social networks is well established, although less has been said concerning the effect of education on their quality and purposes (Emler and Fraser 1999: 267). The biographies revealed that education and learning had been implicated in building, maintaining, dismantling, reconstructing and enriching individuals' social networks. Hence adult education both maintains and disrupts social networks, although the degree to which this occurs is influenced by structural and situational constraints. Education can be seen as a resource used in various forms of cultural and social 'work' involving individual relationships. In this sense, learning is being used as a resource, but not necessarily in building social networks. The dissolution or de-stabilisation of existing social networks could equally be a feature of participation in learning.

Significantly, for some individuals education and learning sites actually became the networks and neighbourhoods of learners. Although this is probably the received perception of students in Higher Education (HE), it was also the case that in Further Education (FE) and Adult Education (AE) these relationships were apparent. For Gareth, a former drug addict who isolated himself from social interaction for many years, the college had led to the acquisition of a sense of community:

> ... there's a pub over the road from the college, where after some of the evening classes that I do, we'll go and have a game of pool and a pint. And, I've become really friendly with the people there. So that's become part of the college community as well. And it's not necessarily people from college.

The role of education and learning as a hub of social networks for young men and women was heavily contingent on other circumstances. In this manner, the cultural and social context of individuals' access to various capitals became apparent. In the case of Ahmed, a single parent in his thirties, childcare responsibilities meant that he could not develop social networks through his course:

> Once I've finished the course I had to ... I had to run as quick as I finished. We finished the course at three o'clock and I had to collect my child at half-past three. So, no socialising whatsoever.

In many cases education led to an extension of social networks, or an enrichment of existing ones. Joe, 40, was bullied at school, left with no qualifications, and since then has had only a few casual jobs. However, adult education has developed his social networks. Joe now goes to the pub, cinema and 'everywhere' with these friends, and states that the class feels like a 'nice family'. Adult education institutions can be a site of network-building, but this is contingent on the possession of other forms of economic capital such as the resources to pay for childcare.

Adult education can also lead to a dissolution and reconstruction of social networks and friendships. Lillian developed her self-esteem through a counselling course, and became aware of the negative features of some of her current relationships. However, given her professional status as a counsellor she may have possessed not only the esteem but the cultural and economic resources to make such an action possible.

LILLIAN: Yes, when I went through my counselling training, obviously you go through a lot of stuff within yourself and I went into therapy and discovered things from the past that were still there and were holding me back from moving on. And so I went through a process of therapy and healing and I moved on. And when I moved on because I became more of the person that I truly am, other people didn't like it because in a certain sense I used to conform in some ways and it used to make me angry because it wasn't really me.

INTERVIEWER: Which people?

LILLIAN: Because they couldn't manipulate me any more. It was friends. And I decided that the way I wanted to live my life through moving on was totally different and I didn't dismiss unkindly the people around me. I just needed a different sort of person around me, a different sort of person around me, a different sort of support system and nurturing and different mentors because I'd moved on a bit . . ..

For these individuals, education has differing functions in structuring their social lives. Learning does not always lead to an expansion of social networks, but can cause their relocation and dissolution. Moreover, the impact of learning on social networks is contingent upon other features of the individual's life. For Ahmed, childcare acts as a major constraint on his ability to engage socially. Lacking both the economic capital to pay for additional childcare and a social network of other carers, social capital is sacrificed. For Lillian, her present cultural resources allow her safely to dismantle an existing social network. Although friendships may appear to be spontaneous and reciprocal, the 'unceasing effort of sociability' required means that the impact of adult education is contingent on other forms of resource. They also relate to different psycho-geographical 'habitus' – understandings of and claims made on space (Raey 2000b; Skeggs 2000). Where we go, and who we associate with, depends upon our histories. Whereas Joe feels comfortable in drawing the boundaries of his friendships within the college, Lillian sees friendship boundaries as transient and transcendable.

As with friendships, informal civic participation such as helping with shopping, participating in childcare circles or being a 'good neighbour' is often not recognised in the same manner as formal community participation. Unsurprisingly then, respondents infrequently mentioned these forms of community action without prompting. However, in line with other observations, the nature of informal community work is both gendered (Smith 2000) and classed (Preston 2002). Particularly applicable in this context is the concept of a 'discourse of care' (Skeggs 1997: 67–69) in the lives of working (and middle-class) women. This involves an internalisation of the dispositions and practices involved in caring. This 'discourse' is employed in maintaining social respectability within the community, although not without its own anxieties and tensions. Tracey, for example, left school with no qualifications and worked in a series of low-paid and 'care' jobs, including markets, a frozen food shop and a number of nursing homes. Her commitment to her own children meant that she spent a lot of time at their school, and used skills gained on an aromatherapy course in giving massages to two special needs children there. Relatedly, Sue, a Belarussian refugee who has been unemployed since mental illness, describes the role of her drama classes in helping her to interact with people including her neighbours. Sue's statement indicates the gendered nature of her involvement ('I listen ... I'll wash up ...'), but also indicates how a shift in values may bring her into conflict with neighbours:

> I sit and listen to people, I mash the tea for them, I'll wash up the cups. I try and make them laugh. Sometimes I get very angry though when some sort of anti-racist comment comes out or sexist comment, and then it's battle stations.

The gendered nature of informal civic participation was apparent from our interviews with men. Whilst working- and middle-class women's learning frequently involved them in care or education-related activities in their communities, working- and middle-class men's courses more often led to them offering physical or technical help to others. Following a series of City and Guilds woodwork and metalwork courses, James (from a middle-class background) built an adventure playground in his area and helped to start other people's cars. This was a public, open display of his participation, as opposed to Comley (from a working-class background), whose participation was less public through the use of his trade skills:

> People that know me, see belonging to a place like the tenants' hall, you have an awful lot of acquaintances and quite a few friends. And people do ask me if I do something, you know, I'll unblock their sink or put a washer on the tap or cistern or something like that. Odd jobs over the time, yeah.

As we have seen, learning has an impact on various kinds of cultural 'work' involving social networks, and also has an effect on informal civic participation. Although gender and class do not act as constraints on these processes, they obviously mediate their effects. From these 'fragments' of social capital, we now move to consider more formally constituted forms of civic participation.

Learning and civic participation

Learning was instrumental for many of our respondents in providing aptitudes which were of use in their civic life. This section examines this notion of work in terms of 'civic skills'. However, as much as these are social competences, they do not represent atomized and de-contextualised statements of skill (Hyland 1996) but are socially embedded *practices* (Bourdieu 1977). That is, they can be understood in terms of the strategies which individuals use in the mobilisation of their capitals over time. This section largely focuses on the practices of women and the ways in which civic skills relate to various aspects of their lives. This is partly as our interviews overwhelmingly showed the gendered nature of community involvement and partly for pragmatic reasons, as it illustrates well the metaphor of civic skill as social practice.

At the most aggregated level of practice, few respondents had achieved an holistic understanding of various generic civic skills, networks and local information through learning (referred to by Hyland 1996 and Schuller *et al.* 2002 as meta-competences). However, these respondents were exclusively female and (as we will see in Chapter 8) there is a danger that such skills are becoming reified as women's work in the community. Many of them were engaged in specific learning activities, such as studying for the Community Development Award (CDA), although it was clear that individuals had already demonstrated community skills. Therefore the purpose of the CDA was to accredit prior learning. This codification and certification of this mental and emotional labour of women has been previously alluded to (Skeggs 1988), although not in a community context. Seema makes reference to the effect of prior learning through counselling, computing and 'make life experience count' courses on addressing community problems:

> We really got ourselves so geared up that we could go off for an hour and sort out the Borough Council and it was a really good learning curve to say that we'd got those skills and hadn't realised. To actually have a problem there and with all the experience we've had with the voluntary sector is to say yes, we know, because it wasn't a blank sheet. If we'd sat there and thought how do we do that? But it's because we were working in a community and we could relate to it. You then thought, yes, we can sort it out.

This pro-active approach to solving community problems links to a sense of personal agency in ways referred to in Chapter 2 in linking personal and collective transformation. In particular, there was an emphasis on these type of courses on self-interrogation:

> There's a lot of personal development on this course. Actually spurring off your own beliefs, your own thoughts, the way your type of work lies about you, where it came from you as a person. And also the fact that there's so much more room to promote, there's so much opportunity to sort of go and do things which will link up with the work which you have been doing.
>
> (Shelley)

A number of generic skills gained from other learning contexts were directly applicable to civic life. Again, it was largely women who were involved in this type of additional community work. Secretarial, IT and teaching skills were employed in civic settings. Jane, for example, used her secretarial and IT skills in order to type letters for a group to raise money for deaf children. Teaching skills were also generically transferred into civic contexts. These may be informally acquired skills, such as being taught in a Bible study class and continuing to teach others, or more formally acquired teaching and training skills. In many of these cases, the integrated nature of labour markets and work in the community is apparent, but implicit. In other cases, there was a more explicit relationship:

> ... you are volunteering for yourself because you are taking your time to go and do something instead of being paid for it, so there's no one earning anything from you being there. It's you and your brain earning something from them ... you don't volunteer for anyone, you volunteer for yourself.
>
> (Maureen)

There are interesting transitions between caring for children and 'care' in a wider, community sense. In this respect, women's adult education is both liberating and seductive in terms of the transition to other, caring roles – particularly for working-class women. Joanne provides a salient example of this process. Originally from a working-class family, Joanne left school at 16 and had two girls in the next two years. She described herself as 'directionless' before enrolling in a computing course:

> It was doing something for me ... you get the adult conversation going, you've got a free lunch, not to worry about the kids, you know, sort of thing, so it helps you relax, getting you back into it slowly ... so when the time came to go back to work I was already used to leaving my children, you know. I was pretty much there and quite confident that they were happy enough before I went back to work anyway.

This confidence and skills meant that Joanne became involved in her children's school as a voluntary assistant, and subsequently employment as a classroom assistant. Again, the role of women's labour in care (Skeggs 1997) and in employment as 'carer' in the welfare state (Smith 2000) is identified.

At the level of what might be called 'survival learning', the ability to speak English for non-native speakers was central in a number of women's biographies. For Haminda, a Somali woman, learning English led to her participation in her children's primary school. For Ebe, from the Philippines, it has meant that she is able to communicate with her neighbours. Surinder, a Tanzanian, was able to translate for others in her community. More generally, being an English speaker may act as a form of cultural capital in helping communities access the welfare state. As Rukban, a Bengali woman, states:

It's all about systems and in order to live in Britain you have to know the systems, explaining systems to people ... If you have knowledge you share it with other people. If you don't have it, you have nothing to share ... If you have, for example, chewing gum, then you share it, like you offer it to other people.

Marifeli, originally from Colombia, also used English to help others to negotiate welfare services:

How many people in this street don't know how to cope? They have trouble and they need to explain that. They don't know. How many people are sick? They went to the doctor: 'I'm sick.' 'What's the matter with you?' 'I don't know how to explain it.' But if you have an interpreter, you do.

Some statements made by respondents concerning the influence of learning on their civic lives did not easily fit into the framework of skills adopted. Rarely, respondents would make analogies between learning episodes and their civic lives. Deirdre was able to make a direct link between organising her work in the Crusaders Church Group for young people and planning an essay:

Well, yeah, again (her English A level course), it just sort of helped me because of like, planning things and the order in which you do things I suppose. Reminds me of like, planning an essay, you know ... you know, you decide how you're going to start and then you're going to have, like, the subject, and then you're going to have the conclusion – you know. How you're going to sort of round it all up and summarise it and all that sort of thing. So, yeah, it's very relevant.

Rather more common were individuals using creative aptitudes in a civic context, although this was somewhat more common for middle- rather than working-class respondents. Music and arts skills were used in the civic or political life of the community. For example, as an indirect result of her English degree Molly now reads poetry for free in local community venues, although such performance required both cultural and identity capital (confidence and self-belief) and economic capital (resources to sustain her outside of the labour market).

I have shown through the interviews that although learning provides various competences (or resources) which individuals use in their civic lives, these are deeply embedded in social context. Although gender has been the main organising concept in this section, through discourses of 'care' and the self-monitoring of a 'caring persona', class and race have also been shown to be of importance. Not all of the civic 'skill' benefits of learning fit into these typologies, and I have also identified ways in which education provides analogies for learners and ways in which creative talents are utilised in the community.

Finally, I have provided a brief illustration of the manner in which the boundaries between learning, employment and civic skills are blurred.

Although this discussion of the role of adult education in practices and skills is somewhat de-contextualised without knowledge of the individual's full biographies, we will see through the case studies in Chapter 8 how the generation of 'bonding' and reciprocal forms of interaction through education requires a particular configuration of educational and personal characteristics. Specifically, education cannot be assumed automatically to generate the collective benefits assumed by social capital theorists (Putnam 2000: 287–349). Class, gender, ethnicity and institutions are important in realising civic participation outcomes, but so too are individual relationships, chance and aspirations. The interrelationships between these bring about various types of civic outcomes of education.

For the time being, it is necessary to restate that the formation of social capital through learning was intertwined with cultural capital (and other capital forms), background characteristics and the influence of social institutions. For Susan, a retired, well-educated, middle-class woman, a multiplicity of courses and civic engagements did not result in bonding with others. Rather, civic participation served the role of both consumption/leisure and the valorisation of remaining cultural capital in interactions with 'people like me'. For Francis, a black unemployed man, civic participation resulted in some participation in cultural activities through learning but did not necessarily result in bonding with others. Despite his interest in and talent for the arts, his cultural capital could not be exchanged for social capital in the groups of which he was a member. Declan and Carol did form social capital, but the barriers against the process of social capital formation in their communities are discussed. We will return to these cases in extensive detail in Chapter 8.

Tolerance, respect and trust

So far, we have dealt with what Norris (2000) calls the structural components of social capital – social networks and civic participation of various kinds. We now turn to more explicit discussion of value formation. In their review of literature on education and values, Halsted and Taylor (2000: 169) use a broad definition of values as referring to:

> ... the principles and fundamental convictions which act as general guides to behaviour, the standards by which particular actions are judged to be good or desirable. Examples of values are love, equality, freedom, justice, happiness, security, peace of mind and truth. The broad term 'values education' encompasses and in practice is often seen as having a particular emphasis on education in civic and moral values. It is very closely related to other terms in current use, including spiritual, moral, social and cultural development.

With this broad definition in mind we allowed respondents to talk freely about how learning had impacted upon their values in general, before asking more specific questions concerning those values particularly pertinent to the formation of social capital: tolerance and trust. This meant that respondents addressed a number of issues, such as respect, inequality and morality, as well as tolerance and trust. Only one respondent refused to answer any questions on values, stating that 'I can't stand political issues', and that she would leave any course which expected her to discuss these.

In this section, I concentrate on the ways in which learning influences values related mainly to tolerance, understanding and respect for others. The distinction between these three is important, as tolerance on its own implies a rather passive acceptance of others. However, understanding and respect imply that individuals have adopted (or at least acknowledged) others' perspectives and perhaps actively engaged with individuals from other communities. These activities are instrumental in 'bridging' social capital between other groups. Indeed, individuals used terms such as 'respect', 'seeing other's perspectives', 'seeing other's points of view' or 'understanding others' to indicate qualitatively different states of tolerance. Although tolerance of other ethnic groups was an emergent benefit of learning, so too was tolerance in respect of social class, gender, sexuality, nationality, religion and often demonised groups, such as young single mothers or asylum seekers.

Tolerance, understanding and respect were all value changes reported by respondents as a result of their learning, and they seemed to have some insight into the mechanisms by which these qualities had been enhanced. We identified five broad mechanisms by which learning influenced tolerant values: social mix and communication, role models, educational activities, subject effects and resistance. In many of these categories, there is an uneasy relationship between consensus and conflict in the production of values. Naturally, resistance implies that values have been influenced in reaction to the educational institution. Values are often formed as a result of 'cognitive dissonance' rather than resistance to educational processes, and conflict, uncomfortable contacts and affective reactions can be seen as mechanisms by which value consensus is achieved. However, in line with the earlier discussion, it would be incorrect to abstract processes of value change from their social context. Although there is evidence that the process of value formation, particularly with regard to racial tolerance, arises through cognitive or socialisation effects, this is not a process empty of the influence of culture (Halman 1994) or class (Roediger 2002: 12–13). A statement of tolerance or intolerance (rather than necessarily its practice), as with other political values, occurs within the nexus of class position (Bourdieu 2003: 411–414).

A mix of pupils or students from different backgrounds on a course appears to be a necessary, but not sufficient, condition for the development of tolerant attitudes. Although background factors (such as social class) were influential, adult education did succeed in bringing together individuals from different social backgrounds. Courses with mandatory social interaction which can be enforced within the discipline, as in the case of creative writing (illustrated above), but also through a professional (nursing, teaching, training to be a therapist) or access (Open University, access courses) context encouraged the growth of tolerance by forcing groups of individuals together. Many individuals commented on the social mix of their courses as changing their attitudes:

> It made me open my eyes a lot more to how people are or how differently they can live.
>
> (Sandra, nursery nurse)

> I met my first battered wife. I couldn't believe it . . .
>
> (Susan, Open University student, retired)

> I suppose one thing that affected me is that I kind of believed a lot of propaganda about asylum seekers, in that I bought the trip about it, you know, about them economic migrants rather than genuine asylum seekers. And being here and . . . there's quite a lot of asylum seekers here and just, you know, they've become people, you know, as opposed to this tag 'asylum seekers' and they're lovely, they're really nice.
>
> (Gareth, access course)

However, social mixing on courses should not necessarily be assumed. Indeed, recent work in adult education has shown that the divisions between those undertaking adult education by class, race and gender have not equalised over time (Sargant and Aldridge 2003). Diane gives an example of how at Art School she was able to mix with individuals from many different social backgrounds, which she would not believe possible now:

> . . . it was brilliant because I met people from many different backgrounds and I think now probably that's not the case because as far as I could see the only people who go to college are people who've got money.

Social mixing is seen as important, but whether this is expressed as 'tolerance' depends upon other conditions, in particular the way in which this is articulated with social class. Paula, a middle-class art therapist, changed her views of Asian young men due to participating in a short course at her local school:

> . . . they do know a lot and it takes you by surprise . . . when you talk to them they're really studious and really studying hard and have already achieved a lot and done a lot. It makes you realise they're not that young and life-inexperienced as you have imagined.

Another change of view, this time towards a working-class man, is also apparent for another middle-class woman interviewed (Jemima, retired) on her creative writing course. However, as shown, the growth of tolerance is mutual and enforced by the routines of the subject in terms of constructive criticism of other's work:

> I go to a creative writing now, at the University of the Third Age. And there's a man there called Danny Brown. I call him Danny B and I hope they hang him in the morning. But his language is absolutely abysmal. Every other word is a swear word and to speak is awful. And I can't stand it. And when he read out one or two of his pieces I actually got up and left the room. I just ... I thought ... And one of the last pieces he wrote was actually blasphemous ... But since then he seems to have got better at the last two meetings we had. We all criticise each other's work you see, and he gave me very constructive criticism to mine. Because I had to write about the 'Gorbals' and I don't know anything about the 'Gorbals' at all. But he does, he's Scottish, very Scottish, and he gave me some quite good constructive criticism about how I'd written about the 'Gorbals' and I found that very good. And he was very constructive and he wasn't swearing or anything. When he actually talks to you he's a very clever man. And then this week which is our last week there were only three of us there. There was this Danny, another fellow called Malcolm who used to be an actor, like one of the old actor college, and he was also in publishing and he feels he's got an edge on everybody and used to talking to lots of people. But there were just the three of us. But I discovered again that there was more to them that met the eye. I made hasty judgements on them. And we actually had quite a nice little session.

Paula and Jemima show that they have gained some form of tolerance for individuals of other ethnicities or classes on their courses. However, one could argue that this tolerance has been granted on their terms. For Paula, the Asian young men are 'really studious' and 'working hard'. For Jemima, when Danny B isn't swearing he is 'actually a clever man' with a unique white, working-class knowledge to be utilised; 'he's Scottish, very Scottish'. The terms by which tolerance is granted are in terms of meeting certain norms of language and behaviour. They also may reflect a further class of judgement in meeting stereotypical depictions of the 'studious' Asian boy or the romanticised 'cultured' working-class man beneath the surface of bad language.

By understanding the relationships between adult education and social class we may also understand intolerance as operating with class and the reasons why education fails to impact upon it. A number of our interviews took place in an almost exclusively white area of Essex. In this area, a number of white, working-class young men expressed intolerant attitudes (although not exclusively – see Declan in Chapter 8). For example, Charles did not gain a clear understanding of race or racism from his PSE lessons. Interestingly, he also conflates racism with homophobia:

INTERVIEWER: And did the teachers deal with the racism?

CHARLES: As I say, I wouldn't really know because there were no coloured or gay people like that in my class. So I couldn't really see if the teachers were acting on the racism.

Later in the interview, though, he says that he is prejudiced against:

CHARLES: Indians, for some reason, or Pakistanis. I don't know why. Just from some silly things that have affected me in the past. In one of the corner shops there was Chomp bars and it says 10p actually on it, but they had scribbled it out and put 15p. I don't think I am ever going to forget how sneaky that is.

INTERVIEWER: Did you learn about Pakistanis at school as a group?

CHARLES: No.

INTERVIEWER: Where has that attitude come from?

CHARLES: Friends, really. All of my friends are homophobic, all of them, every single one, apart from the female ones, obviously. A lot of them are racist against black people and things like that, but then my friends know who they are, really. I don't see that as a fault though. I don't put it against them really.

School or college had obviously not successfully challenged prejudice, nor had it helped Charles understand the difference between racism and homophobia. However, neither had it provided Charles with any sense of race or racism as social formation. Race was not identified as an issue by teachers in almost exclusively white schools and colleges. Later in the interview we see that Charles had informally adopted a sense of identity through identification with the England football team. Another working-class student from Essex, Blake, also felt that education did not influence his views concerning ethnicity and nation, which again were expressed informally through football. Blake did not even consider himself to be white as he felt that it was such a majority group that it did not count as a group at all. Rather disturbingly, the only sense of national identity Blake acquired from school and college was through studying the Nazis.

In the accounts of Charles and Blake, we see manifestations of intolerance. Although this can perhaps be understood in terms of their class, there is then a danger that we interpret white, working-class racism as both determined and as a form of symbolic resistance (Nayak 2002). Indeed, as Chapter 8 will show, some white students did attempt to resist prejudice even in an almost exclusively white area. Although there were few (visible) minority-ethnic students in Charles and Blake's colleges, there seems to have been an assumption that this meant that 'race' and 'racism' was not an issue for teachers and lecturers to confront. Without any other reference points, Charles and Blake make sense of race through 'common-sense' identifiers such as friendships, limited experiences, sporting affiliations and what little discussion of race there is in the curriculum. These are certainly influenced by class position and locality, but colleges must share some part of the blame by assuming that (perceived) white homogeneity implies both an absence of race and systematic racism.

Even in fairly homogeneous settings, teachers and other students can also act as positive role models in terms of tolerance and in challenging prevailing assumptions. Indeed, a common experience for respondents educated outside of the UK was that their teachers were seen as a formative influence on their attitudes. Magda adopted a communitarian viewpoint as a result of her teachers' activity. Her teachers took the time to check that every student was happy with every aspect of their learning and if there were problems, they would ask the parents in to discuss the difficulties. Consuela generalises the actions of individual teachers to the general school ethos:

> It was also an attitude of the school, that although we were individuals, we were all part of a community. And of the country. And we could all put a little dust on the cap of the mountain.

A tutor who represents and is an advocate for a different community can also change values for students and pupils. Charlie had a deaf tutor at college:

> Eventually, talking to him you get another viewpoint on things because he'd grown up in a deaf world and deaf community. Again, it just opens your eyes to a whole new life and there he was teaching people and he'd coped and he'd done really well, so there's hope.

As Charlie's son was deaf, this led her to an understanding of his potential:

> You just sort of realise that this isn't that bad, he can still lead a normal life, there's loads of deaf people in good jobs and it's up to him. It shouldn't be a disability.

In contrast to social mixing and teacher effects, only rarely was it mentioned that increased tolerance emerged through the application of more general reasoning or 'open-mindedness' common to many subjects. Phillipa 'unconsciously feels' that her access course has changed her values:

> It makes me look at people in a different way, really. I suppose I'm not so judgemental either as I was because you tend to think about the reasoning behind things more.

However, whilst more general cognitive skills were not mentioned, certain subject disciplines emerged as particularly influencing tolerance. In particular, subjects such as history and sociology were especially instrumental in changing values. At best, these subjects appear to be associated with the upsetting of conventional historically or culturally specific categories and enable individuals to engage in wider debate with others.

History was reported as enabling subjects to draw parallels between past and current inequalities:

> ... I think not only with the Industrial Revolution, with the Russian Revolution, with all that has happened in history, I think one needs to change his own mentality. We need to change our mentality. And in order to change our mentality, we need to educate ourselves, to look at how other people thought, to look at how things came about, and why they came about, and how in the present, as contemporary, could make a change, could help not make the same mistakes.
>
> (Magda)

History was not always encountered in terms of formal didactic study, though. One of our respondents, Chris, a young, unemployed black man in an area of economic deprivation in Nottingham, had discovered the writings of Malcolm X through engagement in a Music course. This had given him a strong sense of black unity, which had led to his withdrawal from gang activity in the area.

Sociology can also challenge categorisations through its subject matter:

> Challenged my values? Yes, a hell of a lot. I was ... when I came here I was very dogmatic about my beliefs. I didn't approve of single mothers because of my own life experiences. I didn't think they could give a proper – raise a child properly, that is. Having been surrounded by a lot of single mothers, I realise [that] isn't the case. Learning sociology and looking at issues more intently, I found really difficult at first. But obviously, when you look into things more deeper, you know, yeah, you do have to take other things into perspective.
>
> (Gareth, Access course)

The study of sociology may also lead to active debates concerning class or other forms of identity, which may challenge the views of others:

> Well there is a young girl on the Sociology course that believed that all teenage parents get pregnant to get a council house. Being a teenage mother myself I don't share the same opinion. So, no, we had a bit of a ... she's just ... but then she was young. She was only 17, so ... there's the age difference as well. She's just ... because she's seen it on telly or heard it, it's the truth.
>
> (Theresa, Access course)

Tolerant or accepting values were sometimes formed in opposition to the formal (or informal) curriculum of the educational institution. Sometimes teachers resisted debate on controversial or political matters, but informal conversations or debates with teachers outside or incidental to lessons could particularly influence tolerance. Sophie was involved with political arguments with her teachers at school. This reinforced prior views gained through informal learning:

> I've always been interested in the underdogs and it's got me into trouble even now ... I used to watch news and current affairs programmes which means that I probably was too old for my age watching programmes like that, but I just found it very interesting ... I still have the same views now that I did then.

This experience may have influenced Sophie's later entry into voluntary and then paid welfare rights work.

In summary, tolerance is an area of values in which respondents identified particular effects of adult education. Developing tolerance is not necessarily a cognitive process through which one arrives at a position of liberal understanding. It is situated in, although not over-determined by, class factors, and it operates within local sites and conditions. Most of all, tolerance is an active process, with discussion and contestation within adult education arenas being of great importance.

Conclusion

In this chapter I have explored the relationships between learning and social capital. Learning has a relationship with social capital in terms of both its structural and its normative components. Social networks are influenced by learning, which acts as a personal resource, although the extension of networks is not always a consequence of learning. Rather, various forms of cultural work are employed in the construction, reconstruction, reconfiguration and dismantling of social networks within the respondents' current social context. An 'unceasing effort of sociability' is required in this work. Adult education is but one of the symbolic capitals which individuals draw on in their everyday lives. That for some individuals the college represented the new sphere of their friendships, whereas for others the dismantling and reconstruction of friendships was possible, identifies the process as one involving both economic and cultural capitals. Informal civic participation was less likely to be identified as a consequence of learning, and there were clear gender (and class) divisions between learning and the nature of informal civic participation. Although the influence of learning on civic participation will be explored more thoroughly in Chapter 8, the relations between social context, social capital and other forms of capital were introduced. Civic skills are also embedded in social context, and the notion of transferable civic skills should therefore be viewed critically.

Finally, I explored the processes by which adult education affects values, in particular tolerance. Although social mixing is important in realising tolerance, social class relates strongly to these processes. In particular, the ways in which tolerance or intolerance are stated and operated must be interpreted in terms of the social worlds of these respondents. However, values are an arena where contestation, discussion and conflict within adult education can produce changes in position.

Some elements of Bourdieu's work – in particular notions of cultural capital and distinction – as well as more general themes of class, gender and race are implicated in the realisation of what we might call the 'benefits' of adult learning. However, given the nature of the extracts chosen, these were somewhat de-contextualised. In Chapter 8 I examine how these concepts illuminate 'practices' of adult education and more formally constituted civic participations.

Chapter 8

Lifelong learning and civic participation

Inclusion, exclusion and community

John Preston

Chapter 7 examined Bourdieu's conceptual framework of habitus, capital exchange and social distinction as a tool for interrogating the relationships between adult education and social capital outcomes. As full learner biographies are used, there is scope for engaging with the ways in which class, gender and race operate together rather than individually. In particular, the role of individual 'class strategies' are used to explain the ways in which adult education may operate simultaneously as a force for both civic inclusion and civic exclusion.

The term 'class strategies' (Ball 2003) refers to the ways in which individuals act to protect, consolidate or advance their class position whilst consciously or unconsciously excluding members of other social classes. I am therefore not just using class in its economic or occupational sense (although these are important) but also as defined and formed through processes of inclusion or exclusion. This includes the ways in which the benefits of adult education are accumulated.

This chapter contains four biographies of individuals with very different levels and types of civic participation and adult education experiences. In the first two cases (Susan and Francis, both from North London) there are obvious limits, either self-imposed or institutionally imposed, to the types of civic participation arising through adult education. Although their class backgrounds and economic resources could not be more different, I examine the reasons why in each case there is not a straightforward relationship between adult education and civic participation. In the second pair of cases (Declan from Essex and Carol from Nottingham) adult education has led to community involvement in a less problematic manner. However, participation in both Declan's and Carol's cases required negotiation and compromise. I conclude by discussing the implications of these cases for the development of theory, research and policy in this area.

Susan and Francis: inclusion and exclusion

Susan: 'I don't have friends . . . they're a pain in the neck.'

In interview, Susan describes herself as a 'middle-class English woman who likes classical music'. She describes her upbringing as cold and her parents as being remote and uninterested in her. Susan married a senior officer in the RAF and this meant that she moved around the country a great deal, although she worked in a number of temporary clerical and teaching jobs. She was married for 30 years, having five daughters, before her husband's death through a heart attack. Susan is retired. Politically she is conservative in her views, anti-welfare and pro-capitalism.

School was an escape from the isolation of her home life:

> I loved school partly because I didn't enjoy home. I was reading about children who were doing after-school activities and didn't want to go home and I thought that would have been wonderful . . .

Susan has a particular aptitude for mathematics. She has a vocational qualification in Principles of Accounts, but she really furthered her interest through taking an OU degree course in mathematics. Later, she used this course and a certificate in further education teaching to gain employment as a teacher, although she left teaching due to a conflict of views concerning pupil behaviour. Since retirement she has been involved in a number of adult education courses, including economics, genealogy and exercise classes, through the University of the Third Age (U3A). However, by her own admission:

> I don't like getting involved with people. I'm a bit of a loner. I disapprove of calling a teacher by their first name.

Through U3A and her interest in economics, Susan has taken over the running of an investment club and this is her form of civic participation. Aside from the interest in economics and mathematics, she describes the benefits as follows:

> . . . it gets you out of the house. Which is a problem for the elderly. Unless you've got a job which you can carry on until the day you die you get to this point and if you've always worked for other people, which of course I have because we always travelled around all the time, you are unemployable and if you haven't got any time-consuming hobbies . . . And of course you speak to people. I mean these are the main advantages. You get some exercise and stop worrying about your own problems and complaints. Anything that takes you out of your four walls . . .

However, the benefits of participation are individual more than social for Susan:

> Yes well I do my stocks and shares every day. I look on the teletext. It makes you buy a paper at least once a fortnight. I can't believe people don't buy newspapers.

Civic participation, then, does not necessarily mean the same thing as 'bonding' with others in social capital parlance, let alone 'bridging' divides (Putnam

2000). Although Susan describes one of the benefits of participation as forming friendships, it was clear from later parts of the interview that Susan happily lives an isolated existence despite her high levels of participation in courses and groups:

> I go to the classes and I'll talk to anybody ... I like going out and I like meeting people on a friendly casual basis but I don't have friends. They're a pain in the neck. I enjoy mixing and going to things but I don't want to go into a real neighbourhood. I would just like a more casual acquaintance-ship.
>
> Well a community is the people who are around you and basically it means your relationship with that and mine is non-existent.
>
> For myself (community) doesn't mean anything to me ... I don't rely on people for a social basis at all.

INTERVIEWER: What about your role in the community? How's learning affected that, do you think?

SUSAN: Well, it's made me not need it. You see, I'm quite self-sufficient, and I don't need other people, actually, except on, as I've said to you, a casual basis ...

For Susan, then, her course has led to civic participation in the sense of formal memberships, but not to an extension of her social networks or to any reciprocal involvement with others on the course. She is consciously deciding to exclude herself from the wider community. In terms of her class position – retired, respectable and middle class – she may have decided that there is no need for her to make additional friends through her courses. Indeed, she describes one of the functions of her courses as being with '... people like me'. In this way, Susan may be reconsolidating her cultural capital without necessarily requiring it to be converted into social capital. Additionally, it may represent a particular strategy of middle-class whiteness in excluding herself from more socially and ethnically diverse groups. Educationally, school and schoolwork as an escape from her family and an educational career involving mathematical subjects may have been a means of protecting herself from social interaction. This given, the nature of her civic participation does make sense – running an investment club provides a focus for both financial and numerical interest. It also provides a means of transmitting economic capital to successive generations.

Susan's relationship with her civic life can be said to be privatised in that the benefits which arise from education and resulting involvement are couched in terms of her own benefits: '... You get some exercise and stop worrying about your own problems' and the influence of education on community has been '... it has made me not need it'. So there were perhaps private, if not social, benefits of this participation. Indeed, for Susan social interaction and her courses were seen as a leisure activity:

We used to go to summer school and for someone who was widowed and stuck at home with five kids, it was absolute bliss. To go on holiday to a different place. I went to Strathclyde, and Reading and Bath. I'm not a holiday person because I get bored, there's nothing to do on holiday except look [. . . it's] lovely to go away and do summer schools and mix with people of like minds.

The social benefits of participation were also in terms of consolidation of personal position:

Well it does, yes, to a certain extent. Saying well you did Open University in maths, you know. Anything to do with figures, everybody sort of gasps. I mean I had to go to a convenors' meeting and they said everybody give their name and say what group they're doing and I said I'm into stocks and shares and they said 'Oooh!' you know . . . anything you do that boosts your ego gives you confidence to go and do something else, doesn't it?

So although Susan's relationship with civic participation is individuated, reinforced by a solitary and academic education, there are a number of non-pecuniary private benefits arising from her participation – benefits of 'intrinsic satisfactions and edification' (Bourdieu 2003: 287). There are not only benefits for herself, but also potentially economic benefits for her family in terms of investment returns through participation in the investment club. There are also significant familial benefits in terms of a holiday taken with her children, which was made possible through participation in adult education. Susan therefore adopts a socially individuated but economically expansive strategy, which makes sense given her age, race and class history and disposition towards moral conduct. To paraphrase Putnam (2000) she is 'enrolling alone' (Preston 2003), although paradoxically this isolation arises from a position of economic and cultural advantage.

Francis: 'It was just too expensive . . . I didn't have the money for it.'

Francis was in his thirties at the time of the interview. He is black, male, has qualifications below five GCSE passes, and is not living with a partner or dependent children. On the basis of his previous occupations he is working class, and currently he is unemployed. Francis' age falls between the ages of the two cohorts, and we compare him with individuals from the NCDS dataset as opposed to the BCS70 dataset. These individuals were all aged 42 in 2000.

Amongst 42-year-olds in Britain in 2000, about 71 people in every

10,000 were male, non-white, and had qualifications below degree level. Thus, we compare Francis with 42-year-olds who are similar in this respect, but not in terms of current family or occupational status. Amongst this group, a relatively low percentage had participated in learning during the previous nine years (54 per cent as opposed to 61 per cent for all 42-year-olds). Amongst individuals who shared characteristics with Francis and who had participated in adult learning during the previous nine years, a just above average percentage had not gained any qualifications at all (61 per cent as opposed to 57 per cent), and this group had taken just below the average proportion of courses that led to qualifications (27 per cent as opposed to 29 per cent of all 42-year-olds).

People 'like' Francis in the cohort feel slightly less in control of their lives, and are slightly more likely to report high levels of life satisfaction. The proportion of those sharing Francis' characteristics who are members of at least one organisation is similar to the proportion of all 42-year-olds, and the percentage of people 'like' Francis who report an interest in politics is higher than the percentage of all 42-year-olds (55 per cent as opposed to 43 per cent).

Francis' experience is fairly representative of this group. Like 54 per cent of those sharing his demographic characteristics, he has participated in adult learning over the previous nine years. He is not depressed, has positive efficacy and life satisfaction, and is interested in black politics. He is unusual amongst those sharing his demographic characteristics in that he is amongst the one in six who belong to at least one organisation.

In the interview with Francis, a number of themes emerged relating to civic participation. It was clear that *notionally*, arenas for civic participation as well as friendships were open to Francis and that adult education could act as an instrument for increasing involvement. However, the *reality* of civic participation was very different for Francis. The demands of the training state, the expense of adult education, and the exclusionary and self-serving nature of some supposedly cosmopolitan and open civic associations meant that Francis' learning and civic biography was (not by choice) somewhat curtailed, rather than being a linear and developmental narrative. However, this did not prevent him from engaging civically and learning from the goodwill of tutors and the (declining) public good nature of educational activity. For the most part, though, Francis was excluded from full participation in many of these cultural groups.

Francis is working class and in his thirties. His working career has been characterised by lack of occupational choice ('In the mid-eighties I did catering. I just did that because I didn't want to be unemployed. I was given a choice of catering, flower arranging or window dressing, and I just chose catering. The other's I didn't like') and he entered into a number of catering jobs in low-wage, non-unionised premises where explicit and informal racial discrimination was rife. Francis is currently unemployed, having suffered from a work exacerbated spinal injury which has made it difficult to stand for any length of time. He describes his ethnicity as 'British Carib', but also classifies himself as 'black British – I also, I call myself, black European'. He was contacted through a tutor at a North London Learndirect centre where he was involved in a basic skills programme related to the New Deal, and the interview was held at the library where the centre was based.

He describes his situation:

> I don't work. I haven't been able to work for over 10 years because of dis-
> ability – spine disability. Over the years I've just been doing writing courses
> and things, just finding my way, and in 1994 I did a photography course
> and it was for those with learning difficulties. About three years I think
> after that I did an exam but I dropped out because it was just too expensive.
> I didn't have the finance for it so I just went back to doing writing courses.
> In 1998 I was *called up* for a Back to Work scheme but that hasn't worked
> out and now I've gone back to my – I've had a chance to go back to my
> photography and I do that once a week on a Thursday evening.

Lack of economic capital and lack of choice are features of Francis' learning career. He refers at several points in the interview to being 'called up' for various employment schemes and the negative effects which this had on courses which he was taking at the time. Of his photography course, he says:

> ... I left it because I resumed back to work and it meant I had to leave the
> course. I was kind of confused but I was told in January that I needn't have
> done that but when I tried to get back on I couldn't because it was always –
> the classes were always full.

This meant that the friendships Francis had made on the photography course had fallen through:

INTERVIEWER: OK, and did you make many friends or contacts on the course?
FRANCIS: Yes I made quite a few friends.
INTERVIEWER: Can you tell me a bit about those friendships then?
FRANCIS: Everyone bar one, everyone was new. I think there was one lady who
had been there before, a year before. I was sitting with some other – I think
his name was Tom and we would just sit down and we'd talk about what we
have done, what we haven't done and we talked about the kind of cameras
we had. He had like a semi-automatic when it was – and we talked about
the manual and just talking about how you can't get things through using
the automatic. I told him they've got some manual ones there, to ask the

teachers to borrow one of them, things like that. I made friendships like that in that sense.

INTERVIEWER: Have they continued the friendships?

FRANCIS: No I haven't, like I said, I had to drop out.

INTERVIEWER: Oh yes.

FRANCIS: So I haven't seen anyone for three years.

INTERVIEWER: Oh.

FRANCIS: Three, four years.

It was clear that Francis enjoys photography as it involves the exercise of skill. He had good relations with his tutor, and planned activities and compositions for other members of the group. He frequently organised trips to Smithfield market at 4 am to take compositions. However, since being 'called up' for a training scheme he had not found opportunities for taking his photography further:

> I've tried ... there's a Disabled Careers office and we tried but they're all full up ... we tried to join some [photography clubs] ... there was one photographer and the Portrait Gallery but that's for people between the ages of 14 to 18 and so no, it's kind of hard to find anything there.

Although Francis did not find any other photography clubs open to him, the relation between him and his tutor became an avenue through which he could continue his photography in some sense. On leaving the course Francis remarks on his tutor:

> He just said, he gave me some film and said 'go out and do your thing' so I'll do that. I'd say within two, three, months I'll be calm.

As well as photography, Francis also has a passion for literature. He was a member of both poetry and writing groups, although interestingly (given the supposedly inclusive nature of such groups) he did not associate with many of the members outside the context of the groups. He found himself isolated as the 'only black man' in the groups. There were also earlier, institutional antecedents which seemed to act against the development of an interest in literature, as access to certain types of literature were rationed (evidence that the type of institutional racism through educational rationing cited by Gillborn and Youdell (2000) predates educational markets):

> Well I did do literature at school but I think Thomas Hardy was the most difficult one I'd done. Shakespeare, I didn't do that – that was more for O level students. That wasn't for CSE students so I didn't approach Shakespeare in that way. I learned about him in history, but not in literature.

but again any future interest in literature was curtailed by a training scheme:

FRANCIS: Well, my literature course – I just did it just to see what it was like after all those years out – umpteen years out and it was hard to get back into. It's a discipline to get back into it and there's a lot of things I just couldn't understand. I kept with it through the first time but then I felt no, I have a long way to go so I just dropped out but my writing course I always kept up with and I just do my own kind of stories. I was in there in 1998 but then I had to leave because of the Back to Work and I have never been back since.

INTERVIEWER: OK. How do you feel about that?

FRANCIS: I miss that writing because I felt I was coming back to something I knew but then you're told you have to leave so I've missed three years out now.

Francis then was forced to sacrifice both his interest in photography and literature (where one might argue that real and sensuous skills were being developed) for a Back to Work course. The emphasis on this course was on self-presentation and the maintenance of a neutral persona – aesthetic labour (Witz *et al.* 2003) rather than the development of skill:

INTERVIEWER: OK, what does the Back to Work course involve?

FRANCIS: Oh, finding work. It's about writing CVs, preparation of CVs and how not to over-delve in your past. Just write out the basics and it's also about how you dress when going for an interview and then what they do is they give you some advertising things and you look up for some companies and you're given the phone which is at the far end of the room and you phone up for work and that's basically it.

Whereas Francis found in his photography and writing courses a chance for the expression of real skill, the emphasis in the Back to Work course was on both the maintenance of a neutral self ('how not to over-delve in your past', 'just write out the basics') and the presentation of self. Francis does have positive things to say about this course, but the reality of the labour market revealed the inadequacy of this 'deficit model' of improving self-presentation and erasing one's past which the course seemed to be orientated around. Francis did not obtain employment as a result of the training.

In maintaining his photography and literature interests, Francis had to become somewhat of an autodidact. At several points in the interview he mentions how, in the absence of effective public provision, he managed to follow his interests. For example, on television '... maybe on the Open University late at night you might see something and it comes from there' or through book-shops – 'I've read a small book on – I think it's Tolstoy and I've read Thomas Hardy. Up at Waterstones – I just sit there and read.' In particular, Francis had informally explored many aspects of his racial identity through reading and television (*Black Britain* and *Black in the British Frame*) as well as re-discovery of the oral tradition of black history. He had therefore participated in many black cultural events such as poetry readings and discussions. Nevertheless, Francis was excluded from full participation in other cultural activities – both economically and through other more insidious mechanisms of social exclusion.

Francis' story may seem simple to portray in terms of conventional binaries of academic versus vocational. Barriers to studying the 'liberal arts' are blocking the self-fulfillment which he desires. However, the exercise of skill is extremely important to him – photography and, to a lesser extent, literature are methods of realising those skills which the labour market does not wish to reward. In that sense they are as vocational as other craft skills. Additionally, that Francis is prevented from studying those courses is tightly connected with his class (material) position and the demands of the training state.

In conclusion, Francis' biography shows the danger in applying terms such as 'lack of motivation for learning' to depict working-class predilections for learning. Francis is active in civil society in many ways, but the demands of the training state are not supportive of certain types of citizenship ('not over-delving in your past') in favour of offering (reluctant) employers a neutral block of labour. His biography reveals the importance of circuits of cultural and economic capital in achieving certain types of civic participation, but also the institutional racism which is practised by not only schools (Gillborn and Youdell 2000) but also training regimes and social organisations against the minority-ethnic working class. However, on the positive side we can see that adult and informal learning have made participation in various artistic and cultural organisations at least possible.

It is therefore helpful to understand both individuals' relationships between adult education and civic participation together, as both are based upon notions of inclusion (participation) and exclusion and of the importance of various capitals and dispositions in this process. To this end I have conceptualised Susan and Francis' case-structure diagrams together (Figure 8.1). The implication is not that the effects of Susan's trajectory directly influenced that of Francis'. However, at the aggregate, strategies such as those adopted by the middle and upper classes (such as Susan) of engagement with 'people like me' have implications for the working class (such as Francis) in that they act as methods of social exclusion. If we take Susan's trajectory first, from an existing position of status and with a large economic capital in the form of wealth she follows a quite plausible path through the U3A to start an investment club. This is perfectly in accordance with her existing habitus in terms of dispositions towards being with 'people like me' – white, middle class – and her concerns for increasing wealth and self-sufficiency. However, whether consciously or not, her subjective perceptions towards being with 'people like me' are both an internalisation of class and a realisation of class in terms of replicating homogeneous, middle-class, white civic associations. Hence, in the aggregate, actions such as

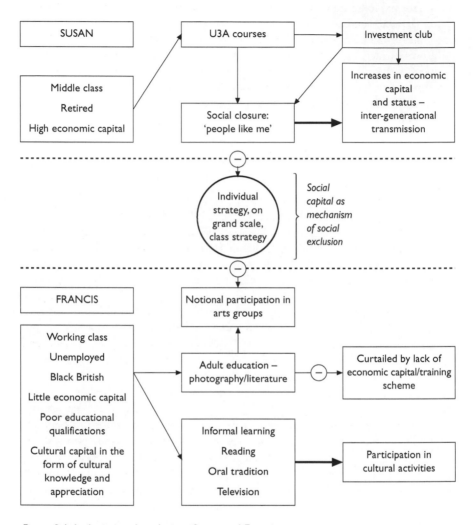

Figure 8.1 Inclusion and exclusion: Susan and Francis.

these are a class strategy, showing how adult education creates social capital but not necessarily the conditions for social inclusion. In Francis' trajectory, we also see adult education in the formation of social capital – this is of benefit both for Francis and his community. However, whilst he is notionally a member of artistic associations he is unable to fully valorise (make valuable) these memberships in terms of extending social networks or deeper involvement in these groups. He perceives them as not being for 'people like him' – black, working class – and indeed there are no other black, working-class members. Despite having a deep knowledge of and interest in culture, he is unable to valorise his cultural capital as symbolic capital – he is frozen out of social interaction within his artistic groups. With only tenuous labour market status and economic capital, he is also unable to accumulate educational capital in terms of photography skills and literature, which might develop his interests in these areas. However, he is very much involved in black cultural groups. Whilst establishing a hierarchy of civic associations is not helpful, it is certainly true that the horizons for action for Francis are much narrower than those of Susan. This is not due to 'cultural deficit' or 'lack of confidence', but rather as a result of economic inequality and the colonisation of valuable civic arenas by the middle classes.

Community action: Carol and Declan

Although Francis and Susan had little in common in terms of ethnicity, class or wealth, both had a similar goal of pursuing individual interests. For Susan, the goal of her investment club was to increase her status and wealth for successive generations. For Francis, a passion for the arts largely drove his involvement. This does not mean that there was no understanding of, or relation to, community in their actions. Even in the case of Susan, her desire to be with 'people like me' was part of her rationale for participation – a community of sorts. However, in other accounts, community (or communities) development or enrichment was a specific aim of the respondent.

Bourdieu has little to say on the subject of social capital as it exists beyond the individual. Although social capital is the product of individual relationships and it can be used as a collective strategy for collectivities or class factions (Bourdieu 1986), he does not place the same emphasis on a 'meso' form of social capital in the same manner as other social theorists (Putnam 1993, 2000). Bourdieu's conception of social capital as an instrument of social competition and comparison has also been critiqued as downplaying the benefits of social capital, namely: '... how social capital can contribute to greater social equity' (Field et al. 2000). However, Bourdieu's concept of symbolic space as a set of social distinctions which can exist through *geographical* space (Bourdieu 2003: 124) and his broad conception of activities which might form 'practices' (Bourdieu 1977) make possible the analysis of this form of activity. For example, voluntary activities within a school and the geographies of such activity can be analysed using Bourdieu's conception that the middle classes use '... the rhetorics of social responsibility', articulated as in the general social good to 'promote their own particularistic interests' (Birenbaum-Carmeli 1999: 88 cited in Ball 2003: 44). However, an emphasis on the middle classes as the generators of social exclusion does not necessarily illuminate analysis of working-class community activity. Rather than adopt a simple middle–working-class binary in relation to adult education and community activity, I therefore examine two working-class respondents – Carol and Declan – as cases. These cases demonstrate the tensions between social capital as both social closure and social panacea, and also the relationships between community activity, class, gender and sexuality.

Carol: 'Two different things there – the caring side and the working side.'

Carol is in her forties. She is white, female, has good A levels, and is living with a partner and dependent children. On the basis of her current occupation she is working class. Since Carol is close to or over 42 years of age, we compare her with individuals from the NCDS dataset as opposed to the BCS70 dataset. These individuals were all aged 42 in 2000.

Amongst 42-year-olds in Britain in 2000, about 57 people in every 10,000 shared all of Carol's characteristics that are mentioned above. Amongst this group, an average percentage had participated in learning during the previous nine years (62 per cent) and of those who had partici-pated, an average proportion (55 per cent) had gained no qualifications – in other words, for 55 per cent of those who had participated in learning during the previous nine years, all of their learning had been unaccred-ited. Amongst this group, the proportion of courses taken that did not lead to qualifications was also in line with the proportion found amongst all 42-year-olds.

People 'like' Carol are much less likely to be clinically depressed than other 42-year-olds. They feel more in control of their lives, and are more likely to report high levels of life satisfaction. A high percentage of people sharing Carol's characteristics belong to at least one organisation when compared to all 42-year-olds (23 per cent as opposed to 18 per cent of 42-year-olds overall), but the proportion reporting an interest in poli-tics is average (43 per cent). It is likely that many of those who share Carol's characteristics belong to organisations which are involved with pre-school organisations and Parent Staff Associations at their children's schools.

Carol is fairly representative of people who share her demographic characteristics in that she has participated in adult learning, gained accreditation, and she is not depressed and has positive efficacy and life satisfaction. She is less representative in that she participates in civic organisations. Carol does not mention her interest in politics during the interview.

Carol is a white British woman with two children. She performed well at school, but decided not to train to be a teacher due to marriage and children. Instead, she worked in the education department and later, after children, worked as a dinner lady and classroom assistant. She stopped working when her father died in order to look after her disabled mother. It was during this time that she became involved in taking adult education courses and community work. She also has a gendered sense of the nature of voluntary activity, and there are parallels with other work on the way in which education may reinforce internal and external discourses of 'care':

> ... it's invariably the women that come and as I say, I think it's because of that voluntary side of it. It's because women have possibly got the time and the men are working. Two different things there – the caring side and the working side.

School was instrumental in building Carol's confidence, but she did not continue with her education due to marrying someone with different values to herself. We can see here how the effective use of confidence and self-esteem are dependent upon economic capital – as 'priorities change' so do Carol's objectives:

CAROL: From school – I think I gained quite a lot of confidence. Obviously, you know, gained knowledge from school and I always enjoyed learning so possibly I gained more knowledge than other children at school because I was just interested in it so I'd perhaps over-do things rather than you know, but I think I gained confidence to go onto other things really. I always wanted to be a teacher, but priorities changed as I say when I met my husband, who by the way, was also from Newcastle.

INTERVIEWER: Yes?

CAROL: He came with his parents and I mean ours was totally different. He left school at 15 and went straight down the pit. He was an electrician at the colliery so we were sort of totally different but that was it. I didn't want to go on with my education then. I wanted to settle down.

Her confidence to change was also constrained by time and her adoption/positioning into a caring role – for children and for her disabled mother: 'I just felt that all I was doing was caring for other people, and I wasn't doing anything for myself.' However, she describes an increase in confidence following an adult education course:

> So as I say, I'd really come down and the confidence and the buzz I'd got from working had totally gone within a matter of nine months I would say, so when I came to this course it took me a few weeks to get back in the rhythm of learning again. I really took off, back in a sort of learning situation, doing my homework, etc., and I really enjoyed it. I thoroughly enjoyed it, and my confidence came back up and from that I then joined a women's group – a women's self-help group and at the time they were organising a big day in Cotgrave – a lifestyle change day and I sort of came into my own then and did loads of things for that.

In relation to confidence and enjoyment the course elicited civic participation – involvement in a women's group and organisation of a lifestyle change day.

Carol also identified that she had the confidence to move outside of the private sphere of her family and use community buildings, such as the Enterprise Centre, and that she finds it easier to meet with others from the council. She described the nature of her work:

CAROL: This is a Women Together group that I co-ordinate, which is a self-help group which tackles isolation/stress within women and promotes self-development through information sharing and education
INTERVIEWER: Is that the main thing you've organised yourself, or have there been other things?
CAROL: The group was already set up and I joined that as I say, not long after doing the Every Women's Health course and I joined that and basically at the time that I joined it, it was a drop-in for a coffee and a chat and share your experiences, but it's developed from there. It's moved on and the women that go wanted to do a little bit more so we started doing these courses as it were, a little bit of education and training and whatever and it seems to be working quite well. We do a session a month and if there's anything in particular that anybody wants to know about, we'll try and find out about it.

However, her husband was not fully supportive of these activities:

... As I say, he's not fully accepting. He'll go through the stage of 'you've been out doing your voluntary work today – the housework isn't done' – 'well the housework can get done anytime can it?' you know, so a little bit like that which – my values have changed a little bit I suppose then, because I don't do my housework first before I go and do it. I do what I enjoy.

Her family were more accepting of her community work and recount a personal experience early in her marriage where her husband would not let her go to a school reunion. Carol would not stand for that now, and her husband would probably come with her.

Through Carol's biography we see a change in the ways in which her confidence was articulated. After leaving school, she was confident enough to enter the labour market as a teacher, but this was suppressed by marriage, 'care' and lack of economic capital. 'Regaining' confidence through adult education helps her to challenge her husband, but also orientates her towards a wider caring role in terms of helping the community. Hence her horizons for action changes over time, but she is positioned towards labour in the form of care, albeit in different social forms (family, extended family, and now community). This has involved wider involvement with community health and the NHS:

It moved on from there because I then became co-ordinator for Women Together and we started looking at women's health issues and we were trying to organise a women's health group which at the time failed miserably actually, but we were really keen on setting that up and looking at – we also set up a group on the menopause and a group of us went to – somebody had heard about it on the radio, and there was a place in Leicester that actually did bone scans, so one of the ladies got in touch with them, we got all the information back on it, we shared with the group and a group of us went down there for a bone scan and that started the women's health issues . . .

A sense of internal efficacy and confidence were important in generating the links between education and altruistic civic engagement. She is engaged both in personal and community transformation. However, confidence is not a socially

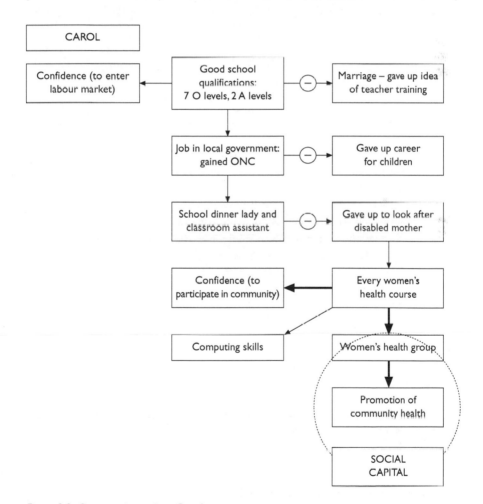

Figure 8.2 Community action: Carol.

abstracted trait, but is bound up with class and gender. Carol is involved in a 'discourse of care', but she works not only for her family (Delphy and Leonard 1992) but also for the wider community and even for the welfare state more generally. The generation of community social capital is dependent upon Carol's labour and her disposition to care in addition to her investment in adult education.

Figure 8.2 shows the ways in which Carol's labour market position has been eroded by various caring positions over time. I have distinguished between two types of confidence – that gained through school (to enter the labour market) and that gained through adult education (to participate in community activities). The final result is the generation of community social capital and, probably, of community benefits. This social capital should not be reified as having an essence of its own – it rests upon (Carol's) material labour.

Declan: 'There's no set pattern of events: the individual can influence events.'

Declan is white, in his early twenties and gay, working as a mobile security inspector and as a volunteer both for a charity for homeless young offenders in Nottingham and for a gay helpline. At the time of the interview he was living away from home due to '... family problems, emotional problems'. In terms of acquiring qualifications, Declan's education had been a positive experience: he had a number of GCSEs and A levels, and was acquiring NVQ as part of his training as a security inspector. During his education, he participated in many formal organisations – Cubs and Scouts, and the ATC.

In Declan's biography there is a tension between college as a site in which he developed confidence and self-efficacy, but also where he was subject to bullying because of his sexuality and where homophobia was the norm. To defend himself, Declan took up martial arts and sports – a not untypical strategy of accommodation (Epstein and Johnson 1998: 166–168). Hence his sense of agency can be seen as both a product of and reaction to the college. I have chosen Declan's biography to illustrate the role of post-compulsory and adult education in the development of a particular form of self-esteem which resulted in community participation, but not without cost.

Through school, and particularly through college, Declan developed a strong belief in his own agency. Although school was more routinised than college, Declan received a great deal of support from school in organising and running a basketball team. However, college life was a major revelation for Declan:

> When you actually got to college, you could actually be yourself. Within reason, you could do what you wanted. There's no pressure to do what you're told to do.

College was also a site where individual identity was explored in the context of other's searches for their own identity. Individuation was a strong theme in this interview – identity and efficacy development were seen as individual, not collective processes:

> I think ... the main thing I learnt at college was how everybody is different, how everybody is entitled to be themselves. Even though society is like 'This is how it should be' at college it's not. 'No, this is how we want to be' as the individual ... You control ... this is going to sound really weird, but you control your own fate. Fate does not control you. People's influences and decisions don't have to determine what you are going to become, what you are going to do.

He cites the process of learning (the environment) rather than specific courses as being the main influence behind this sense of agency. However, history and business studies A level are later cited (actually from a question on tolerance) as being areas where the importance of agency was emphasised:

> It teaches you the system can go up and down, left and right. There's no set pattern of events. The individual can influence events ...

However, despite this positive influence on efficacy and agency, school and college were not positive arenas for Declan to explore his own identity:

> ... there were no avenues, there was no way of exploring how I was feeling at the time. You couldn't go and talk to anybody because, if you tried, they were all like 'No. no. no. That's a big taboo. I don't want to talk about it ...' If anything they [school and college] take me more into the closet

and he was bullied at school due to his sexuality. Therefore, despite claims that college shows you that '... everybody is different ... everybody is entitled to be themselves', this was neither the formal or hidden curriculum of the college.

Despite the institutionalised prejudices of educational establishments, the sense of internal efficacy and agency inculcated by school and college did give Declan the confidence to participate civically – he describes his community as 'the gay community', and volunteered to help run a gay helpline. He describes himself as wanting to 'give back to society', and this reciprocity had been built up through positive experiences of teachers at college:

INTERVIEWER: Do you think that attitude has come at all from school, college environments, teaching environments ...
DECLAN: In a way, yeah, it has because you see the lecturers coming in day after day, putting up with the same monotonous thing every day, year after year. And to me it was a case of 'Oh, they must be enjoying it, doing it because

they want to do it' because it was a way of them putting back in what they got out of the system.

INTERVIEWER: And so them being like that ... how has that made you ...?

DECLAN: It was a good influence on me. They were like setting an example, if you like. You don't have to be like this, you can be a boring old professor or teacher. You can still enjoy yourself and at the same time put something back into it.

He described 'old-fashioned teachers' (not necessarily didactic) as contributing to this sense of reciprocity due to their experience and their 'knack of making it interesting'. Some of the learning dichotomies which are conventionally adopted, such as traditional vs non-traditional didactic teaching vs groupwork, are artificial for Declan. Traditional teachers adapt to the group, and groupwork is 'centred' on the lecturer:

Just because the years of experience they've got, they just know what they're doing. They know what they're telling you is the right way to do something. They've tried ... they've been on the highway. They've taken the low and high roads and they know what's best for each individual. They can adapt, for a class of 30 kids, they can adapt lessons for each individual.

... the lecturer helps co-ordinate the group. They're like the pinpoint, the pivot, the balance, the centre. They are middle, so you start off by learning ... throwing an idea at them. And then, by the end of two years, the lecturers no longer ... because they've given all the information, all of a sudden the questions start flowing between the group.

For Declan, then, not only a sense of agency but a sense of reciprocity was transferred through his college education. The agency arose through the college as an institution in which independent decisions could be made, and through the manner in which his subjects were taught (although sociology was also found to be a subject where students studying it reported an increased sense of insight and efficacy). The reciprocity arose not as a result of institutional or curricular factors, but through observation and positive experience with the 'gifting' aspect of education – that '... you can still enjoy yourself and put something back in'. As with the case of Carol, though, there are contradictions and costs involved in developing certain forms of confidence and individuation through adult education and the lived experience of individuals. Declan's experience of being bullied and his sexuality being ridiculed at college were not necessarily the defining experiences of his life (as his sexuality is not necessarily his defining personal characteristic). However, the contradictions of a post-compulsory education which stresses agency and action whilst simultaneously rejecting diversity are not necessarily comfortable ones for educators. In Figure 8.3 we can see that college had a dual effect on Declan: the development of an agentic

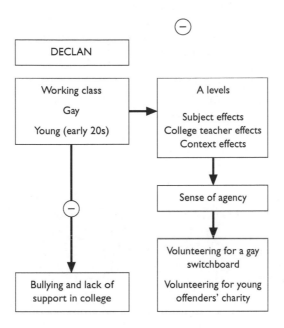

Figure 8.3 Community action: Declan.

subject and citizen in terms of teacher influence, subject content and ethos, and the bullying and harassment which he suffered as a young gay man in college. Although the overall result of Declan's education was therefore positive in terms of civic participation, this occurred despite some of the treatment which he received in education.

Conclusion

The relationship between adult education, civic participation and community activity is complex. The results here do not necessarily contradict those of earlier quantitative work or other theorists (Putnam 2000) in that adult education means that individuals are more likely to join associations, to volunteer and to take a more active role in their community. What these biographies show is that we need to go deeper into what this association actually means in terms of individuals' lives and their practices.

First, in terms of both theory and policy, the role of social capital both as symbolic capital and class strategy needs to be taken seriously. As the cases of Susan and Francis have shown, social capital can be a means to an end, being the realisation of real and symbolic profits. Social exclusion is not just incidental to this process but integral to it. Susan could not achieve the symbolic rewards of status or (perhaps) the economic rewards of investment without a 'continuous effort of (un)sociability' – being with '... people like me'. More-over, even given adult education and cultural capital Francis could not translate these resources into the symbolic capital required to participate fully in cultural groups. His participation was also limited by participation in training and basic literacy courses, notionally an area which is designed to produce active cit-izenship.

This means that we must see different types of civic participation as joint (but related) products of adult education. When repeated on an aggregate scale, actions such as Susan's and situations such as Francis' are class strategies. The non-participation of the working-class or ethnic minorities in certain activities is thus a result not necessarily of deficit of that class or community, but of delib-erate or unconscious strategies of the other classes. Adult education designed to meet the 'deficits' of these groups (through basic literacy, self-esteem, training in community activity) may raise participation in certain areas, but not impact on the class mix of civil society in general. Indeed, evidence from the UK is that class is an increasingly important factor in civic participation (Hall 1999).

Social capital theorists might argue that such class distinctions are unimpor-tant. Putnam (2000) states that social capital without social mixing is better than no social capital at all as a 'second-best' solution. Hence, separate schools, churches and associations for different class and ethnic groups are seen as bene-ficial in building a fraternal society (Putnam 2000: 362), although these institu-tional divides have been widely accepted as contributing to lack of community cohesion (Home Office 2002) and even institutional racism (Gillborn and Youdell 2002) in the UK. Moreover, the operation of supposedly open civil society in including and excluding individuals serves both to legitimize social inequality and to obscure the material basis of such exclusion.

However, this process is not so determined by class or other social structures that it leaves no room for agency. The biographies of each of these participants show that there are spaces for civic participation of many diverse forms, and that there is an important role for lifelong learning. For practitioners this may mean a re-engagement with critical traditions in adult education (Tobias 2000) which challenge contemporary notions of the active citizen as mere voter or consumer. Practitioners should also take note that not only the extraordinary activities of adult educators (supporting Francis even when he had finished the course) but also their everyday activities (showing Declan the power of critical discussion, including Susan in a surrogate form of community) have real effects on the lives of their students.

In policy terms, this means concerns with social justice and inequality should be taken seriously. There is a strong relationship between educational inequal-ity, income inequality and social cohesion in terms of societal trust and community safety at least when observed cross-nationally (Green and Preston 2001; Green et al. 2003). Adult education aimed at increasing the civic activity of the least well off in society may be well intentioned, but both economically and strategically the middle and upper classes are better positioned to maximise real and symbolic profits from civil society. At the very least, this analysis implies redistribution of resources.

Second, like 'human capital' (Rikowski 1999: 80–81), the concept of social capital itself reveals something concerning the ways in which social life is being re-conceptualised. Social capital may support the notion that community and associational life is a trans-historical property and asset, rather than a social process (Fine and Green 2000: 85–87). As the biographies of Carol and Declan have shown, the creation of (community) social capital is premised on human labour (Bourdieu 1986). In particular, Carol's labour of working and care, together with the evidence in the preceding chapter, shows how women's work is being deployed in the service of the community (Delphy and Leonard 1992; Smith 2000). Although adult education may indeed be central to the building of social capital, whose labour this involves and who benefits from such work should be the object of any future enquiry and of critical importance to adult educators.

Part C

Drawing together

The benefits of adult learning

Quantitative insights

John Bynner and Cathie Hammond

The case studies that supplied our evidence in Part B give rich insights into the processes that underpin the role of learning in making a difference to people's lives. Our approach enabled us to locate learning in a wide range of individual biographies, pointing to its critical roles in life changes of varying dimensions and kinds. Such transitions generally, but by no means exclusively, represent positive steps forward in the life course, in the domains of employment, family life, health and civic activity. Taken in aggregate, our cases shared patterns of experience relating learning to personal and social benefits, through which our core organising principle of *transforming* and *sustaining* effects emerged.

Locating these patterns in our triangle symbolising different forms of capital brought home another fundamental point: that the benefits of learning – also seen as the cornerstone of *capability* – are accumulative. Thus enhanced capability (in Sen's (1992) terms) improves the potential for realising long-standing, or newly acquired goals concerned with *functioning* in the different domains of life. Learning makes the prospect of achieving such individual (and community) goals more likely, as learning leads typically to more learning. Learning and its benefits are therefore dynamic in the sense that benefits gained in one domain such as health impact on functioning in other domains, such as family and community. And the effects that follow are either transformative in the reconstruction of personal and community life, or sustain or enrich the status quo.

Case study material goes a long way towards revealing the depth and complexity of the functions learning performs in people's lives. However, it leaves certain questions unanswered. These are questions fundamental to social scientific enquiry. To what extent are our conclusions generalisable to the population at large? To what extent does our evidence for causal interpretations of observed relationships stand up against the standards of scientific proof?

It is not the place here to go into the details of what generalisability implies, but the overall idea is intuitively straightforward. The individual lives we have uncovered through our cases may or may not be typical of a population comprising individuals like them. We need to know to what extent their particular set of experiences of the benefits of learning is common to this population as a whole. Without some degree of confidence that our findings are generalisable in this sense, there is the risk of going up theoretical blind allies. The evidence base is also insufficient to launch new policies or change existing ones.

The social science tool used for this purpose is the social survey, which when based on the principles of representative sampling can be used to make inferences about population characteristics with confidence intervals attached. That is to say, we can infer that a particular correlation between learning and, say, a health outcome, observed in a sample of the population, extends to the population from which the sample comes and that its size is likely to vary between specified limits.

The other unresolved question, how to determine causality, raises even bigger challenges. As noted in Chapter 1, establishing the 'counter-factual' in typical social enquiry is virtually impossible without an experimental research design. Such a research design eliminates the problem of selection bias by comparing individuals who appear to have gained a particular benefit from learning with a perfectly matched group who have not had the learning experience. The most rigorous form of such an enquiry involves randomised allocation of individuals to a 'learning' as opposed to a 'non-learning' (control) group or groups.

Randomised experiments are rare in social science for obvious reasons, and, in relation to adult learning, are virtually non-existent in the UK. Accordingly we need to turn to other research strategies that in part reflect experimental methods, but only through the observation of individuals whose lives are not manipulated in any way as in an experiment. In our analysis we have turned to the longitudinal survey, involving follow-up of sample members through a series of surveys at different stages of their lives.

Large-scale longitudinal survey datasets, when based on representative samples, have the merit of embracing large numbers of individuals – meeting our generalisability requirement. The temporal sequencing that we are able to capture in longitudinal data also enables us to establish, with quite a high degree of certainty, which learning outcome follows which learning input. The large sample sizes and wide range of variables included also offer the opportunity to match individuals in terms of their characteristics reasonably closely post hoc. Thus the methods of statistical modelling substitute for experimental controls by, in effect, holding constant the effects of other variables on the learning outcome with which the learning experience might be confounded. We can therefore be reasonably sure that our learners are not fundamentally different from people who have not participated in learning – i.e. that our results are not subject to selection bias.

Finally, we are not putting up quantitative approaches as having any kind of superiority over case study work, because they can help resolve certain methodological issues of the kind we address in this chapter. Both approaches are complementary in the sense that each has its strengths, depending on the research question we want to ask. Our strategy is founded on multi-method approaches in which conclusions from one data source can be *triangulated* against conclusions from another data source (Bynner and Chisholm 1998). That is to say, where conclusions from qualitative and quantitative sources converge, our confidence in them increases. Where there is divergence, then further research follows to find the reason why. Typically, we will move from qualitative to quantitative and back to qualitative in building our evidence base.

In this chapter we pursue our understanding of the benefits of learning mainly through quantitative methods using a particular longitudinal data source, the 1958 birth cohort study, or National Child Development Study (NCDS). This study, which was introduced in Chapter 2, is reported in full in Feinstein et al. 2003. It is based on a large sample of almost 10,000 individuals who participated in the last two sweeps and who have been followed up from birth with subsequent surveys taken at ages 7, 11, 16, 23, 33 and 42. The measure of adult learning available in the survey at age 42 is self-reported attendance in taught courses between the ages of 33 and 42. The question we address to the data is a tightly constrained one: to what extent do learning experiences between the ages of 33 and 42 in cohort members' lives relate to various kinds of wider benefit?

It might be expected that participation in learning over the period 33 to 42 is a relatively rare phenomenon. However, this turns out to be only partly the case (see Figure 9.1). Although 42 per cent of the 1958 cohort did not experience any learning of a formal kind in this period, 58 per cent did, with participation in additional numbers of courses following the pattern of a declining gradient. A small proportion of cohort members claimed participation in more than 14 courses over the period; over 4 per cent had taken more than 10.

The types of courses taken were also most revealing, as were the qualifications that had been gained from them (Figure 9.2). The great majority of

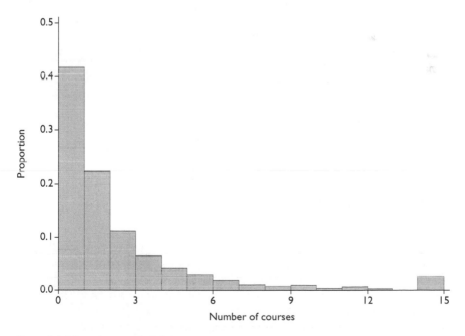

Figure 9.1 The take-up of adult learning.

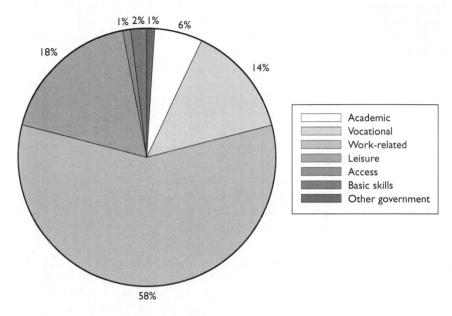

Figure 9.2 Average number of courses taken of each type.

courses taken (58 per cent) were unaccredited work-related training provided by employers. These were followed by leisure courses, with no obvious academic or vocational output in terms of a qualification gained (18 per cent). Accredited academic courses then followed at 14 per cent and vocational at 6 per cent. Small proportions, 1–2 per cent in each case had also engaged in basic skills remedial courses, other government training courses and access courses.

Outcomes: changes between 33 and 42

The NCDS dataset contains much information about health-related behaviours, physiological functioning, social and political participation, and social and political attitudes. The variables available do not of course map precisely into the qualitative accounts of learning benefits, but within our broad triangular capitals and capabilities framework can be seen as offering some degree of functional equivalence. In other words, we use the variables as indicators of the kinds of benefits revealed by the case study analysis, and use the same interpretive framework as a means of making sense of them. The variables we focus on particularly are those within the identity and social capital domains. Broadly these reflect capabilities central to functioning concerned with on the one hand the *quality of life*, and on the other *social capital* and *social cohesion*.

Rather than assess the wider benefits (or disbenefits) of learning in absolute terms, e.g. the level of life satisfaction reported at the end age of 42, or the amount smoked, we assess *changes* in these levels. For variables measured on a 'continuous' scale, such as life satisfaction, we take as our criterion measure the change in life satisfaction over the nine-year period, standardised on a scale of standard deviation units.[1] For the other 'binary' variables signifying presence or absence of an attribute such as smoker/non-smoker, we use the percent change in the sample with respect to the attribute as the criterion, e.g. the percentage of those who smoked at the beginning of the period who had subsequently given up.

Table 9.1 lists all the outcome variables that we used in the analysis differentiated in this way, and gives the observed change in the sample between ages 33 and 42 years (measured as percentage change, or in terms of standard deviation units). The full specification of the variables is given in Appendix 2. The quality of life outcomes comprise three health measures (giving up smoking, change in alcohol consumption, taking more exercise) and three well-being

Table 9.1 Changes in outcomes between ages 33 and 42

Outcome	Level at age 33	Change between 33 and 42	Sample size
Quality of life			
Gave up smoking (B)	17%	28%	2,961
Change in units of alcohol drunk (C)	11.06	−0.71	7,944
Increased exercise (B)	3.96	41%	7,997
Change in life satisfaction score (C)	8.00	−0.22	9,266
Onset of depression (B)	7%	9%	9,102
Recovery from depression (B)	were depressed	41%	616
Social capital/cohesion			
Change in race tolerance score (C)	3.79	0.19	9,374
Change in political cynicism score (C)	2.82	0.44	9,348
Change in support for authority score (C)	3.56	0.26	9,372
Increased political interest (B)	2.38	19%	8,372
Increase in civic memberships (B)	0.26	12%	9,756
Voted in 1997 general election having abstained in 1987 (B)	n.a.	50%	2,116

Notes
For continuous variables (C), the measure of change in the third column is given in standard deviation units based on the distribution of the variable at age 33, with a mean value of 0 and a standard deviation of 1; '+' signifies increase in the measure, '−' signifies decrease in the measure. The level at 33 in the second column is the mean value on a psychometric scale that ranges from 0–5 for attitudes and between 0 and 10 for life satisfaction. In relation to alcohol consumption, the value is the average number of units drunk per week.

For binary variables (B), the value in the second column represents the proportion of the total population who at the age of 33 had the attribute, with the exception of level of exercise. For this variable, the value represents the level of exercise taken on a six-point ordered categorical scale where those who take the highest level of exercise are given a value of one. The varying sample sizes reflect the number in the sample, who had the attribute at the beginning of the nine-year period, i.e. when they were aged 33.

measures (changes in life satisfaction, and onset and recovery from depression). The social capital and social cohesion outcomes comprise four social and political attitude measures (changes in race tolerance, political cynicism and support for authoritarian attitudes, and increased political interest) and two measures of civic participation (increase in civic memberships and increased likelihood of voting).

Analytic approach

A relationship between any one of these changes in outcome and participation in learning over the period gives some indication of a possible causal or functional link. However, we need to be sure that any such correlation is not simply telling us that people who participate in learning also experience changes in their lives over the age period 33 to 42 years, with no direct connection between the learning and the outcome. To control for such 'selection biases', we use multi-variate statistical analysis methods. That is, we investigate the relationship of learning to the outcome variable, controlling statistically for the effects of all other variables with which the key relationships of interest could be confounded.

The control variables we employed were selected on the grounds that they related to one or more of the outcome variables and to participation in learning. They comprised measures of the outcome variables at age 33, academic and vocational qualifications obtained by age 33, socioeconomic status at age 33, and gender. These acted as proxies for a much wider range of potentially confounding variables, including home ownership, family income, social class at birth, reading and maths scores at age 11, and parents' interest in child's education at age 11. Appendix 2 gives a full specification of the control variables that were used.

Basically, the hypothesis under test is that engaging in adult learning between the ages of 33 and 42 does enhance life in the various ways indicated. Using statistical regression methods, we are able to estimate differences in outcomes between those who participated in adult learning and those who did not. We refer to these estimated differences as marginal effects.

For 'binary' variables, which take only two values (e.g. change/no change), we estimate the marginal percentage change. For example, for those who were smoking at age 33, we estimate the difference between the percentage of adults who took courses and gave up smoking and the percentage of adults who took no courses and gave up smoking. We attribute this difference to participation in adult learning. For the 'continuous' variables, measured in terms of standard deviation units, our regression estimate tells us the marginal increase (or decrease) in standard deviation units that can be attributed to learning experiences, i.e. over and above the increase or decrease that occurred over the same period for those who did not participate in adult education. Very roughly, a change of one standard deviation unit is the equivalent of a shift of 33 per cent.

Usually, as Table 9.2 shows, the change is much smaller than this, so the estimate appears as a proportion of a standard deviation: a 0.1 estimate for one of the outcome variables would signify roughly a 3.3 per cent marginal improvement.

In interpreting the results we need to take one other factor into account: statistical significance. This is the issue of whether a given estimate could have arisen by chance, due to the vagaries of sampling, and is in reality zero. We set as the criterion for statistical significance a probability of 0.05. This means that the chances of the estimate having arisen by chance are less than 5 in 100 (95% confidence) or 1 in 20.

Overall, the analysis supplies striking evidence that taking courses during adulthood leads to a wide range of benefits. Table 9.2 shows the estimated marginal effects of taking one or two courses as opposed to none for each of the outcome variables. Although on first glance the estimates appear to be rather small, when set against the shifts that occurred in the sample as a whole they can be viewed as substantial. The right-hand column of the table, headed 'Contextualised effect size', gives the ratio of the estimated marginal shift (attributable to learning) to the observed change in the sample as a whole.

Notably, with a few exceptions, the estimates are statistically significant at the 0.05 level, shown by asterisks in the left-hand column of the table. Thus we can see that in relation to quality of life outcomes, participants in adult learning are more likely to have given up smoking and increased their level of exercise, and to have increased their life satisfaction (positive value) relative to a downward shift in the sample as a whole (negative value – Table 9.1). Although a

Table 9.2 Interpretation of the estimated effects of taking one or two courses

Outcome	Marginal effect 1–2 courses	Contextualised effect size (%)
Quality of life		
1 Gave up smoking*	3%	10.7
2 Change in units drunk	−0.44 units	63.4
3 Increased exercise*	2%	4.9
4 Change in life satisfaction*	0.034sd	−15.5
5 Became depressed	−0.3%	−3.3
6 Recovered from depression	4%	9.8
Social capital/cohesion		
7 Change in race tolerance*	0.047sd	24.7
8 Change in political cynicism*	−0.046sd	−10.5
9 Change in authoritarianism*	−0.067sd	−8.1
10 Increased political interest*	2%	10.5
11 Change in memberships*	3%	25.0
12 Voted in 1997, abstained in 1987*	6%	12.8

Notes
sd = standard deviation units.
*Estimates statistically significant at the 0.05 level.

statistically significant learning effect could not be established for drinking alcohol, the minus sign for it was in the direction of a reduction. Similarly, for depression the results pointed to the possible function of learning as a brake on becoming depressed (negative sign) and enhanced likelihood of recovering from depression (positive sign).

In the case of the social capital and social cohesion outcomes, there is clear evidence of effects of learning in increased race tolerance, a reduction in political cynicism, less authoritarian attitudes and heightened political interest. There is also evidence of increased take-up in memberships of organisations and an increased tendency to vote in the 1997 as compared with the 1987 election. Overall it appears that participation in courses, even at the relatively low level analysed here, encourages more democratic value orientations and stimulates an interest in civic engagement.

Extrapolating these findings to the population as a whole puts another perspective on them. Even a marginal effect of only 3 per cent in increased memberships points to a substantial rise in this indicator of social capital in terms of numbers engaging in civic activity in the population of 30–40-year-olds. In the case of voting, a marginal shift of 6 per cent points to an even larger democratic return to learning. Health and other quality of life improvements draw in the added benefit of a possible economic return. Thus the 3 per cent of the population who are likely to give up smoking as a consequence of participation in learning could represent a substantial reduction in pressure on the health service, as well as a return to the taxpayer and to the economy more generally.

Such benefits resonate with the reports of individual experience through the case studies. Consistently we gain a picture of enhanced life satisfaction and improved health together with greater participation within the community, taking place following and alongside participation in learning. These accounts also help us to uncover another facet of the effects of learning. The quantitative analysis could not establish unequivocally the sequencing of participation in learning and its possible benefits. Biographical analysis of the case study data demonstrated the accumulative effects of learning in reinforcing sequences. For example, Donette took a course in childcare, which changed her attitudes, behaviours, relationships and state of well-being. These changes motivated her to take more challenging courses in childcare and numeracy, which in turn fed into her individual and social development. Such a sequence is not detectable in the cohort data.

Some of the benefits investigated therefore precede, as well as follow on from, adult learning. Positive feelings about life may motivate the desire to learn. Participation in courses enhances life satisfaction further, as well as motivating further learning. Thus adult learning is an important element in positive cycles of development and progression.

Taken together, the evidence from the case studies and the longitudinal survey data converge on the same conclusions. Educational participation has a range of non-economic benefits that extend beyond the classroom into personal life and the community. These results may be seen as encouraging to government strategies for promoting lifelong learning and suggest that adult learning might do better than it tends to in the battle for education resources. They also suggest that government departments with responsibility for the outcomes considered here, such as the Home Office and Department of Health, might look to adult learning as an important policy lever for achieving their goals.

Besides demonstrating the dynamic nature of the relationships between learning and its wider benefits, the case studies also highlight the importance of context on the impacts of learning during adulthood. The effects of learning will be shaped by the learner's family background and current circumstances. The quantitative analyses provide additional evidence of the importance of such contextual variables through the controls that are employed, such as socio-economic status, qualifications at age 33, and gender. Including them in the analysis has the effect of reducing the size of the estimated learning effects, which suggests that these variables relate directly and indirectly to both participation in learning and the outcome variables.

Effects of different levels of participation in adult learning

The evidence examined so far has been restricted to a rather crude measure of participation – one or two courses as opposed to no courses. The full analysis went much further than this, estimating the effects of not only any form of participation and different levels of participation within this level, but also the kind of course taken. These more detailed appraisals of the wider benefits are subject to the problems of small sample sizes, which reduces the precision of the estimates and the chances that they are statistically significant. Comparability of size of effects across different types of learning can also not be assumed because sample sizes differ. However, the analyses do offer a more elaborate picture of the effects of different kinds of learning on our outcome variables, pointing to numerous areas for further research.

Figure 9.3 demonstrates the marginal effects of different levels of participation on the outcome variables: one or two courses, three to ten courses, and over ten courses. Only outcome variables for which there were statistically significant effects at the 0.05 level are included. In each bar diagram, the vertical axis represents the size of the effect and the horizontal axis represents the level of participation. It can be seen that that for most of the outcome variables the marginal effects for the first few courses taken are greater than those generated from higher numbers of courses. In other words diminishing returns set in, suggesting that it is the move from non-participation to participation rather than amount of participation per se that lies behind the benefits. The exception is effects on civic participation and political interest.

To avoid such 'washing out' of the benefits with increased participation, progression in or from learning is probably an important factor, as many of our case

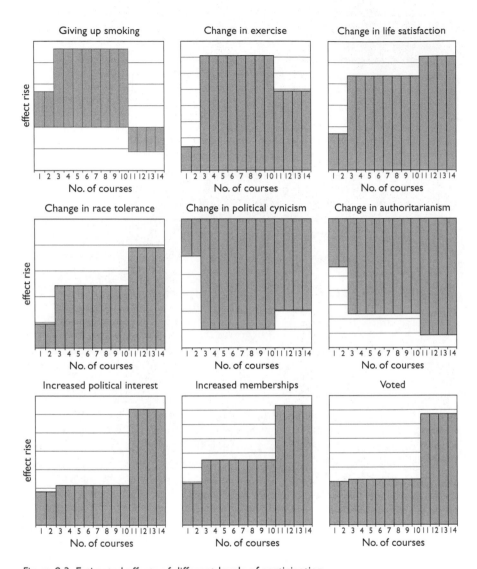

Figure 9.3 Estimated effects of different levels of participation.

studies show. To return to our example, Donette's learning contributed to a positive spiral of progression. Initially she helped on a voluntary basis in her daughter's nursery. This constituted a learning experience, which strengthened her confidence to take her first course, an introduction to childcare. This led to a more challenging diploma course in childcare, which transformed her identity, efficacy, attitudes and family relationships. As part of this personal and social development, she decided to master basic numeracy, taking a family numeracy course, which once again had important effects on her sense of self-worth and on her family relationships. At the time of the interview, Donette planned to obtain an A level in mathematics.

However, we need to be aware that what constitutes progression in learning for an individual may not be progression in the conventional sense. Following a diploma course with a basic skills course might not be considered progression in learning, but for Donette it was. She had failed in maths at school, and was only able to face returning to the subject once she had built up confidence in her abilities through the diploma course. Taking the basic numeracy course was a greater challenge to Donette than taking the diploma course in childcare. Similarly, for Denise, who had a degree in science, taking courses at lower levels in counselling and IT represented important progressions in her learning that facilitated her personal and social development, and led to her employment.

To gain *transforming* value, progression in learning may be a necessary factor. In contrast, some case study informants had taken large numbers of courses as adults, with positive *sustaining* value, i.e. helping them to cope during periods of difficulty in one or more domains of their lives. For example, Jean took leisure courses, initially to help her to recover from a psychological breakdown, and continued to take courses because they sustained her psychological health. Jo had mild learning difficulties, and participation in adult learning provided structure, social contacts, and the opportunity to contribute in civic activities. Elizabeth took courses during her retirement to get out of the house, speak to people, get some exercise, and stop her worrying about her own problems and complaints. In contrast, Donette and Denise demonstrated more of the features of 'learning careers', transforming their lives by moving from one course to another at different levels and in different subject areas.

Effects of adult learning on health-related behaviours

Investigation of the effects of learning on the adoption of positive health practices was not a specific objective of the fieldwork programme. Nevertheless, some respondents described how taking courses led to their making new contacts and friends with whom they went swimming and visited the gym. Such activity may be seen as lying behind the statistical finding that adult learning leads, on average, to adults taking more exercise.

Effects on exercise were found for all types of courses, except those leading to vocational qualifications. The marginal effects were largest for courses leading to academic qualifications and for leisure courses. Notably, the effects of taking leisure courses on changes in exercise were particularly marked for those with below Level 2 qualifications at age 33, who took less exercise to start with. The same pattern of effects was found for civic participation (see below).

The quantitative analysis also showed that taking leisure courses during mid-adulthood increased the chances of giving up smoking. Taking either leisure or vocational accredited courses was associated with reduced alcohol consumption. Although none of the case study informants talked about changes in their smoking or drinking behaviours, many described how participation in learning had developed their sense of self-value and had empowered them in other areas of their lives. This would appear to support the health promotion practice that emphasises the importance of such psychological attributes in helping people to lead healthier lives.

Taking only a small number of leisure courses appeared to have positive impacts on smoking and alcohol consumption but, taking over ten courses had the reverse effect, reducing the tendency to give up smoking and increasing alcohol consumption. Similarly, only the first vocational course taken was associated with reduced alcohol consumption. Taking more employer-provided training courses was associated with *increased* alcohol consumption. Such findings point again to the social role of courses, especially employment-related ones, of which smoking and drinking may play a part. For example, Gareth reported:

> There's a pub over the road from the college, where after some of the evening classes that I do, we'll go and have a game of pool and a pint. And, I've become really friendly with the people there. So that's become part of the college community as well.

This illustrates a more general point arising from the case studies. Positive experiences of learning may engender increased levels of social activity and participation. The type of activity depends on the individuals' background, contacts and opportunities – i.e. the context in which they live. Thus greater levels of activity may be reflected in increased exercise, further learning, community activities, employment, extending social networks and deepening friendships, or in smoking, drinking and taking other drugs.

Effects of adult learning on well-being

The quantitative findings suggest that although adult learning has positive effects on well-being, it may also carry an element of risk. The effect of adult learning (averaged over course types) on life satisfaction is positive, but this reflects the effects of academic courses leading to qualifications, and to a lesser extent, employer-provided training courses. These positive effects were found for men but not for women. Yet women informants in the case studies gave very positive accounts of the effects of the academic courses they had taken. In addition, it is surprising that no effects were found for taking leisure courses for either sex.

The difficulty in reconciling these quantitative findings with the findings from the case studies may be an artifact of the measure of life satisfaction used. This measure combined satisfaction with 'life so far', with satisfaction with 'life in the future'. Many female respondents in the fieldwork described learning during adulthood in terms of empowerment, and this involved the realisation that their earlier lives had been unfulfilled. For example, Parveen, from an Asian family, left school at 16, got married when she was 18 and had three children. Because she had been brought up and educated in England, she took on the role of informal interpreter for her extended family. She also carried all the domestic and childcare responsibilities. When her children started school, Parveen lost her sense of purpose and direction and came close to depression. At this point she enrolled on a course at the local college, which she enjoyed and which built up her personal and social confidence. The course led to more courses, and eventually to employment. As a result, Parveen felt more in control of her life than before and had a greater sense of self-worth. She felt that her husband treated her with greater respect, and she felt confident enough to put her own needs and those of her immediate family before those of the extended family. She felt more positive about her life in the moment, but was aware that her past was not all it could have been.

Probably because of the relatively small numbers identified as depressed at age 33 (616), the effects of adult learning on recovery from depression were not statistically significant. Against expectation, however, onset of depression was *positively* associated with taking leisure courses, and with courses leading to academic qualifications for those with below Level 2 qualifications at age 33.

Many of the fieldwork respondents had started to take leisure courses at times of difficulty or when their lives were at a low ebb – a possible source of selection bias. Leisure courses, as opposed to accredited courses, were taken because they were less challenging. Adult learning provided a distraction, but also could bring personal and domestic problems into sharper relief. Donna was caring full time for her two daughters, one of whom had ADHD and other emotional and behaviour problems. She said:

> I can't handle what's going on now without having an interest for myself. I would be stuck [...] and being isolated thinking, 'I'm stuck' [...] I think I had to get out and do something for myself. I felt bogged down at times and you can't really carry on like that forever because I get stressed and can't cope with it.

Those who enrol on leisure courses may not be typical of the population as a whole because they are more likely to become depressed, and have low levels of life satisfaction. Within this special population, generally participation in leisure courses was reported by case study informants as having a positive impact upon their well-being. Such benefits would be masked when comparing such learners with non-learners in the population at large.

The association between taking academic courses and increased chances of becoming depressed for those with below Level 2 qualifications raises further questions. In contrast, taking vocational accredited courses was associated with decreased chances of becoming depressed for the same group. No effects were found for those with Level 2 and above qualifications at age 33.

Both vocational and academic courses may be beneficial for many individuals, as the case study evidence affirms. However, from the quantitative evidence it appears that taking academic courses does not generally lead to these benefits for those with below Level 2 qualifications to start with. For this group, taking academic courses may undermine psychological health, possibly as a consequence of the stress associated with high demands that outstrip participants' skills and knowledge, and with fears of failure. Many of those with below Level 2 qualifications at age 33 will have experienced academic failure already during their initial education.

Donna left school at 16 without qualifications, and when her children were small took an academic Arts foundation course at the Open University. This course sapped her confidence, which was low to start with. She couldn't make every session because the kids were young and her husband wasn't always available to look after them:

> I used to feel like a deadhead. [...] [The teacher] would go around asking questions and what I said was totally opposite to what everyone else was saying. Totally wrong. And I thought, 'I can't cope with this. I haven't got a clue about this.' And I felt really, really dim. [...] After I had done this essay and only got a C on it, I looked at it and thought that that was terrible. I felt really like a failure. [...] I thought that I had done a fairly good job, but I felt really dim.

Effects of adult learning on social and political attitudes

The quantitative analysis pointed to pervasive effects of adult learning on social and political attitudes in democratic directions. These applied to both men and women for each type of course, regardless of prior levels of qualifications. However, the effects of academic courses were by far the strongest and most consistent.

Several respondents described the processes through which education challenged fixed beliefs and taught them to listen to other viewpoints. These include Declan, who attended an FE college and was one of the case studies we met in Chapter 8:

> College is the best way, I think, of learning how to interact with groups of people. Because you're put – you put yourself in an environment of learning ... you then choose the subjects you want to choose – you – what you're interested in, what you most want to learn from ... they then put all these people, therefore creating a group of like-minded people. Okay, they may be like-minded people, but they've got their own ideas about what they want to do ... their own ideas on how to do things. Therefore you learn to – the lecturer helps co-ordinate the group. They're like the pinpoint, the

pivot, the balance, the centre. They are middle, so you start off by learning
... throwing an idea at them. And then, but the end of two years, the lecturers no longer ... because they've given all the information, all of a
sudden the questions start flowing between the group.

Declan identified the importance of learning with others who shared similar
interests but who had different ideas. The teacher facilitated discussions based
on listening and responding to other people's viewpoints. Consuela also mentioned the role of education in helping her to listen to other people's views:

> It's amazing that everybody has so many different ideas. And you learn to
> be not so biased or – to be more objective, not to take things personally.
> Because in these discussions, you know, people can get pretty personal. But
> then, it's like a good practice for your future career, for when you're at uni-
> versity, not to take things personal, just to – it just shapes your character,
> really, education.

Other respondents felt that education had led to greater understanding of
people from other backgrounds, against whom they had been prejudiced. The
fact that these effects were most evident for academic courses suggests that the
content of such courses in 'opening minds' and challenging previously held
beliefs may also have been a factor.

Such results are also in line with those from a survey of FE practitioners in
England and Wales. Interactions between students were thought by the practitioners to be central to the formation of tolerant attitudes (Preston and
Hammond 2003). The survey also found that teachers of humanities and
health subjects were more likely than teachers of other subjects to report
such changes in values, as these subject areas were said to provide students
with 'the opportunity to locate their own experiences within wider frameworks'.

Effects of adult learning on civic participation

The quantitative analysis showed that taking courses between the ages of 33
and 42 predicted greater levels of civic and political participation. The effects
were largest in relation to taking leisure courses, but there were also substantial
effects on civic and political participation from taking employer-provided training. The effects of taking leisure courses on civic participation were particularly
strong for those with below Level 2 qualifications at age 33.

Although taking academic courses was associated with the largest shifts in
social and political attitudes, the effects were, if anything, more modest for civic
and political participation. Presumably, students learned to think critically and
adopt or learn to express more liberal views, but this did not necessarily translate into increased civic behaviour. Roediger (2002: 12–13) suggests that shifts

in attitudes towards race tolerance, for example, may not be reflected in changes in racist practices, and cites segregated housing as an example.

Case study informants who had taken courses leading to academic qualifications were on the whole fairly active and confident already. Taking academic courses may have led to increased activities, but not in the ways that were measured in the statistical analyses. In contrast, it is the accounts of those who were initially isolated and lacking in confidence and who took less demanding unaccredited courses that describe significant (in the non-statistical sense) changes in levels of activity.

The cases of Lisa and Lucy illustrate effects, or the lack of them, on civic participation of taking academic courses. Lisa is white British and was in her late twenties when she was interviewed. She had a degree and MA in politics, and had recently embarked on a diploma course in opera. This had not affected her levels of civic participation, because she described herself as a loner and too busy already.

Lucy was also white British and highly qualified, with an MA in Contemporary Theatre Practice. At the time of the interview she was studying for a diploma in drama. She had a strong commitment to contributing to the community, and felt that participation in the drama course had led to very close relationships and to the development of better communication and leadership skills. The course had not led to increases in the levels of civic participation, but her communication and leadership skills, improved through the course, seem likely to lead her to take on community roles more effectively in the future.

Effects of vocational courses leading to accreditation

An intriguing finding from the quantitative analyses was that vocational courses leading to qualifications led to very few quality of life and social capital benefits. The only outcome for which a statistically significant effect was found was with respect to race tolerance. This may perturb policy-makers, particularly in the context of other findings, using the same dataset, that vocational qualifications obtained between 33 and 42 have no identifiable wage returns (Jenkins et al. 2002). In contrast, taking employer-provided training courses not leading to qualifications appeared to lead to a wide range of quality of life and social capital/cohesion benefits.

These findings indicate the need for further research, for example to elucidate the different effects of different pedagogies and selection procedures that are encompassed within the categories of vocational accredited and employer-provided training courses. Vocational accredited courses include both national vocational qualifications (NVQs) and vocationally-related qualifications (VRQs), and involve very different styles of pedagogy and assessment: NVQs are obtained through providing a portfolio of evidence of competency at work, whereas VRQs are obtained through participation in classes, usually at college (Green 2003). In addition, the extent to which adults feel coerced into obtaining a vocational qualification is likely to affect how learning is experienced and therefore its impact, and the level of coercion probably varies across courses.

Some individual cases illustrate how different the benefits of different types of vocational courses can be. Surinder was of Asian origin and grew up in Tanzania. She emigrated to London to join her sister, but was initially timid about going out. She took a course in interpreting, which involved attending weekly classes at a lively and friendly Asian community centre. She built up her confidence, made friends, and took some one-off interpreting jobs. For the first time, she began to use London Transport alone. She says:

> It makes me happy. When I went in England I never knew that I would be able to go in hospitals, such big hospitals [. . .] For the very first time I was a confident person.

A tutor teaching courses in interpreting explained that these courses involve discussion and reflection, as well as the acquisition of both linguistic knowledge and understanding of British administration, such as medical, welfare and legal services.

In contrast, Francis, whom we met in Chapter 8, was prevented from continuing in courses in creative writing and photography, which provided vehicles for self-expression and creativity and led to social activity, because he was 'called up' to a Back to Work course. The pedagogy of the course sounds prescriptive, the content superficial, and the course objectives seem to be about hiding deficits rather than recognising and promoting individual strengths. It does not appear that Francis got much out of this course.

Analysis of the case study evidence suggests that education leads to wider benefits when provision matches the interests, strengths and needs of the learner. Courses that are taken of one's own volition are much more likely to result in such a match than courses taken through compulsion.

Conclusions

Could we combine the findings in a more systematic way? Is there a model implicit in the approach used, which could be made more explicit and be improved on? In relation to the main findings, we have a high level of convergence across the different methodological approaches. We obtain a much fuller picture through consideration of both types of evidence together, and have added confidence in our conclusions. In relation to the more detailed findings, the results converge less often. Nevertheless, case study evidence informs the interpretation of detailed findings, and where interpretations are not straightforward this raises questions for future research.

The outcomes measured in the quantitative analyses did not match in all areas those investigated in the case studies. For example, self-efficacy and self-confidence were central features of the case study findings, but they were not included in the quantitative work. Similarly, health-related behaviour was not pursued explicitly in the case studies, though it occasionally arose unprompted. These differences reflect research design decisions taken by different teams at different times, which makes it all the more surprising that there was so much common ground in the coverage between them. Overall, therefore, we can see a synthesis emerging, which is strengthened through the opportunity to draw on both quantitative and qualitative data. Learning plays an integral part in shifting population characteristics in positive directions. For individuals and groups, it also plays a key part in moving the life course in directions that improve quality of life and contribute to the building of social capital and social cohesion. The latter may involve complex processes in which learning triggers a particular pattern of activity in a particular domain of life such as health or family, which triggers activities in other domains such as the civic arena. The overall picture is of a learning career or pathway with multiple diversions and multiple continuities. The remarkable point is that, over and above the individual complexity, clear returns to learning in the economist's sense of the term can be identified in the population at large, in social and psychological as well as economic domains. We can conclude that learning certainly *works*.

Note

1 The exception is change in units drunk, for which the values in the table represent the numbers of units consumed per week. The standard deviation is a measure of the variability of the values of a variable for a population of individuals. Broadly, for a normal distribution, which is commonly found, one standard deviation represents approximately one-third (33 per cent) of the sample.

Chapter 10

Reappraising benefits

Tom Schuller, Cathie Hammond and John Preston

We have reported in this book the results of the WBL Centre's first major piece of original fieldwork, against a background of other analysis of large-scale datasets. We have combined the presentation of empirical results with reflection on the conceptual and methodological issues involved in tackling the impact of learning on people's lives We have aimed to convey a sense of work which is still in progress, but without hedging our bets so much that we cannot offer firm results. In this concluding chapter we revisit the main findings, but at the same time we open up themes for future exploration and debate. We take further the discussion of the triangle of capitals which underpinned the analysis; and stress the significance of the matrix in Chapter 2 which developed the notions of sustaining and transformative effects. We focus particularly on issues to do with the breadth and interconnectedness of learning's effects.

Wider still and wider

In Chapter 1 we described two senses of the term 'wider' as it applies to our research: beyond the economic, and above the level of the individual. However, the field cannot be tidily segmented into discrete sectors and levels. We deal here with some of the blurred boundaries.

Beyond the economic

Economics matter, but neither men nor women can live by bread alone; and bread needs to be buttered and eaten in the company of others if life is to be fulfilling to any degree and not merely lived at the modern equivalent of sustenance level. We have focused on health, family life and social capital as key domains where learning has an impact, beyond the capacity to gain a living (for the individual) or increase performance (for the organisation or nation). Of the three, social capital most obviously spans the economic and the social spheres, but even the most reductionist approach must acknowledge that economic competence entails reasonable levels of health, and that employees have personal lives which impinge on their performance at work (see Dow 2002 for a discussion of classical economists on this point). Conversely, the quality of people's employment affects the other parts of their lives, and not only in the sense that the material rewards it brings shapes their lifestyles and relationships. It is impossible to separate the economic from the social; base and superstructure interpenetrate.

We can explore this directly using the triangle which we presented in Chapter 2, and which has formed the basis of our study. Human capital is usually interpreted in terms of the skills and qualifications which people can deploy in gaining employment and developing a career. However, in some influential conceptions of human capital, notably in the work of Gary Becker, health is an integral part of human capital and not a consequence or dependent variable. This has interesting consequences for estimating costs and benefits. For example, the introduction of paid holidays as a quasi-universal right in the 1930s was justified in part on the grounds that recreational time was needed for workers to refresh themselves sufficiently to be able to perform effectively for the rest of the year. It was in this sense just as much an investment in human capital as public expenditure on schooling or the allocation of a company training budget. We can develop the analogy in relation to our own concerns via the notion of paid educational leave as an investment as well as an occupational benefit (see OECD 1976; Boulin and Hoffman 1999). We pick up the notion of investment in different forms of capital later in this chapter.

Sickness and absenteeism are major features of modern societies. Millions of working days are lost every year in the UK, at an estimated cost of over £11 billion. Sickness now hugely outweighs industrial disputes as a cause of lost output. It is also distributed in a way which strikingly reflects wider social divides, with those in poor quality jobs or insecure labour market circumstances having both less access to learning and worse sickness records. In short, employment circumstances are heavily implicated in the relationship between health and learning, both as an influence and as an outcome.

We paid considerable attention to mental health and well-being in our analysis in Part B. Stress at work is a major factor in mental well-being, only imperfectly revealed in sickness and absenteeism data. Recent evidence from the ESRC's Future of Work programme shows disturbing trends in workplace attitudes, which add a different dimension to the point just made (Taylor 2003). Overall, satisfaction at work is declining, in strikingly bimodal fashion: the negative trend is most apparent at the lower end of the occupational scale, but also at the top. So it is not only those in ill-paid and insecure jobs who report declining satisfaction, but also professionals and managers who work generally in far safer environments. The main reason for this is the loss of autonomy, of a sense of being in charge of one's own working life, which has until now been a defining feature of the professional existence (in addition, of course, to higher remuneration). This links directly to the second point in our triangle, identity capital, which is defined in terms of self-esteem and the ability to plan and control one's life. In other words, the picture is one of people in well-paid jobs who are nevertheless experiencing a loss of control. The latest evidence from the Adult Learners Survey confirms this. It shows that higher occupational classes, whilst still enjoying a relative advantage in access to learning, are decreasing their engagement (Sargant and Aldridge 2003). The most obvious explanation is that the pressure of work, mixed with other commitments, is making it more difficult for them to make time for learning. Identity capital is clearly linked to effective access to learning and the accumulation of human capital; barriers to this access may be financial or attitudinal, but control over one's own time is also a major factor.

Our third capital, social capital, relates to learning and work in rather different ways. Membership of networks (inside as well as outside the workplace) and the ability to mobilise social capital provide access to employment opportunities and enhance people's ability to do the job effectively. This is one reason why a body such as OECD, primarily concerned with economic policy, has endorsed the concept of social capital, recognising that human capital alone will not deliver the goods or the services (OECD 2000). If people do not have the capacity to deploy their skills in collaboration with others, to exhibit and develop trust in their working relationships, it does not much matter how well qualified they are. Economic success depends, generally, on a modicum of social competence as well as opportunity; solipsistic nerds are not likely to make it big, for themselves or the organisation. (There are of course some major exceptions to this rule.)

In addition, work settings are increasingly the source of personal friendships and social activity (Sanders 2002). Learning as a social activity may correspondingly be located in and dependent on the workplace, even where it is not job-related. The more the work culture and the social or peer culture overlap, the more learning of all kinds, vocational and liberal, will be shaped by this relationship. Finally, the notion that civic engagement in the form of volunteering actually enhances employment-relevant skills is gaining ground, so that enhanced social capital feeds in to economic performance.

This increasing interconnectedness between work, family and social life accentuates divisions and inequalities, as well as providing new links and bonds (see Carnoy 2000). In the UK, where workless households form an unusually high percentage of the total, the incidence of social exclusion is correspondingly higher. Both acquiring and deploying capital of any kind is harder by far if you belong to a group which has no ties to income-generating activity.

One last point on the relationship between the economic and wider spheres: one of the fundamental dynamics in individuals' lives is the interaction between producer and consumer roles. Do we work to live, or live to work? How much do we need to earn in order to do what we want? Learning impacts on both sides of this equation, in ways which may be assuming increasing importance. First, a learner is not only a more skilled and productive producer, but also one who is more capable of taking into account the wider social and environmental impact of his or her work, contributing to what is becoming known as the triple bottom line (see www.sustainability.com/philosophy/triple-bottom). This perhaps sounds utopian, but it is not fanciful to expect more highly educated people to be aware of the wider implications of what they produce. What they do with that knowledge is of course another question, and depends heavily on the norms and institutional structures that surround them – their social capital. On the other side, learning will influence the way people behave as consumers. Faced with tidal waves of pressure to consume, they should be more discriminating and more able to assert their rights. One way is through litigation. However, learning may also enable them to go beyond the notion of purely individual consumerism, and to exercise collective leverage to improve the quality of goods or services rather than expressing themselves solely through the market or seeking personal compensation. Becoming an effective and socially aware consumer is a major potential benefit of learning, to the individual and also to the community.

(Re)socialisation

We have shown how strong a role learning can play in integrating people socially, or in sustaining their social integration. The socialising role of education is a familiar one in relation to children. There is no surprise in the notion that schools should teach young people social rules, from punctuality to consideration and empathy for others. However, this function has been much less explored in relation to adults – maybe because adults are assumed to have completed their socialisation processes (see Hopper and Osborn 1975 for a rare example). Our evidence shows how participation in learning continues to influence the ways in which people relate to each other socially, whether directly to fellow students or more generally.

There are two aspects to this. The first, as implied above, is the continuing resocialisation of adults as they take part in learning. 'Resocialisation' is not a beautiful term, but it adequately suggests the similarity between what happens to children in schools and what happens to adults in classes or other learning contexts. The intensity of the socialisation of course varies greatly – we are certainly not suggesting that there is some universally effective process of norm imposition – and will on average be less for adults than it is for children, but the process is of the same order. Second, however, adults participate in shaping norms as well as adopting them. They are not passive recipients; nor are children, but adults generally exercise greater power in establishing normative rules. Adults' involvement in learning enables them – again, in varying measure – to redefine what is acceptable or desirable behaviour. This may apply to themselves alone, as individuals, or to them and their families, or to them as part of the wider society. In short, learning is part of a process of continual development and reshaping of norms, and not of a one-off process of instillation or enforcement.

Above the individual

Our analysis has aimed to combine the impact of learning on individuals with the effects on social units at a more collective level. This raises, obviously, the question of how far such a distinction is possible; after all, households, communities and nations are made up of individuals. Is the collective effect anything more than the mere aggregation of individual effects?

A first approach to this revolves around the notion of *critical mass*. At what point are there sufficient individuals engaged in learning to have a detectable impact on the wider community? We have the example of Carol in Chapter 8, whose learning led her to mount a programme to involve her fellow citizens in a campaign to improve the health of her local environment. On her own this is unlikely to succeed (though even as a solo individual she may be a very influential role model), but if she is able to convince a number of neighbours to work with her the chances of making a mark are considerably enhanced. We have no independent evidence on the actual outcomes of her efforts, but the logic is reasonably clear. This is the whole basis of community learning: the recognition that it is cultural practices and collective behaviours which need to change. However, there is still much work to be done to explore how the notion of a critical mass actually applies in a variety of social contexts.

A different line of argument concentrates on the *distributional* implications of learning. If we focus only on increasing overall levels of education, and ignore the way in which such increases affect different social groupings, we may miss highly significant policy outcomes which run counter to intended goals. This is an essential and under-regarded aspect of the debate. Other work from the Centre has addressed this at the national level, examining the link between education and social cohesion (Green et al. 2003). Individual level correlations between education and social capital indicators of trust and tolerance do not hold when using aggregated data at the societal level. Although we know that people with higher levels of education tend to exhibit higher levels of trust and tolerance, this does not in itself justify the assumption that nations with relatively high levels of education in the aggregate will also exhibit correspondingly superior levels of social cohesion. There are major methodological as well as conceptual difficulties associated with data and analysis at this level; but this initial work certainly illustrates the possibility that pumping up the overall volume of human capital is no guarantee of social improvement.

One aspect of this which has particular policy salience, especially in the UK context, concerns education as a positional good. If I achieve a higher level of qualification, it produces benefit in the sense that I am more competent, therefore more productive and hence more likely to be rewarded for this productivity. The assumption here is of a direct relation between my educational achievement and the enhanced reward, and that the reward more or less reflects my increased value, whether that be to a private company or a social service. However, my increased level of qualification may simply serve to put me ahead of others in the queue for jobs (or a particular job), or in gaining access to other beneficial outcomes. Getting a university degree increases my chances of gaining good employment, and certainly in this sense at least is of benefit to me, but it may be largely at the expense of someone else who would have done the job just as well. Collectively there is no gain in this, even though the outcome will show up in conventional analyses as a 'return' from educational investment.

The line between the 'highly educated' and the rest is constantly changing, especially as a consequence of the universal expansion of higher education. What used to be a highly distinctive level of educational achievement is no longer so. The distributional point is that this has an impact not only on those who gain degrees, but also on those who still do not. Their position is actually worse than it was before, perhaps significantly so. Whereas being without a degree might previously still have allowed you to be in the top 20 per cent of educationally qualified people, it now means that you are probably below the 30 or even 40 per cent mark. In other words, in the aggregate assessment (which is what we are interested in here) the effects of learning may be beneficial for some – those who have been drawn in as a result of expansion – but positively harmful for others who find themselves excluded from opportunities for which they would previously have been well placed.

Positional goods are linked to, but distinguishable from, *trade-offs*. Trade-offs occur at the level of the individual – most obviously in the time and the resources which people commit to learning when they might have been otherwise enjoying themselves. Consciously or not, people make sacrifices to achieve the benefits of learning. However, above the level of the individual trade-offs also occur. At the household level, partners and other family members may pay the price for the educational commitment of a student, in the shape of rushed meals, cheaper holidays or remortgaging the house. In our study we had no examples of the latter but several of the former, and of other ways in which costs are incurred. One person's benefit may be another's loss, in a zero-sum or even negative-sum game. In quite a serious sense, a nation of committed students who have no time for each other is not an appealing prospect, however much it may constitute a 'learning society'.

At the group or class level, divergences of interest and reward take us into issues of power and potential conflict. We have shown, notably in Chapters 7 and 8 on social capital, how the impact of education can often only be understood by reference to the location of the individual within a particular social milieu. There is no suggestion that the individuals concerned consciously frame their goals or aspirations to align them with class interests, but the reproductive power of education operates in relation to adults as it does with schooling. It fosters social mobility, but at the same time consolidates patterns of social advantage and division. Although we argue strongly for the potential of education to foster social cohesion, it is naïve to see it as automatically operating to counter all forms of social division.

In this section we have developed the two senses of 'wider', going beyond the economic and above the individual level. This leads us now to take a second look at our triangle, with its three capitals. We recognise that people behave as economically minded individuals up to a point, but argue that their behaviour and attitudes can only be understood as part of a broader pattern of interactions.

Interaction, 'investment' and rationality

The three capitals do not exhaust all possible angles. Different and proliferating forms of 'capital' jostle with each other in the academic and professional literature; we hear nowadays of intellectual capital, organisational capital, emotional capital and so on (see, for example, Boisot 1998; Thomson 2002). These cause greater or lesser degrees of apoplexy amongst some economists, who tend to claim ownership rights to the concept and to insist on a particular definition.[1] Our task is not to define a pure version of capital. The core of the notion is that capital represents some kind of asset, which can be more or less consciously built up, and from which a stream of material or non-material benefits flow. Here we look again at the relationships between the different capitals, and at how the use of them affects our understanding of educational participation.[2]

In thinking about the notion of capital, the interesting issues for us fall into two clusters. First, what are the mechanisms by which one form of capital converts into another; and how far does the accumulation of one form of capital assist (or impede), the accumulation of another? Piling up qualifications indicates growth in human capital, but if the individuals with the qualifications have no networks through which they can find jobs, or cannot operate effectively in the workplace if they have a job, the benefits will be limited. Having better-educated mothers is a major benefit for children, but the impact of this too will be relatively limited if parents cannot link up in some form of collective association. Individual tutorials by a doctorally qualified mother are likely to increase one aspect of a child's development, and the probability of initial educational success, but may well not help overall if they occur in pressurised social isolation.

The interactions are complex. Take first the links between social and human capital. There is a growing literature on the way in which social capital allows human capital to grow in ways which otherwise would not have occurred, by providing the necessary contacts, information and peer support. However, there are also some findings on how the norms and networks which make up social capital can inhibit the accumulation of human capital (Field and Schuller 2000). Similarly, the extent to which someone's identity capital is bound up with the networks to which they belong – their social capital – is not something which can be easily read off in any mechanical way. We can acknowledge that raising self-esteem is probably the single most significant effect of education, but also that it may not always lead to greater sociability, where the social and normative structures are not in place. These kinds of interaction between different forms of capital merit further exploration, theoretically and empirically. A third example, to complete the set of links between capitals: accumulating qualifications (human capital) is on balance more likely than not to strengthen one's self-confidence (identity capital), but this is no certainty. Our fieldwork has several cases of individuals who felt that they were constrained to go beyond the level of education they were comfortable with, at least at the point in their lives at which it happened, and as a result they lost rather than gained in their sense of identity.

One possible key to understanding these interactions is the notion of capability, developed by Sen (1992). Sen's capability approach is distinct from other approaches to the conceptualisation of well-being, notably that of Rawls (1972), who concentrates on primary goods, or Dworkin (1979), who concentrates on resources. Capabilities are defined by Sen as 'the various combinations of functionings (beings and doings) that the person can achieve' (Sen 1992: 39); in other words, capabilities relate to the means people have to achieve desired goals. This linkage to functioning has two implications: first, if achieved functionings constitute a person's well-being, capability constitutes the capacity, and hence the *freedom*, to achieve well-being. Second, in so far as choice and the ability to choose are self-evidently valuable, then achieving well-being itself depends on capability. What makes the approach particularly relevant to our concerns is the notion that we should pay attention to potential which is there to be mobilised. Our three capitals all denote assets which can be mobilised to improve functioning in different domains and ultimately well-being, in an individual and a community sense, as a whole. The relationship between capitals and capabilities is one which has considerable political potential and deserves further exploration.

There is also an important set of issues to do with rationality, and the process of individual and collective decision-making and evaluation. The human capital approach is sometimes criticised for implying that people take (or should take), decisions through a process of explicit calculation, as if they were investing in stocks or shares as a kind of personal professional broker. They are expected to weigh up the investment costs of their education, factoring in financial and other considerations (such as family stress), assess the likely returns, and make their decision accordingly. In practice, and our evidence certainly shows this, people rarely behave in this way, at least to the extent implied in the model. We are naturally all limited in the extent to which we attempt fully to work out the consequences of our actions or inactions. This is not to say that the model should be discarded, since people commonly have definite, if perhaps not very specific, expectations about an improvement in professional as well as personal circumstances as a result of education. However, for many the goals are only loosely defined, and are based on very approximate information. More importantly, the criteria for measuring returns to the investment change over time as people's experience of education shapes their expectations and their values, so any original calculation of anticipated benefit may bear little resemblance to the final verdict on the value of the investment (if there is such a verdict). They may have set out to gain a qualification to improve their career and earnings potential, but finished by valuing the course for its intrinsic enjoyment, even though the hoped for labour market advantages have dissolved into thin air (Schuller *et al.* 1999). This kind of flux and uncertainty is inherent in the educational process.

In some sectors of education, notably in the more vocationally oriented fields and in higher education, decisions are characterised by a greater degree of this kind of economic rationality. Prospective higher education students are more likely to be conscious of the benefits to themselves of investing time and money in their own education. More evidence already exists on the superior returns to higher education over secondary education, the gap being particularly high in the UK (Blundell *et al.* 2000; Chevalier *et al.* 2002). It is important not to discard the model altogether, as if decisions were not made at all or were made almost randomly or without reference to financial reward. However, it is just as important to underline the fuzzy way in which decisions to engage in, or continue in, education are made: the low level of information that is genuinely available to potential participants; the fact that the reasons are often not articulated by participants even to themselves; and the changing nature of the framework within which they make their judgements about the costs and benefits of learning. This is especially true of those for whom education as an adult is a relatively new experience. Given that these people are often on relatively low incomes or in poorer economic circumstances, and are therefore more vulnerable to events which might disrupt such plans as they have made, the extent to which a rational investment model, of the kind that might appeal to an insurance broker or an actuary applies, is quite limited.

This has two implications which are central to our discussion. The first is that the reasons which people might have for taking part in education, and the expectations they have about the benefits that education might bring, are strongly shaped by their culture and circumstances, and change over time. This includes the extent to which they present options to themselves, and map their progress accordingly. In general, the pathways learners follow are not straight but jump around, take sharp turns, go round in circles, and end up in very different places to those originally envisaged (McGivney 2002). Learners themselves may not follow their own progress in any conscious sense. They may start with clear ideas about the outcomes – though, as we have just argued, many do not – but find these changing as the learning goes on, or discover only later that the ideas have changed.

Second, if putative rationality is low in relation to decisions about personal costs and benefits, at least compared to the assumptions of rational choice theorists, it is still less evident when it comes to outcomes beyond the learner's own immediate circle. There are cases where people will take part in some form of learning specifically in order to generate a benefit to others, notably in respect of family life. Parents will enrol in classes in order to be able to bring their children up more competently, as well as to satisfy their own desires to be good parents. Some citizens study in order to be able to be more effectively engaged in civic activity on behalf of the community, as well as to fulfil their personally felt needs, but most people are driven to learn by expectations about resultant improvements to their own circumstances (even though often not of an economic kind), and not to the wider community.

In short, our three capitals serve, in different ways and in interaction with each other, as metaphors to explain behaviour and outcomes. As metaphors they can be accompanied by other language which draws on economic models of investment and returns, and by concepts which derive from other disciplines to explain behaviour. However, this should not be taken to suggest unrealistic levels of conscious individual calculation. In deploying our capitals we are not signing up to the neo-classical school, nor reducing learning to matters of economic interest, but seeking to broaden the framework within which the debate about benefits can be held.

The time dimension

Our work grapples with the complexities of people's lives and the role learning has played in it. Time is a key dimension of this. Incorporating time adequately into social analysis is a permanent challenge, practically and philosophically (see, for example, the seminal works of J.T. Fraser (1990) and Michael Young (1988)). We deal here first, and in very schematic form, with some of the methodological challenges time presents in our field, and then briefly with the substantive interaction between education and time.

Temporal research matters

The following are not just technical problems; the extent to which they are acknowledged as challenges can strongly affect the way in which policies are formulated and evaluated.

Lags

One of the enchanting but also frustrating features of the way people learn is the length of time it can take before results show through. We have shown – encouragingly, for teachers – how individuals who have been patently unsuccessful at school can nevertheless retain positive memories, perhaps buried quite deep, which years later help them to return to learning and benefit from it. Later learning may also have outcomes which are long delayed. Lagged effects are inherently difficult to assess, but it is crucial to recognise that they do occur, especially so that the impact of educational provision is not judged on too short-term a basis.

Payback period

Some learning has not only an immediate impact but also a concentrated one, so that it shows in a short period of time. Other effects filter through only gradually, but are sustained over a long period. Sometimes the effect may be negative at first, and only later turn positive. Our biographical approach enabled (or at least encouraged), our respondents to trace effects over however long a period seemed appropriate, but it would have been inappropriate to attempt to specify this in any exact numerical sense. Some of the effects we have described permeate people's lives such that they arguably have an almost continuous direct impact, quite apart from the transformative effects we outlined earlier in the book. Awareness of the variability of payback periods is important, especially to counter some of the more crude calculations which suggest that all educational investment should continue to be made early on in people's lives.

Sequencing

Life-course analysis always wrestles with the literally infinite number of permutations which can occur over an individual's lifespan. To take just one example, Rindfuss *et al.* (1987) looked at the pathways young Americans took in moving from adolescence into adulthood. From quite a limited number of key episodes, such as military service, marriage, first job, leaving home, first child, they identified literally thousands of actual sequences. If things can occur in any order, tracing cause and effect is problematic. In Chapter 9 we discussed some of the difficulties this presents in respect of our quantitative analysis. We have been striving to close on the elusive quarry of causality, which (given the fundamental status of cause–effect) requires an understanding of the order in which events occur. However, sadly for us as analysts (though not in any other sense), lives do not present themselves in straightforward linear sequences with significant events neatly juxtaposed. Even when respondents are telling their own stories and offering explicit causal chains, we cannot necessarily be sure that the whole sequence is present.

Ages and cohorts

It is difficult to disentangle the effects of people getting older from the influence of where they find themselves in the historical process, but it is important for a number of reasons to bear the distinction in mind. Many of our respondents went to school in an age when selection at the age of 11 was dominant and access to higher education extremely restricted; this certainly shapes their stories. This has changed dramatically in succeeding generations, whose experiences will therefore be quite different. We include a wide range of ages in our sample. Some of the effects recounted to us are a function largely of the individual's personal ageing process; others are heavily influenced by the historical specificity of their generation. Glenn Elder's pathbreaking work on children of the Great Depression shows how strong the generational effect can be, but it is cross-cut with other effects (Elder 1974). Time streams on, carrying us all with it, but not in a neat convoy (see Phillipson *et al.* 2001).

Time structures lives

Time is involved in all three of the domains we have explored: health, family life and social cohesion. This is the way in which learning gives people a sense of horizon, agency and purpose in their lives. One way of thinking about this is to consider the relationship between time and choice. Our relationship to time is a source of unending speculation, at all kinds of levels (Adam 1990). On the one hand we live in a world in which time is ever more closely measured, divided and controlled. Few workplaces now operate clocking on, with punch-cards recording starting and stopping times, but our actions are monitored with extraordinary precision. The sending and receipt of email messages, logging on and off computers, working on documents – all these are recorded to the second. On the other hand, the customary structures of day and week are increasingly dissolving into an undifferentiated stream of activity. People shop – and therefore other people work – 24 hours a day, 7 days a week. Entertainment, notably through television screens, is constantly available, instead of being restricted to evenings and weekends. Educational provision itself is part of this trend, though it is not yet so continuously accessible. For the most part this signals increased choice in a positive sense (leaving aside the whole debate about whether what is on offer to the consumer is more or less homogeneous), but alongside this is a sense of a de-differentiation of time: time loses its structure and we are caught up in a constant flux of activity with little sense of direction or shape. One thing education does is provide people with this sense, by offering future perspectives and the possibility of choosing between options.

The goals may be very specific, such as the completion of a course or the achievement of a qualification, and perhaps therefore the possibility of moving onto a new career trajectory. However, they can also be quite general, such as the hope of a new departure in life. They will vary in the extent to which they are realistic, on any objective criteria, but the fact that they exist can be very important to individuals and their sense of what is possible for them. Whether or not education is the original cause of the goal-setting, or an instrument for making progress towards a goal derived from some other source, is another matter. The important function it provides is enabling people to have a sense of a future for themselves, for their families and perhaps also for their communities, which they can to some extent control or influence. Several of our respondents spoke about having a sense of agency which they did not have before. In other words, education provides a kind of choice in life which parallels the consumer choice which money provides. The choice may be narrow or broad, it may be well informed or not, but at least the notion of choice (and therefore some degree of personal autonomy) is present in ways which did not previously exist and horizons are extended beyond what might have been imagined.

Once again, the effect is not solely an individual one – a crucial point given that our concern is with benefits that go beyond the individual. The more some individuals in a given community have aspirations and longer-term horizons, the easier it is for others to do likewise. The converse is certainly also true: where members of a community or a peer group generally lack aspirations or horizons, it is extremely difficult for an individual to buck the trend (arguably a major factor in the concern about boys' under-performance in schools). In other words, the effect of education in raising people's sights is to be felt not only in terms of their own lives and careers but also more widely, as a positive influence on the cultural norms which encourage others to do the same.

Signing off

This has not been a forensic exercise extolling the virtues of learning. As we said in Chapter 1, in analysing the results we have not taken a completely neutral approach but have focused primarily on beneficial effects, yet this has not prevented us from pointing to ways in which participation in learning can have ambivalent or even damaging consequences. Life is risky, and whilst learning can pre-empt some of the risks and cushion others, it undoubtedly also introduces new ones. This is true for the learner and sometimes for those who sponsor learning, which is why autocratic rulers tend to be less enthusiastic supporters of popular education. That said, we can confirm that learning does make a material difference to many people's lives, as individuals and as members of a wider community. Our quantitative work shows this, even after controlling for just about every factor imaginable; and the fieldwork reported here spells it out in some detail without capturing the full range of effects. One possible reaction to this as a conclusion is that we hardly needed 200 pages to reach it. However, we have been extremely heartened by the number of practitioners to whom we have reported our various findings and who have said that this confirms what they knew and yet have found it extremely affirming to have this done. The key point is to make progress in systematically sorting out the different kinds of effect.

Second, we believe that our distinction between the sustaining and the transformative effects of learning has real political significance because it highlights the sustaining value of adult education. It calls for much greater understanding of how education endows people with the resilience to cope with minor problems as well as major challenges, and to prevent the former swelling into the latter. We need also to show the interactions between different effects, and their cumulative impact. Both sustaining and transformative effects run across all three of the domains we have examined in detail here, and into others such as criminal activity.

Third, the causality conundrum remains: just how many layers of the onion do we have to peel before, eyes watering, we can conclusively point to causal relations between learning and social domains? We have taken our respondents' accounts at face value, other than where inconsistency or implausibility has thrust itself at us. We have matched our findings, as far as we could, with quantitative evidence. However, we are well aware that there is more imaginative work to be done, especially in triangulating evidence, so we intend in future fieldwork to seek views from those associated with learners as well as from the learners themselves, in order to have some kind of cross-check.

Fourth, we would like the debate on what we mean by 'significance' to take a fresh turn. We mean by that not a re-examination of the statistical sense of significance, but two other aspects: the need to distinguish between cases where education is largely responsible for a small change and where it is a small factor in a large change, and to push forward normative discussion of which changes really make a difference, whether at individual level or above. All three senses of significance are apt for debate, but are rarely brought into the same frame.

Finally, our results have a number of policy implications. Some of these are relatively new, and many of them confirm previous findings. We do not have space here for detailed policy discussion (see Schuller *et al.* 2002), but conclude with just three points:

1   Learning has value at every age. As the demography of an ageing society comes into play, and families and communities include a higher average number of generations and age-groups, concentration of educational resource on the young looks more and more irrational. Demography gives the sustaining effect of education added salience, not just for older people but for all of us caught up in changing family and social structures.
2   Learning outcomes should be assessed within a framework which goes far beyond the acquisition of qualifications, and includes the learners' capacity to sustain and develop themselves and their communities across a range of domains. It follows that learning opportunities should be broad and diverse in content, mode and pedagogy, and driven by personal need and motivation more than top-down specification.
3   Huge costs are incurred when learning is absent. Poor physical and psychological health, malfunctioning families, and communities lacking in social glue: all these are at least partial consequences of inadequate education. Converting our cost–benefit tools to encompass these facts is an urgent policy challenge. Of greater importance even than this technical requirement is the need to develop a more holistic, imaginative and generous attitude to education's benefits.

We have said relatively little about the actual processes of learning in which our respondents engaged. The science of education, and what makes for effective learning at different points in the life course, is still in its infancy (OECD 2002). Our evidence, however, illuminates the obvious point that more benefits are generated when there is a good match between learning provision and the learners' strengths, interests and needs. However well tailored the provision, its effects will always be mediated by a whole range of social and psychological factors. A society of healthy, active citizens and happy family members is more likely if many of them are engaged in learning, but it needs many other conditions to hold as well.

Notes

1 Nobel Laureate Kenneth Arrow, for example, urges abandonment of the metaphor of capital and the term 'social capital', primarily on the grounds that it involves no deliberate sacrifice in the present for future benefit (in Dasgupta and Sarageldin 2000: 4). Contrast this with Fine (2001), who argues that social capital is a kind of Trojan horse which enables neoclassical economics to tighten its grip on social and political analysis generally.
2 This section is further developed in Schuller et al. 2003.

Appendix 1: Background characteristics of respondents

Background characteristics		Frequencies		
Background characteristic	Value	Social cohesion project	Transitions project	Total across projects
Gender	Female	54	48	102
	Male	34	9	43
Ethnic group	White British	56	34	90
	White other	15	7	22
	Black African	4	5	9
	Black Caribbean	4	1	5
	Black British	3	1	4
	Mixed race	2	none	2
	Indian	1	1	2
	Pakistani	2	2	4
	Bangladeshi	1	2	3
	Asian other	none	4	4
Age	16–19	15	none	15
	20–24	5	1	6
	25–34	20	20	40
	35–50	31	34	65
	51–64	10	2	12
	65 plus	6	none	6
Occupational status	Working class occupation			38
	Middle class occupation			26
	Student			45
	Housewife/husband			22
	Retired			15
	Unemployed			9
Highest qualification[1]	No qualifications	10	5	15
	Level 1	11	3	14
	Level 2	24	16	40
	Level 3	25	15	40
	Level 4 and above	18	18	36

Marital status	Married	32	34	66
	Cohabiting	9	4	13
	Single	36	9	45
	Separated/divorced/ Widowed	7	8	15
Area of residence	Nottingham	38	22	60
	North London	28	26	54
	Rural Essex	22	9	31
Time commitment to current course	Part time	64	52	116
	Full time	24	5	29
Number of children (data available for transitions project only)	1		16	
	2		17	
	3		12	
	4 and more		12	
Age of youngest child (data available for transitions project only)	Under 4		1	
	4		9	
	5		11	
	6		8	
	7		10	
	8		7	
	9		4	
	10		1	
	11		4	
	Unknown		1	
Totals for each background characteristic		88	57	145

Note
1 Level 1 – basic skills; Level 2 – 5 GCSEs A–C, NVQ2 and equivalents; Level 3 – A levels, NVQ3 and equivalents, Level 4 – degree and equivalents.

Appendix 2: Specification of outcome and control variables

Outcome variables with answer category codes/values

Quality of life

Health

Gave up smoking (smokers at age 33 only):	Smoked one or more cigarettes at age 42=0 Smoked less than one cigarette a day at age 42 = 1
Change in units of alcohol drunk:	Values ranging from −145 to +96 and a mean of zero; change score equals age 33 value subtracted from age 42 value
Increased exercise (respondents who were not taking exercise at the maximum level at age 33):	Serious exercise not taken more often at 42 than at 33 = 0 Serious exercise taken more often at 42 than 33 = 1

Well-being

Change in life satisfaction score:	Values obtained from averaging ratings for two self-report items rated on scale of 0–10: 'how satisfied are you about the way life has turned out so far?' 'how satisfied do you expect to be in 10 years' time?' Change score equals age 33 value subtracted from age 42 value
Onset of depression (respondents who were not depressed at age 33 only):	Score of 7 or less on the Malaise scale (comprising 24 items indicating depression) at age 42 = 0 Score of 8 or more at age 42 = 1
Recovery from depression (respondents who were depressed at age 33 only):	Score of 8 or more on the Malaise scale (comprising 24 items indicating depression) at age 42 = 0 Score of 7 or less at age 42 = 1

Social capital/cohesion

Social attitudes

Change in race tolerance:

Values obtained by averaging scores across five opinion statements rated on a five-point scale (strongly agree = 5, agree = 4, undecided = 3, disagree = 2, strongly disagree = 1)
'It is alright for different races to get married'
'I would not mind if a family from another race moved in next door to me'
'I would not mind if my child went to a school where half the children were of another race'
'I would not mind working with other races'
'I would not want a person from another race to be my boss'
Change score equals age 33 value subtracted from age 42 value

Change in political cynicism:

Values obtained by averaging scores across three opinion statements rated on a five-point scale (strongly agree — 5, agree = 4, undecided = 3, disagree = 2, strongly disagree = 1)
'None of the political parties would do anything to benefit me'
'It does not really make much difference which political party is in power in Britain'
'Politicians are mainly in politics for their own benefit and not for the benefit of the community'
Change score equals age 33 value subtracted from age 42 value

Change in support for authority:

Values obtained by averaging scores across three opinion statements rated on a five-point scale (strongly agree — 5, agree = 4, undecided = 3, disagree = 2, strongly disagree = 1)
'The law should be obeyed even if a particular law is wrong'
'For some crimes the death penalty is the most appropriate sentence'
'Censorship of films and magazines is necessary to uphold moral standards'
'People who break the law should be given stiffer sentences'
'Young people today don't have enough respect for traditional British values'
'Schools should teach children to obey authority'
Change score equals age 33 value subtracted from age 42 value

Change in political interest:

Interested in politics did not increase between 33 and 42 = 0
Interest in politics increased between 33 and 42 = 1

Civic participation

Increase in civic membership:

Number of memberships (political party, charitable organisation, voluntary group) at age 33 subtracted from number of memberships at age 42
Increase in number of memberships between 33 and 42 = I
No increase in number of memberships = 0

Voted in 1997 general election having abstained in 1987 (respondents who abstained in 1987 only):

Not voted in 1997 election = 0
Voted in 1997 election = I

Control variables with answer category codes/values

Gender

Male = 0, Female = I

Socio-economic status at age 33

Six dummy variables reflecting social classes i, ii, iii non-manual, iii manual, iv and v.

Academic level at age 33

Seven dummy variables indicating NVQ levels I to 6, and no academic qualifications

Vocational level at age 33

Five dummy variables indicating NVQ levels I to 4, and no vocational qualifications

References and bibliography

Acheson, D. (1998) *Independent Inquiry into Inequalities in Health*, London: The Stationary Office.

Adam, B. (1990) *Time and Social Theory*, Cambridge: Polity Press.

Alheit, P. and Dausien, B. (2002) 'The "double face" of lifelong learning: two analytical perspectives on a "silent revolution"', *Studies in the Education of Adults* 34: 13–22.

Allison, K.R., Adlaf, E.M., Ialomiteanu, A. and Rehm, J. (1999) 'Predictors of health risk behaviours among young adults: analysis of the national population health survey', *Canadian Journal of Public Health* 90(2): 85–89.

Anthony, E.J. (1974) 'The syndrome of the physiologically invulnerable child', in E.J. Anthony and B.J. Cohler (eds) *The Child in his Family: Children at Psychiatric Risk, International Yearbook* (Vol. 3), New York: Wiley.

Antikainen, A. (1998) 'Between structure and subjectivity: life-histories and lifelong learning', *International Review of Education* 44(2–3): 215–234.

Antikainen, A. and Harinen, P. (2002) 'Living and learning in a changing European periphery', *Lifelong Learning In Europe* 3: 183–194.

Arrow, K. (2000) 'Observations on social capital', in P. Dasgupta and I. Serageldin (eds) *Social Capital: A Multifaceted Perspective*, Washington, DC: World Bank, pp. 3–5.

Asplund, R. and Pereira, P. (1999) *Returns to Human Capital in Europe: A Literature Review*, Helsinki: ETLA (The Research Institute of the Finnish Economy/Taloustieto Oy).

Ball, S. (2003) *Class Strategies and the Education Market: The Middle Classes and Social Advantage*. London: Routledge-Falmer.

Bandura, A. (1997) *Self-efficacy: The Exercise of Control*, New York: W.H. Freeman and Company.

Barocas, R., Seifer, R., Sameroff, A.J., Andrews, T.A., Croft, R.T. and Ostrow, E. (1991) 'Social and interpersonal determinants of developmental risk', *Developmental Psychology* 27: 479–488.

Baron, S., Field, J. and Schuller, T. (eds) (2000) *Social Capital: Critical Perspectives*, Oxford: Oxford University Press.

Battle, J. (1978) 'Relationship between self-esteem and depression', *Psychological Reports* 42: 745–746.

Beck, U. (1992) *Risk Society: Towards a New Modernity*, London: Sage.

Becker, G. (1964) *Human Capital: A Theoretical and Empirical Analysis, with Special Reference to Education*, New York: National Bureau of Economic Research.

Beeker, C., Guenther Gray, C. and Raj, A. (1998) 'Community empowerment paradigm and the primary prevention of HIV/AIDS', *Social Science and Medicine* 46: 831–842.

Behrman, J., Crawford, D. and Stacey, N. (1997) 'Introduction', in J. Behrman and N. Stacey (eds), *The Social Benefits of Education*, Ann Arbor: University of Michigan Press, pp. 1–10.

Birenbaum-Carmeli, D. (1999) 'Parents who get what they want: on the empowerment of the powerful', *Sociological Review* 47(1): 62–90.

Black, D., Morris, J., Smith, C. and Townsend, P. (1982) P. Townsend and N. Davidson (eds) (1982) *Inequalities in Health – The Black Report*, Harmondsworth: Penguin.

Blackwell, L. and Bynner, J. (2002) *Learning, Family Formation and Dissolution*, Research Report 4: Centre for Research on the Wider Benefits of Learning, London: Institute of Education/Birkbeck.

Blaxter, L. and Hughes, C. (2000) 'Social capital: a critique', in J. Thompson (ed.) *Stretching the Academy: the Politics and Practice of Widening Participation in Higher Education*, Leicester: NIACE, pp. 80–93.

Blöndal, S., Field, S. and Girouard, N. (2002) *Investment in Human Capital Through Post-Compulsory Education and Training: Selected Efficiency and Equity Aspects*, Paris: Organisation for Economic Co-operation and Development.

Blundell, R., Dearden, L., Goodman, A. and Reid, H. (2000) 'The returns to higher education in Britain: evidence for a British cohort', *Economic Journal* 110: 82–99.

Boisot, M.H. (1998) *Knowledge Assets*, Oxford: Oxford University Press.

Boulin, J.-Y. and Hoffman, R. (eds) (1999) *New Paths in Working Time Policy*, Brussels: European Trade Union Institute.

Bourdieu, P. (1977) *Outline of a Theory of Practice*, Cambridge: Cambridge University Press.

Bourdieu, P. (1986) 'The forms of capital', in J.E. Richardson (ed.) *Handbook of Theory for Research in the Sociology of Education*, Westport, CT: Greenwood Press.

Bourdieu, P. (2003) *Distinction: A Social Critique of the Judgement of Taste*, London: Routledge.

Bourdieu, P. and Passeron, J.C. (1977) *Reproduction in Education, Culture and Society*, London: Sage.

Bowlby, J. (1953) *Child Care and the Growth of Love*, London: Penguin Books, 1990.

Bowlby, J. (1969) *Attachment and Loss. Vol. I: Attachment*, London: Penguin Books, 1978.

Bowlby, J. (1988) *A Secure Base: Parent–child Attachment and Healthy Human Development*, New York: Basic Books.

Branden, N. (1969) *The Psychology of Self-esteem; A New Concept of Man's Psychological Nature*, Los Angeles: Nash Publications Corporation.

Brassett-Grundy, A. (2002) *Parental Perspectives of Family Learning*, Research Report 2: Centre for Research on the Wider Benefits of Learning, London: Institute of Education/Birkbeck.

Brassett-Grundy, A.J. and Hammond, C. (2003) *Family Learning: What Parents Think*, Wider Benefits of Learning Papers: No. 4, London: Institute of Education/Birkbeck.

Bretherton, I. (1985) 'Attachment theory: retrospect and prospect', in I. Bretherton and E. Waters (eds), Growing points of attachment theory in research. *Monographs of the Society for Research in Child Development* 50 (1–2, Serial No. 209).

Brown, G. and Harris, T. (1978) *The Social Origins of Depression: A Study of Psychiatric Disorders in Women*, London: Tavistock Publications.

Buffton, J. (1999) *Family Learning: Taking the Work Forward*. Working paper. Second Report, National Advisory Group for Continuing Education and Lifelong Learning, London: Department for Education and Skills.

Burnette, B. and Mui, A.C. (1994) 'Determinants of self-reported depressive symptoms by frail elderly persons living alone', *Journal of Gerontological Social Work* 22(1–2): 3–19.

Bynner, J. and Chisholm, L. (1998) 'Comparative youth transition research: methods, meanings and research relations', *European Sociological Review*, 14, 131–150.

Bynner, J., Ferri, E. and Wadsworth, M. (2003) 'Changing lives?', in E. Ferri, J. Bynner and M. Wadsworth (eds), *Changing Britain, Changing Lives: Three Generations at the Turn of the Century*, London: Institute of Education, pp. 295–312.

Bynner, J., Joshi, H. and Tsatsas, M. (1999) *Obstacles and Opportunities on the Route to Adulthood: Evidence from Urban and Rural Britain*, London: Smith Institute.

Bynner, J. and Parsons, S. (1998) *Use it or Lose it?*, London: Basic Skills Agency.

Bynner, J. and Steedman, J. (1995) *Difficulties with Adult Basic Skills*, London: Basic Skills Agency.

Campaign for Learning, NIACE and Scottish Council Foundation (2000) *A Manifesto for Family Learning*, London: Campaign for Learning.

Carnoy, M. (2000) *Sustaining the New Economy: Work, Family and Community in the Information Age*, New York: Russell Sage Foundation/Harvard University Press.

Castells, M. (1997) *The Power of Identity*, Oxford: Blackwell.

Chevalier, A., Conlon, G., Galinda-Rueda, F. and McNally, S. (2002) *The Returns to Higher Education Teaching*, Centre for Economics of Education, London: London School of Economics.

Clausen, J.A. (1993) *American Lives: Looking Back at the Children of the Great Depression*, New York: Free Press.

Cohen, P. (1997) *Rethinking the Youth Question: Education, Labour and Cultural Studies*, London: Macmillan.

Coleman, J.S. (1988) 'Social capital in the creation of human capital', *American Journal of Sociology*, 94, S95–S120.

Costa, P.T., Zonderman, A., McCrae, R.R., Cornoni-Huntley, J., Locke, B.Z. and Barbano, H.E. (1987) 'Longitudinal analyses of psychological well-being in a national sample: stability of mean levels', *Journal of Gerontology* 42(1): 50–55.

Côté, J. (1997) 'An empirical test of the identity capital model', *Journal of Adolescence* 20: 577–597.

Côté, J.E. and Levene, C.G. (2002) *Identity Formation, Agency and Culture: A Social Psychological Synthesis*, New Jersey: Lawrence Erlbaum.

Cox, R. and Pascall, G. (1994) 'Individualism, self-evaluation and self-fulfilment in the experience of mature women students, *International Journal of Lifelong Education* 13(2): 159–173.

Crossley, M.L. (2000) *Rethinking Health Psychology*, Buckingham: Open University Press.

Dale, A. and Egerton, M. (1997) *Highly Educated Women: Evidence from the National Child Development Study*, London: HMSO.

Dasgupta, P. and Serageldin, I. (2000) *Social Capital: A Multifaceted Perspective*, Washington, DC: World Bank.

Davie, R., Butler, N. and Goldstein, H. (1972) *From Birth to Seven*, London: Longman.

Delphy, C. and Leonard, D. (1992) *Familiar Exploitation: A New Analysis of Marriage in Contemporary Western Society*, Cambridge: Polity Press.

Department for Education and Employment (1998a) *The Learning Age: A Renaissance for A New Britain*, Green Paper, London: HMSO.

Department for Education and Employment (1998b) *National Adult Learning Survey 1997*, Research Report 49, Sudbury: Department for Education and Skills.

Department for Education and Skills (1999) *Learning to Succeed: Post-16 Funding*. Second Technical Consultation Paper, London: HMSO.

De Ruyter, D. and Conroy, J. (2002) 'The formation of identity: the importance of ideals', *Oxford Review of Education* 28(4): 509–525.

Diaz, R.M., Neal, C.J. and Vachio, A. (1991) 'Maternal teaching in the zone of proximal development: a comparison of low- and high-risk dyads', *Merrill-Palmer Quarterly*, 37: 83–108.

Diener, E., Suh, E. and Oishi, S. (1997) 'Recent findings on subjective well-being', *Indian Journal of Clinical Psychology* 24(1): 25–41.

Dow, S. (2002) *Economic Methodology*, Oxford: Oxford University Press.

Dworkin, R. (1979) *Taking Rights Seriously*, London: Duckworth.

Easterlin, R.A. (2003) *Building a Better Theory of Well-Being*, IZA Discussion Paper No. 742, Bonn: Institute for the Study of Labor. Available at <http://ssm.com/ abstract=392043> (accessed 23 June 2003).

Ekinsmyth, C. and Bynner, J. (1994) *The Basic Skills of Young Adults*, London: Adult Literacy and Basic Skills Unit.

Elder, G.H. (1974) *Children of the Great Depression: Social Change in Life Experience*, Chicago: University of Chicago Press.

Emler, N. (2001) *Self-esteem: The Costs and Causes of Low Self-worth*, York: Joseph Rowntree Foundation.

Emler, N. and Fraser, E. (1999) 'Politics: the education effect', *Oxford Review of Education*, 25(1 and 2): 271–272.

Epstein, D. and Johnson, R. (1998) *Schooling Sexualities*, Buckingham: Open University Press.

Eraut, M. (2000) 'Non-formal learning, implicit learning and tacit knowledge in professional work', in F. Coffield (ed.) *The Necessity of Informal Learning*, Bristol: Policy Press, pp. 12–31.

Feinstein, L. (2000a) *Quantitative Estimates of the Social Benefits of Learning, 2: Health (Depression and Obesity)*, Research Report 6: Centre for Research on the Wider Benefits of Learning, London: Institute of Education/Birkbeck.

Feinstein, L. (2000b) *Quantitative Estimates of the Social Benefits of Learning, 1: Crime*, Research Report 5: Centre for Research on the Wider Benefits of Learning, London: Institute of Education/Birkbeck.

Feinstein, L., Hammond, C., Woods, L., Preston, J. and Bynner, J. (2003) *The Contribution of Adult Learning to Health and Social Capital*, Research Report 8: Centre for Research on the Wider Benefits of Learning, London: Institute of Education/Birkbeck.

Ferri, E., Bynner, J. and Wadsworth, M. (eds) (2003) *Changing Britain, Changing Lives*, London: Institute of Education.

Ferri, E. and Smith, K. (1997) 'Where you live and who you live with', in J. Bynner, E. Ferri and K. Smith (eds.) *Twenty-something in the 1990s*, Aldershot: Ashgate, pp. 53–76.

Field, J. and Schuller, T. (2000) 'Networks, norms and trust: explaining patterns of lifelong learning in Scotland and Northern Ireland', in F. Coffield (ed.) *Differing Visions of a Learning Society*, Bristol: Policy Press, pp. 95–118.

Field, J., Schuller, T. and Baron, S. (2000) 'Social capital and human capital revisited', in S. Baron, J. Field and T. Schuller (eds) *Social Capital: Critical Perspective*, Oxford: Oxford University Press, pp. 243–263.

Fine, B. (2001) *Social Capital versus Social Theory: Political Economy and Social Science at the Turn of the Millennium*, London: Routledge.

Fine, B. and Green, F. (2000) 'Economics, social capital and the colonization of the social sciences', in S. Baron, J. Field and T. Schuller (eds) *Social Capital: Critical Perspectives*, Oxford: Oxford University Press, pp. 78–93.

Fox, J. and Pearce, D. (2000) '25 years of population trends', *Population Trends* 100: 6–31.

Fraser, J.T. (1990) *Of Time, Passion and Knowledge: Reflections on the Strategy of Existence*, Princeton: Princeton University Press.

Galindo-Rueda, F. and Vignoles, A. (2003) *Class-Ridden or Meritocratic? An Economic Analysis of Recent Changes in Britain*, Centre for Economics of Education, Discussion Paper 32, London: London School of Economics.

Gamarnikow, E. and Green, A. (1999) 'The third way and social capital: education action zones and a new agenda for education, parents and community', *International Studies in Sociology of Education* 9(1): 3–22.

Garmezy, N. (1971) 'Vulnerability research and the issue of primary prevention', *Journal of Orthopsychiatry* 41: 101–116.

Gillborn, D. and Youdell, D. (2000) *Rationing Education: Policy, Practice, Reform and Equity*, Buckingham: Open University Press.

Gilleskie, D.B. and Harrison, A.L. (1998) 'The effect of endogenous health inputs on the relationship between health and education', *Economics of Education Review* 17(3): 279–296.

Glaeser, E.L. (1999) *The Formation of Social Capital*, Paper delivered at OECD/Canada Statistics Conference on Human and Social Capital, Quebec.

Glennerster, H. (2000) *British Social Policy since 1945*, 2nd edn, Oxford: Blackwell.

Goleman, D. (1996) *Emotional Intelligence: Why it can Matter More than IQ*, London: Bloomsbury.

Gorard, S., Rees, G., Renold, E. and Fevre, R. (1998) *Family Influences on Participation in Lifelong Learning*, Working Paper 15, Cardiff: Cardiff University.

Green, A. and Preston, J. (2001) 'Education and social cohesion: re-centering the debate', *Peabody Journal of Education* 76(3 and 4): 247–284.

Green, A., Preston, J. and Sabates, R. (2003) *Education, Equity and Social Cohesion: A Distributional Model*, Research Report 7: Centre for Research on the Wider Benefits of Learning, London: Institute of Education/Birkbeck.

Green, J. (2003) 'Vocational qualifications (including NVQs)', DfES Briefing Sheet, London: Department for Education and Skills.

Grossman, M. and Kaestner, R. (1997) 'Effects of education on health', in J.R. Behrman and N. Stacey (eds) *The Social Benefits of Education*, Ann Arbor: University of Michigan Press, pp. 69–124.

Gundelach, P. and Torpe, L. (1996) 'Voluntary Associations: New Types of Involvement and Democracy', Paper prepared for the ECPR Workshop on Social Involvement, Voluntary Associations and Democratic Politics, Oslo.

Habermas, J. (1987) *The Theory of Communicative Action*, Cambridge: Polity Press.

Hall, P. (1999) 'Social capital in Britain', *British Journal of Political Science* 29(3): 417–461.

Halman, L. (1994) 'Variations in tolerance levels in Europe. Evidence from the Euro-barometers and European Values Study', *European Journal on Criminal Policy and Research* 2–3: 15–38.

Halsey, A.H., Lauder, H., Brown, P. and Wells, A. (eds) (1997) *Education: Culture, Economy, and Society*, Oxford: Oxford University Press.

Halsted, J. and Taylor, M. (2000) 'Learning and teaching about values: a review of recent research', *Cambridge Journal of Education* 30(2): 169–202.

Hammond, C. (2002a) 'What is it about education that makes us healthy? Exploring the education–health connection', *International Journal of Lifelong Education* 21(6): 551–571.

Hammond, C. (2002b), *Learning to be Healthy*, Wider Benefits of Learning Papers: No. 3, London: Institute of Education/Birkbeck.

Hammond, C. (2003) 'How education makes us healthy', *London Review of Education* 1(1): 61–78.

Hart, J.T. (1971) 'The inverse care law', *Lancet* I: 405–412.

Hartog, J. and Oosterbeek, O. (1998) 'Health, wealth and happiness: why pursue a higher education?', *Economics of Education Review* 17(3): 245–256.

Haskey, J. (1987) 'One-person households in Great Britain: living alone in the middle years of life', *Population Trends* 50: 23–31.

Haskey, J. (1996) 'Families and households in Great Britain', *Population Review* 85: 7–24.

Haskey, J. (1998) 'One-parent families and their dependent children in Great Britain', *Population Trends*, 91: 5–14.

Heinrich, J., Popescu, M.A., Wist, M., Goldstein, I.F. and Winchmann, H.E. (1998) 'Atopy in children and parental social class', *American Journal of Public Health* 88(9): 1319–1324.

Hess, R.D. and Holloway, S.D. (1984) 'Family and school as educational institutions', in R.D. Parke (ed.) *Review of Child Development Research*, Chicago: University of Chicago Press.

Hobcraft, J. (2000) *The Roles of Schooling and Educational Qualifications in the Emergence of Adult Social Exclusion*, CASE Paper 43, London, London School of Economics: Centre for Analysis of Social Exclusion.

Home Office (2002) *Community Cohesion: A Report of the Independent Review Team*, London: HMSO.

Hopper, E. and Osborn, M. (1975) *Adult Students: Education, Selection and Social Control*, London: Frances Pinter.

Howard, S., Dryden, J. and Johnson, B. (1999) 'Childhood resilience: review and critique of literature', *Oxford Review of Education* 25(3): 307–323.

Hubbs-Tait, L., McDonald Culp, A., Culp, R.E. and Miller, C.E. (2002) 'Relation of maternal cognitive stimulation, emotional support and intrusive behaviour during Head Start to children's kindergarten cognitive abilities', *Child Development* 73: 110–131.

Hyland,T. (1996) *Competence, Education and NVQs*, London: Cassell.

Jackson, B. and Marsden, D. (1962) *Education and the Working Class: Some General Themes Raised by a Study of 88 Working-class Children in a Northern Industrial City*, London: Routledge and Kegan Paul.

James, K. (2001) *Prescribing Learning: A Guide to Good Practice in Learning and Health*, Leicester: NIACE.

James, W. (1890) *The Principles of Psychology*, London: Macmillan.

Jenkins, A., Vignoles, A., Wolf, A. and Galindo-Rueda, F. (2002) *The Determinants and*

Effects of Lifelong Learning, CEE Discussion Paper No. 19, London: London School of Economics.

Johnes, G. (1993) *The Economics of Education*, London: Macmillan.

Karabel, J. and Halsey, A.H. (1977) *Power and Ideology in Education*, New York: Oxford University Press.

Kawachi, I., Kennedy, B.P. and Glass, R. (1997) 'Social capital and self-rated health: A contextual analysis', *American Journal of Public Health* 89: 1187–1193.

Keep, E., Mayhew, K. and Corney, M. (2002) *Review of the Evidence on the Rate of Return to Employers of Investment in Training and Employer Training Measures*, SKOPE Research Paper 34, Warwick Business School, Coventry: University of Warwick, pp. 60.

Kiernan, K. (1997) 'Becoming a young parent: a longitudinal study of associated factors', *British Journal of Sociology* 48: 406–428.

Kiernan, K. (1999) 'Childbearing outside marriage in Western Europe', *Population Trends* 98: 11–20.

Klebanov, P., Brooks-Gunn, J. and Duncan, G. J. (1994) 'Does neighbourhood and family poverty affect mothers' parenting, mental health and social support?', *Journal of Marriage and the Family* 56: 441–455.

Knack, S. and Keefer, P. (1997) 'Does social capital have an economic payoff? A cross-country investigation', *Quarterly Journal of Economics* 62 (4): 1251–1288.

Krais, B. (1993) 'Gender and symbolic violence: female oppression in the light of Pierre Bourdieu's Theory of Social Practice', in C. Callhoun, E. LiPuma and M. Postone (eds) *Bourdieu: Critical Perspectives*, Cambridge: Polity Press: 156–177.

Lazarus, R.S. and Folkman, S. (1984) *Stress, Appraisal, and Coping*, New York: Springer.

Lin, N. (2001) *Social Capital Theory: A Theory of Social Structure and Social Action*, Cambridge: Cambridge University Press.

Lomas, J. (1998) 'Social capital and health: implications for public health and epidemiology', *Social Science and Medicine* 47(9): 1181–1188.

Lynch, L. (2002) 'Too old to learn? Lifelong learning in the context of an ageing population', in D. Istance, H. Schuetze and T. Schuller (eds), *International Perspectives on Lifelong Learning: From Recurrent Education to the Knowledge Society*, Buckingham: SRHE/ Open University Press, pp. 63–75.

Manlove, J. (1997) 'Early motherhood in an intergenerational perspective: the experiences of a British cohort', *Journal of Marriage and the Family* 59: 263–279.

Marcia, J.E. (1966) 'Development and validation of ego identity status', *Journal of Personality and Social Psychology* 3: 551–558.

Masten, A. S. and Coatsworth, J. D. (1998) 'The development of competence in favorable and unfavorable environments: a tale of resources, risk and resilience', *American Psychologist* 53: 205–220.

McGivney, V. (1992) *Tracking Adult Learning Routes: A Pilot Investigation into Adult Learners' Starting Points and Progression to Further Education and Training*, Leicester: NIACE.

McGivney, V. (2002) *A Question of Value: Achievement and Progression in Adult Learning*. A Discussion Paper, Leicester: NIACE.

McGivney, V. (2003) *Staying or Leaving the Course*, Leicester: NIACE.

McMahon, W. (1999) *Education and Development: Measuring the Social Benefits*, Oxford: Oxford University Press.

McRae, S. (1999) 'Introduction: family and household change in Britain', in S. McRae (ed.) *Changing Britain: Families and Households in the 1990s*, Oxford: Oxford University Press.

Morgan, D.H.J. (1996) *Family Connections: An Introduction to Family Studies*, Cambridge: Polity Press.

Morrow, G. (2003) 'Conceptualizing Social Capital in Relation to Children and Young People: Is it Different for Girls?', Paper presented at Gender and Social Capital Conference, Manitoba, Canada.

Mortimore, P. (1998) *School Matters: The Junior Years*, Wells: Open Books.

Mruk, C. (1999) *Self-esteem Research, Theory and Practice*, London: Free Association Books.

Nayak, A. (2002) 'Pale Warriors': skinhead culture and the embodiment of white masculinities' in A. Brah, M. Hickman and M. Mac an Ghail (eds.) *Thinking Identities: Ethnicity, Racism and Culture*, Basingstoke: Macmillan.

Nettleton, S. (1995) *The Sociology of Health and Illness*, Cambridge: Polity Press.

Nie, N., Junn, J. and Stehlik-Barry, K. (1996) *Education and Democratic Citizenship in America*, Chicago: University of Chicago Press.

Norris, P. (2000) *Making Democracies Work: Social Capital and Civic Engagement in 47 Societies*, Paper presented at the EURESCO conference on social capital: interdisciplinary perspectives, University of Exeter, 15–20 September.

Nurmi, J. (1989) 'Adolescents' orientation to the future: Development of interests and plans, and related attributions and affects in the life-span context', *Commentationes Scientiarum Socialum* (No. 39), Helsinki: Finnish Society for Sciences and Letters.

Nurmi, J. (1991) 'How do adolescents see their future? A review of the development of future orientation and planning', *Developmental Review* 11: 1–59.

OECD (1976) *Educational Leave of Absence*, Paris: Organisation for Economic Co-operation and Development.

OECD (1998) *Human Capital Investment*, Paris: Organisation for Economic Co-operation and Development.

OECD (2000) *The Wealth of Nations: The Role of Human and Social Capital*, Paris: Organisation for Economic Co-operation and Development.

OECD (2002) *Understanding the Brain: Towards a New Learning Science*, Paris: Organisation for Economic Co-operation and Development.

Office for Standards in Education (2000) *Family Learning: A Survey of Current Practice*, London: Ofsted. Available at http://www.ofsted.gov.uk.

Parfit, D. (1984) *Reasons and Persons*, Oxford: Clarendon Press.

Parkes, C.M. (1971) 'Psycho-social transitions: a field of study', *Social Science and Medicine* 5: 101–115.

Parry, G., Moyser, G. and Day, N. (1992) *Political Participation and Democracy in Britain*, Cambridge: Cambridge University Press.

Parsons, S. and Bynner, J. (1998) *Influences on Adult Basic Skills*, London: Basic Skills Agency.

Paterson, L. (1994) *The Autonomy of Modern Scotland*, Edinburgh: Edinburgh University Press.

Phillipson, C., Bernard, M., Phillips, J. and Ogg, J. (2001) *The Family and Community Life of Older People*, London: Routledge.

Plewis, I. and Preston, J. (2001) *Evaluating the Benefits of Lifelong Learning: A Framework*, Wider Benefits of Learning Papers: No. 2, London: Institute of Education/Birkbeck.

Portes, A. (1998) 'Social capital: its origins and applications in modern sociology', *Annual Review of Social Sciences* 24: 1–24.

Preston, J. (2002) 'White Trash Vocationalism', Paper presented at the Discourse, PowerResistance in Post-Compulsory Education Conference, 12–14 April, Plymouth.

Preston, J. (2003) 'Enrolling alone? Lifelong learning and social capital in England', *International Journal of Lifelong Education*, 22(3), 235–248.

Preston, J. and Hammond, C. (2002) *The Wider Benefits of Further Education: Practitioner Views*, Research Report 1: Centre for Research on the Wider Benefits of Learning, London: Institute of Education/Birkbeck.

Preston, J. and Hammond, C. (2003) 'Practitioner views on the Wider Benefits of Further Education', *Journal of FE and HE* 27(2): 211–222.

Pulkkinen, L. and Rönkä, A. (1994) 'Personal control over development, identity formation, and future orientation as components of life orientation: a developmental approach', *Developmental Psychology* 30(2): 260–271.

Putnam, R.D. (1993) *Making Democracy Work: Civic Traditions in Modern Italy*, Princeton: Princeton University Press.

Putnam, R.D. (1995) 'Bowling alone: America's declining social capital', *Journal of Democracy* 6(1), 65–78.

Putnam, R.D. (2000) *Bowling Alone: The Collapse and Revival of American Community*, New York: Simon and Schuster.

Raey, D. (2000a) 'A useful extension of Bourdieu's conceptual framework? Emotional capital as a useful way of understanding mothers' involvement in their children's education', *Sociological Review* 48(4): 568–585.

Raey, D. (2000b) 'Children's urban landscapes: configurations of class and place', in S. Munt (ed.) *Cultural Studies and the Working Class: Subject to Change*, London, Cassell, pp. 151–164.

Ramey, C.T. and Ramey, S.L. (1999) *Right from Birth: Building Your Child's Foundation for Life*, New York: Goddard Press.

Ramey, S.L. and Ramey, C.T. (1992) 'Early educational intervention with disadvantaged children: to what effect?', *Applied and Preventive Psychology* 1: 131–140.

Rawls, J. (1972) *A Theory of Justice*, Oxford: Clarendon Press.

Rikowski, G. (1999) 'Education, capital and the transhuman', in D. Hill, P. McClaren, M. Cole and G. Rikowski (eds) *Postmodernism in Educational Theory: Education and the Politics of Human Resistance*, London: Tufnell Press, pp. 150–184.

Rindfuss, R.C., Swicegood, G. and Rosenfeld, R. (1987) 'Disorder in the life course: how common and does it matter?' *American Sociological Review* 52(6): 785–801.

Roberts, E., Bornstein, M.H., Slater, A.M. and Barrett, J. (1999) 'Early cognitive development and parental education', *Infant and Child Development* 8: 131–140.

Roediger, D.R. (2002) *Colored White*, Berkeley: University of California Press.

Rosenberg, M. (1965) *Society and the Adolescent Self-image*, Princeton: Princeton University Press.

Ross, C.E. and Mirowsky, J. (1999) 'Refining the association between education and health: the effects of quantity, credential, and selectivity', *Demography* 36(4): 445–460.

Rutter, M. (1990) 'Psychosocial resilience and protective mechanisms', in J. Rolf, A. Masten, D. Cicchetti, K. Neuchterlein and S. Weintraub (eds), *Risk and Protective Factors in the Development of Psychopathology*, New York: Cambridge University Press.

Sampson, R.J., Morenoff, J.D. and Earls, F. (1999) 'Beyond social capital: spatial dynamics of collective efficacy for children', *American Sociological Review* 64: 633–660.

Sanders, P. (2002) *Friendship Works*, London: Penna Sanders Consultancy.

Sargant, N. (2000) *The Learning Divide Revisited*, Leicester: NIACE.

Sargant, N. and Aldridge, F. (2003) *Adult Learning and Social Division: A Persistent Pattern*, Leicester: NIACE.

Sargant, N., Field, J., Francis, H., Schuller, T. and Tuckett, A. (1997) *The Learning Divide*, Leicester: NIACE.

Schlossberg, N.K. (1981) 'A model for analyzing human adaptation to transition', *Counseling Psychologist* 9(2): 2–18.

Schlossberg, N.K., Waters, E.B. and Goodman, J. (1995) *Counseling Adults in Transition: Linking Practice with Theory*, 2nd edn, New York: Springer.

Schuller, T. (2000) 'Social and human capital: the search for appropriate technomethodology', *Policy Studies* 21(1): 25–35.

Schuller, T., Baron, S. and Field, J. (2000) 'Social capital: a review and critique', in S. Baron, J. Field and T. Schuller (eds.) *Social Capital: Critical Perspectives*, Oxford: Oxford University Press, pp. 1–38.

Schuller, T., Brassett-Grundy, A., Green, A., Hammond, C. and Preston, J. (2002), *Learning, Continuity and Change in Adult Life*, Research Report 3: Centre for Research on the Wider Benefits of Learning, London: Institute of Education/Birkbeck.

Schuller, T. and Bynner, J. (2001) Measuring the Benefits of Learning: Theoretical and Conceptual Considerations, Conference Paper, European Society for Research in the Education of Adults, Lisbon.

Schuller, T., Bynner, J. and Feinstein, L. (2003) Capital and Capabilities. WBL Discussion Paper 1, London: Institute of Education.

Schuller, T., Bynner, J., Green, A., Blackwell, L., Hammond, C., Preston, J. and Gough, M. (2001) *Modelling and Measuring the Wider Benefits of Learning: A Synthesis*, Wider Benefits of Learning Papers: No. 1, London: Institute of Education/Birkbeck.

Schuller, T., Raffe, D., Morgan-Klein, B. and Clark, I. (1999) *Part-time Higher Education*, London: Jessica Kingsley.

Schultz, T.W. (1961) 'Investment in human capital', *American Economic Review* L1 (1): 1–22.

Sen, A. (1992) *Inequality Re-examined*, Cambridge: Harvard University Press.

Sen, A. (1999) *Development as Freedom*, Oxford: Oxford University Press.

Skeggs, B. (1988) 'Gender reproduction and further education: domestic apprenticeships', *British Journal of Sociology of Education* 9: 131–149.

Skeggs, B. (1997) *Formations of Class and Gender*, London: Sage.

Skeggs, B. (2000) 'The appearance of class: challenges in gay space', in S. Munt (ed.) *Cultural Studies and the Working Class: Subject to Change*, London: Cassell.

Skeggs, B. (2002) 'The Re-branding of Class: From Economics to Culture', Paper prepared for Conference 'Discourse, Power, Resistance in Post-Compulsory Education and Training', 12–14 April, Plymouth.

Smith, D. (2000) 'The underside of schooling: restructuring, privatization and women's unpaid work', in S. Ball (ed.) *Sociology of Education: Major Themes*, Vol. 2, London: RoutledgeFalmer, pp. 698–716.

Stams, G.J., Juffer, F. and van Izendoorn, M. H. (2002) 'Maternal sensitivity, infant attachment, and temperament in early childhood predict adjustment in middle childhood: the case of adopted children and their biologically unrelated parents', *Developmental Psychology* 38: 806–821.

Stockdale, J. (1995) 'The self and media messages: match or mismatch?', in I. Markova and R. Farr (eds) *Representations of Health, Illness and Handicap*, London, England: Harwood, pp. 31–48.

Taylor, R. (2003) *Skills and Innovation in Modern Workplaces*, Future of Work Programme report, Swindon: Economic and Social Research Council.

Thomson, K. (2003) *Emotional Capital: Maximising Intangible Assets at the Heart of Business and Brand Success*, London: Wiley Europe.

Tizard, B., Blatchford, P., Burke, J., Farquhar, C. and Plewis, I. (1988) *Young Children at School in the Inner Cities*, London: Lawrence Erlbaum Associates.

Tobias, R. (2000) 'The boundaries of adult education for active citizenship – institutional and community contexts', *International Journal of Lifelong Education* 19: 418–429.

Trommsdorff, G. (1983) 'Future orientation and socialization', *International Journal of Psychology* 18: 381–406.

Tuckett, A. and Aldridge, F. (2003) *A Sharp Reverse – NIACE Survey on Adult Participation*, Leicester: NIACE.

Turner, H.A. and Turner, R.J. (1999) 'Gender, social status, and emotional reliance', *Journal of Health and Social Behavior* 40(4): 360–373.

Unicef (2002) *The State of the World's Children*, New York: United Nations Children's Fund.

Waterman, A. and Archer, S. (1990) 'A life-span perspective on identity formation: development in form, function, and process', in P.B. Baltes, D.L. Featherman and R.M. Lerner (eds), *Life-span Development and Behavior*, 10: Hillsdale, NJ: Erlbaum, pp. 29–57.

Wessely, S., Hotoph M. and Sharpe, M. (1998) *Chronic Fatigue and its Syndromes*, Oxford: Oxford University Press.

West, L. (1996) *Beyond Fragments: Adults, Motivation and Higher Education, A Biographical Analysis*, London: Taylor & Francis.

White, M. and Hill, H. (2003) *New IT and Work Innovations*, in R. Taylor (ed.) *Skills and Innovation in Modern Workplaces*, Swindon: Economic and Social Research Council, p. 25.

Whitty, G., Aggleton, P., Gamarnikow, E. and Tyrer, P. (1998) 'Independent Inquiry into Inequalities in Health: Input Paper 10 to the Independent Inquiry into Inequalities in Health', *Journal of Education Policy* 13(5): 641–652.

Wilkinson, R.G. (1996) *Unhealthy Societies: The Afflictions of Inequality*, London: Routledge.

Witz, A., Warhurst, C. and Nickson, O. (2003) 'The labour of aesthetics and the aesthetics of organization', *Organization* 10 (1), pp. 33–54.

Woolcock, M. (1998) 'Social capital and economic development: toward a theoretical synthesis and policy framework', *Theory and Society*, 27, pp. 151–208.

Young, M. (1988) *The Metronomic Society: Natural Rhythms and Human Timetables*, London: Thames and Hudson.

Index

The index is in word-by-word alphabetical order. Names of individual study respondents have only been indexed in cases where reference is made to them in more than one place in the text.

accreditation of courses 176–7
alcohol consumption 171–2
alienation at school 66, 74
Angela: confidence 45; disruptive effects of family 95
aspirations, unmet 50
attachment theory 82
attitudes: effect of learning 174–5; of family *see under* families

Back to Work courses 144
Becker, Gary 180
behaviour, health-related 171–2
Bourdieu, Pierre 17–18, 119–21, 147
BSC70 (British Birth Cohort Study 1970) 24

capabilities 12–13, 161, 186
capital, human: critique 14–16, 186; and health 180
capital, identity: definition and scope 19–21; effects of the workplace 180–1
capital, social: and class 155–7; critique 16–19; and health 38–9; networks and informal interactions 121–4; theory of Pierre Bourdieu 119–21, 147; and the workplace 181
capitals, the three 12–14, 179–80; interactions 185–8; outcomes 21–2
career guidance, lack of 66
caring work as women's labour 126
Carol: case study 148–52; confidence 43; formal civic participation 183

Catherine: children's influence 85; enhancement of family learning 87; transfer of knowledge 90–1
causality 162
Centre for the Economics of Education 7
Centre for Research on the Wider Benefits of Learning 6–7
childcare, problems of 106–7, 112; and social capital 122, 123
civic participation: attitude of family members 150; effect of learning 175–6; formal 124–8, 137–40, 153–4; informal 123–4
class *see also* socio-economic status: and academic achievement 82–3; class gradient in diagnosis 70
class strategies 137, 156
Cliff: attitude of children 92–3; role-model for children 87
cognitive dissonance 129
cohort studies 24
Coleman, James 17
communication and competencies 51–3, 64
Community Development Award 125
community work *see* civic participation
competencies *see* communication and competencies
confidence 41–5, 53, 107–8, 149–52; loss 51 *see also* failure, impact of
conflicts 32, 47
Consuela: case study 71–7; exchange of views 175; impact of teachers 133

consumerism 182
context, learning 117
coping 40–1; and self-understanding 47–8; sense of purpose 50
Côté, James 19–20
critical mass of learning 183

deafness, attitude to 133
decisions on education 186–8
Declan: case study 152–5; confidence 42; exchange of views 174–5; identity 46; self-esteem 44
Delia: case study 99–105; importance of learning context 117; life-long learning 118
Denise: case study 66–71; communication skills 52; coping 43; independence 48; knowledge and understanding 52–3
depression 173–4; positive effect of learning 101–2; and resilience 38; and unmet aspirations 50
discourse of care 123–4, 149
Donette: progression in learning 168, 170–1
Donna: domestic stress 173; experience of failure 174
Doris: confidence 41; identity 46–7; need for recognition 45
drugs: addiction and rehabilitation 59–63

economic rationality 187
Ede: independence 49; knowledge and understanding 52; role-model for children 87–8
effects of learning see matrix
Elder, Glenn 189
Elsa: confidence 43; involvement in children's school 86
Elsbeth: catharsis 47–8; influence of parents 88–9; pride in creativity 91; self-expression 48–9
emotional resilience see resilience, emotional
empowerment 30–1, 173
English language skills 126–7, 127
Enid: family support 92; fear of changing too much 96; support from husband 93–4
Essex 131–3
exclusion, social 145–7, 181
exercise 171

failure, impact of 42, 43, 44–5, 174

Faith: attitudes of children 93; influence on son's schooling 86; parenting ability 90
families see also parents: and attainment 81–3; attitudes to adult learning 88, 91, 92–3, 108; definition and scope 83–4; impact of learning on relationships 93–4, 96–7, 102, 112–14; learning as fun 89; and motivation to learn 84–5, 107; mutual reciprocation 88–9; as obstacles to learning 95, 110–11, 112; recent trends 80–1; and role-models 87–8; source of valuing and support 86–7; as sources of learning 100–1; time pressures 96
Francis: case study 140–7; formal civic participation 128; lack of economic capital 142; vocational learning 177
Fraser, J.T. 188
future, orientation towards 49–51, 190–1

Gareth: case study 58–63; self-esteem 44; social mixing 130, 172; social networks 122; values 134
gender bias 49–50; and civic participation 125
generalisability 161–2
generational effect 189
Gloria: support from children 88; time pressures 96; transformation 94

health: access to services 38, 52–3; and aspects of identity 47–8, and behaviour 171–2; and communication and competencies 52–3; effect of class on diagnosis 70; effects of workplace 180; and human capital 180; psychosocial mediators 54–6; and self-esteem 42–4; and a sense of purpose and future 50, 51; and social capital 38–9; and social integration 53–4; and socio-economic status 37–8
Health Action Zones 39
Hermione: children's influence 85; independence 48
Hester: case study 110–16; importance of learning context and parent status 117
homophobia 132, 152
human capital see capital, human

identity: and coping 47–8; mechanisms of development 48–9, 152–3; pros and cons of self-discovery 46–7, 112–13

identity capital *see* capital, identity
immigrants: English language skills 126–7; negative experiences at school 74; social integration 52
independence 47, 49
integration, social: and health 53–4; of immigrants 52; networks and informal interactions 121–4; resocialisation 182
interactions, informal 121–4
Internet as learning source 107
inverse care law 38

Kali: support from husband 93; time pressures 96
Kashani: role-model for daughter 87; support from daughter 88
knowledge: and understanding 52
knowledge, transfer of 91

lags in learning 188
language skills 126–7
life course 189; and effects of learning 57–8, 78–9; and relevance of learning 66–7, 116–17
lifelong learning 118
lifestyles 50
longitudinal surveys 162

Magda: communitarian attitude 133; effect of history course 134
Mandisa: gender bias 50; parenting ability 90; son benefits from her education 91
matrix of learning effects *25, 26–33*
methodology: outcome and control variables 196–8; principles 161–3; of the study 23–4, 39–40, 166–7; study respondents 194–5

Nadine: feelings of failure 43; mixed attitudes of children 93
Naomi: family relationships 96; feelings of inferiority 42; parenting ability 90; role-model for children 87; time pressures 96
National Adult Learning Surveys 9–10
National Child Development Study (NCDS) 24; courses taken at ages 33-42 163–4; effects of learning 164–71; health and well being 171–4
networks and informal interactions 121–4
non-accredited learning 58

OECD (Organisation for Economic Co-operation and Development) 18, 181

parenthood 100–1, 111
parents *see also* families: impact of education 82; importance of parent status 117; interactions with children's learning 85–9, 103, 114; parenting ability 89–92, 111; return to work 91–2; as role models 87–8, 108
participation: focus of policy and research 5–6
paybacks of education 188–9
Phyllis: case study 105–9; importance of parent status 117
policy: focus on participation not outcomes 5–6; implications of study results 192
positional good, education as a 183–4
poverty, impact of 142
prejudice 131–3
purpose, sense of 49–51
Putnam, Robert D. 120, 147, 156

racism 132
rationality, economic 187
recognition, need for 45
reinforcement effects 168
relationships: impact of learning 93–4
research: focus on participation not outcomes 5–6
resilience, emotional 38, 74–5, 76 *see also* coping
risks of education 8–9, 55; unmet aspirations 50
role models: parents 87–8, 108; teachers 51, 133, 153–4

school: negative effects 59, 63, 66, 67, 74; positive effects 71–3
self-efficacy *see* self-esteem and self-efficacy
self-esteem and self-efficacy: effect on mental health 43–4; mechanisms of development 45–6; as outcome of learning 41–3
Sen, Amartya 12, 161, 186
"sleeper" effect 63
smoking 172
social capital *see* capital, social
social change 27
social cohesion and education 183

social integration *see* integration, social
social mix, importance of 129–31
social surveys 162
socio-economic status *see also* class: and
   health 37–8
stress 38, 180; and academic courses 174
subjective well-being (SWB) 40
Surinder: English language skills 126;
   vocational learning 177
surveys: longitudinal 162; social 162
Susan: formal civic participation 128,
   137–40; social mixing 130
sustaining effects of learning 25–6, 26–7;
   in parents 29–30

teachers: as role models 51, 133, 153–4;
   supportive role 45–6, 64
time, the dimension of 188–91

tolerance 128–35, 175
trade-offs 184
transformation through learning 26, 94,
   102 *see also* social change

values and value judgements 7–8, 28;
   tolerance 128–35
vocational education 176–7

well-being 40, 172–4
work: negative effects of workplace 180–1;
   return to work 91–2; and social capital
   181
World Bank 18

Young, Michael 188
youth, reconnection 46